THE HISTORY OF EUROPE

The Rise and Fall of the Classical World

2500BC–600AD

The Rise and Fall of the Classical World

2500BC–600AD

The History of Europe

Published in 2006 by Mitchell Beazley,
an imprint of Octopus Publishing Group Ltd
2–4 Heron Quays, London E14 4JP
Copyright © Octopus Publishing Group Ltd 2006

Executive Editor	Vivien Antwi
Executive Art Editor	Yasia Williams-Leedham
Senior Editor	Peter Taylor
Copy-editor	Naomi Waters
Designer	Tom Green
Picture Researcher	Jenny Faithfull
Production	Faizah Malik
Indexer	Sue Farr

ISBN 1 8453 3162 1
A CIP catalogue record for this book is available from the British Library.

General Editor Dr John Stevenson

Contributors	
Ancient Greece	Dr Peter Liddel
Ancient Rome	Dr Josephine Crawley Quinn
Byzantium	Dr Peter Heather

Typeset in Adobe Garamond, Gill Sans, Frutiger, Univers

Printed in China

Contents

6   Introduction

10   **Ancient Greece**

Early Greece: 2500–750 BC
Prehistoric Greece
Homer and the Trojan War
The Formation of Greek Identity
Panhellenic Games

The Archaic and Classical Periods: 750–336 BC
Greeks on the Move
The Ancient Economy
Spartan Politics and Society
Democracy Established
Greek Warfare
Warfare in the 5th Century BC
Philosophy and Religion
Greek Poetry
Athenian Drama
Greek Art
Greek Drama
Philosophy and Religion
Science and Medicine
Histories

The Hellenistic Period: 336–146 BC
Philip and the Rise of Macedon
Alexander the Great
Greece Between Alexander and the Romans
Greece as a Roman Province
Hellenistic Society and Politics
Hellenistic Culture

66   **Ancient Rome**

The Roman Republic: 509–44 BC
The Foundation of Rome and the Period of
  the Kings
The Early Republic and the Struggle of the Orders
Rome in Italy
The Conquest of the Mediterranean
Politics and Discontent in Rome and Italy
The Age of the Generals
Republican Culture

The Roman Empire: 44 BC–476 AD
Augustus Caesar
Augustan Culture
The Early Empire
Imperial Life and Literature
Architecture and Urbanism
Religions and Rome
New Religions
The Decline and Fall of the Roman Empire

90   **Byzantium and the Rise of the West**

Byzantium: Apogee and Decline
The Renewal of Empire
Art and Architecture
The Arab Conquests

The Barbarian Kingdoms
Kingdoms of the Mediterranean Rim
Northern Worlds 500–700
The Rise of the Slavs
Culture and Society

Introduction

A fresco from Naples depicts the Greek myth of Europa, a Phoenician princess who was wooed by the god Zeus in the form of a bull and carried off to Crete. On that island, she became his queen and the mother of the Minoan kings, founding the earliest civilization on European soil.

Although not the cradle of civilization, Europe was the inheritor of the pioneering developments in statecraft, literacy, and urban life, which had begun in Egypt and the Near East. From these would emerge the philosophical and intellectual advances of Greece and their enduring legacy for Europe and the world. The civilizations of Sparta and Athens, and figures such as Homer, Plato, and Aristotle would shape Europe's contribution to world culture and the way Europeans thought about themselves for centuries to come.

Even as the Greek city-states went into decline, Aristotle's pupil, Alexander, from the hitherto obscure kingdom of Macedon, blazed across the historical firmament to create, in a few short years, the largest empire ever seen, reaching from the Balkans to India. With Alexander's death and the break-up of his empire a new and more durable power emerged. The rise of the Roman Republic and its domination of the Mediterranean world provided the basis for the creation of an empire that would eventually stretch from Scotland to the Sahara and from the Atlantic to the Euphrates. The reach of Rome was not merely geographical; the empire left a permanent imprint on European civilization in its law, institutions, and culture. As the Roman Empire declined, its successors in the East and the West adopted many of its features, not least of all Christianity. What had begun as a small, persecuted sect from the distant Roman province of Judea had become the official religion of the later Empire. Amidst the onslaught of barbarian, Slav and Arab invasion, Rome's legacy helped to shape early medieval Europe.

Defining Europe

How Europe got its name is unknown. Herodotus, the Greek historian, wrote of three continents – Europe, Asia, and Africa. The division of the world into three landmasses was therefore very ancient, but Herodotus confessed that he did not know why they had been given these names. In Greek mythology, Europa was the daughter of a Phoenician king with whom Zeus fell in love. Disguising himself as a bull, Zeus enticed Europa onto his back and galloped into the sea, taking her with him to Crete. So the Greek word "Europa" may derive from the Phoenician for "evening land" – the land of the setting sun or, to them, the West.

The Greeks themselves initially used "Europe" to mean central Greece, but soon it meant the whole of the Greek mainland and the entire landmass to the north. The boundary between Europe and Asia was usually fixed at the River Don in Russia, but knowledge of lands north of Greece and west of Sicily was sketchy. Gradually, however, the Mediterranean seaboard of Europe was explored. Early seafarers, possibly Neolithic, but certainly Greeks and Phoenicians, ventured beyond the Straits of Gibraltar to the Atlantic coast of Europe.

The land exploration of Europe was carried out by the Romans, who brought Spain, Gaul, and Britain into the early Roman Empire. The Balkans, the Alpine massif, and the Danubian lands were opened up by the conquests of later emperors. Roman traders rediscovered the amber route from Vienna to the Baltic, and the conquests of Trajan penetrated into the Carpathian lands; however, Roman knowledge beyond the Elbe was minimal, and Scandinavia virtually unknown. The great sea beyond the Straits of Gibraltar was still believed to encircle the whole world. The oldest medieval map – from the early 7th century – shows the three-part division of the world bounded by a great ocean. The first separate map of Europe dates only from the early 12th century, long after the period covered by this volume.

Europe in the geographical form that we think of it today was formed in the aftermath of the last Ice Age over 10,000 years ago. At the western end of the great Eurasian landmass, its geographical boundaries were bounded largely by the sea, in the west by the Atlantic, to the North by the Arctic Ocean, and to the South by the Mediterranean. By 6000 BC, rising sea levels separated the British Isles from the western mainland of continental Europe, though only by a relatively narrow sea, and had defined the Baltic and Mediterranean coastlines. The Mediterranean now contained numerous islands, some large, like Crete and Sicily, which to were to play an important part in the history of European civilization, while even many of the smaller islands, like Rhodes and Malta, were to acquire enormous strategic significance in the ebb and flow of later empires.

In the East, however, the boundaries of Europe were less geographically distinct, the great forests and marshes of what became known as western Russia, provided natural barriers, as did the Ural Mountains. But the sheer distances involved, with much of eastern Europe further from the sea than any part of the western Eurasian landmass, created its own barriers. The world beyond the Urals, the vast trackless wastes of Siberia, became a by-word for remoteness and the very edge of European civilization.

The first Europeans
The earliest Europeans left no written records, and lived long before the last Ice Age. Physiologically recognizable "modern" human beings (*homo sapiens*) had evolved by what is called the Upper Palaeolithic, the period from *c*.50,000 to *c*.10,000 BC, part of the Old Stone Age culture. Europeans were already distinct in their lighter skin pigmentation and facial characteristics from other groups of *homo sapiens*, such as the Negroids of Central Africa and the Mongoloids of Asia. They had speech, though we know nothing about their languages, could make fire, and were toolmakers. These societies depended on hunting, fishing, and the gathering of edible roots and berries. Finds of a huge variety of animal and fish bones, shells, and the remains of edible plants give us some insight into their diet. Needles and beads, often of worked pebbles, amber, or shale, indicate that they made their own clothes and sought personal adornment.

While we can learn little in detail about their beliefs, we know that they sometimes buried their dead with artefacts and natural objects. But, most importantly, these early populations have left us the first European art. Almost 120 sites with cave paintings have been discovered – the most famous, at Lascaux in southern France, dating from *c*.15,000 BC were only uncovered by accident in 1940. They depict in spectacular colours and great craftsmanship the animals these early Europeans hunted, bison, wild aurochs, horses and deer. As well as paintings we have early statues, possibly cult or votive objects, such as the female figurine known as "The Venus of Willendorf". Whatever their growing artistic sophistication, these populations were relatively scattered and sparse, living in the caves in which they had survived the Ice Ages, or, as the climate became more tolerable, in huts or tents made of skin or brushwood. Estimates would suggest a population of little more than 250,000 for the whole of Europe by 7500 BC.

The "first agricultural revolution"
The rise of more complex societies in Europe was primarily associated with the development of farming. Some form of early farming appears to have been practised in more than one site in Mediterranean Europe by 6000–5500 BC, reaching north-western France around 5000 BC, southern England and Ireland by 4500 BC and the extreme north of the British Isles, by 3500 BC. During this period new cereal crops had begun to penetrate Europe from the Near East. Wild grains gave way to cultivated varieties, greatly increasing productivity. Domesticated animals, including cattle, may also have appeared as early as 6000 BC. Farming was accompanied by growing sophistication in other areas, the fabrication of more elaborate tools, the development of weaving, the development of pottery, and the first metalworking.

But it was agriculture, in what is sometimes known as the "Neolithic revolution" that had the most dramatic impact. Farming was accompanied by permanent settlement, and excavations at places such as Koln-Lindenthal, near Cologne, and Bylany in the Czech Republic, reveal villages of substantial timber buildings, a pattern repeated across much of central and western Europe. Such conditions made a population explosion possible, with as many as five million Europeans by 2000 BC. It was also possible for surpluses to be generated and stored, which could be utilized for other purposes than mere subsistence. The process was not a simple one; hunter-gatherer and more settled peoples may well have co-existed. Nor should we assume that the former lacked sophistication. We know that some hunter-gatherer groups celebrated the deaths of their members with ritual burial, and had their own belief-systems, probably revolving around hunting cults and magic.

But the food resources that sown crops and large-scale animal husbandry generated, and the social structures that went with them permitted much larger scale activities. We have evidence of elaborate systems of land ownership and the large-scale organization of wealth-generating resources. Trade developed across Europe in precious metal goods, flint, and fine stone axes, carried by boats, dugout canoes and pack animals. Amber from the Baltic and stone axes from Central Europe have been found in Britain, while Phoenician traders from the Mediterranean penetrated beyond the Straits of Gibraltar to trade for copper, tin and gold from Britain and Ireland. This trade was associated with the emergence of higher status social groups and large-scale community projects, allowing grand structures to be built, such as great barrows and megaliths, which were constructed even before the first towns and cities. Although events did not move at the same pace across different parts of Europe, the "Neolithic revolution" would eventually lead to the first recorded civilizations and their first palaces, temples and cities.

Europe's population was not only growing indigenously. It was also regularly reinforced by new immigrants, many of them from the east. Some of these immigrant groups have been distinguished by the artefacts they left in their graves. The so-called "Beaker" peoples, with their distinctive funnel-shaped pottery came from Iberia and spread widely into northern Europe, including the British Isles, the Low Countries and Northern Germany. The "Battle Axe" culture seems to have spread from Russia into Eastern and Central Europe, Scandinavia, and Romania. These people also produced distinctive pottery decorated by cord impressions, and tamed and bred horses. It has been suggested that such groups formed the first aristocratic and warrior societies. It is not yet entirely certain whether these distinctive cultures always or necessarily involved the large-scale movement of peoples. We may be seeing the diffusion of a culture and its artefacts, possibly introduced by relatively small numbers of people as conquerors or peaceful settlers.

The most striking evidence we have of these new farming and animal-raising peoples are the archaeological remains of the huge projects of which they were capable: elaborate wooden track-ways and burial barrows, "henges" – circles of earth, wood, and stone – and great stone alignments, tombs and pillars, the so-called "megaliths" (Greek for "large stone"). Thousands of stone monuments exist in a great arc of sites from the islands of the central Mediterranean, Malta, Corsica, and Sardinia, through the Iberian penninsula to Brittany, the British Isles and Scandinavia. The very earliest are immensely old: an early monumental tomb at Ireland's Donegal Bay, yields a Carbon 14 date in the seventh millennium BC, making it as old as some of the oldest stone structures in the Near East. Many more, such as the chamber tombs of Iberia and Brittany, and the temples of Malta, predate the Egyptian pyramids by up to a thousand years.

Some of these projects were clearly functional, such as the wooden track-ways of several kilometres length, built c.3200 BC across the marshy areas of the Somerset Levels in southern England. Others were obviously ritual or ceremonial sites, associated with important burials or significant astronomical events. Sites were often remodelled on an extensive basis, over hundreds if not thousands of years, producing a complex archaeology which is still being explored.

The downland of southern England, largely undisturbed since the prehistoric period, is amongst the richest in megalithic monuments. Silbury Hill, near Avebury, Wiltshire in southern England, built about 2000 BC is the largest prehistoric man-made mound in Europe. Its construction is estimated to have involved the equivalent of 500 men working every day for ten years. Nothing, however, rivals the greatest stone monument of prehistoric Europe, Stonehenge. Starting as a simple cremation site, surrounded by an earth bank, it went through successive phases, including a major remodelling c.1700 BC, which produced much of what we see today. Although later classical writers were to ascribe these monuments to the work of the quasi-mythical "druids" of the Celtic tribes they encountered, they were the creation of much older, stone- and bronze-age peoples.

Scythians, Celts, and the dawn of history

Into this already sophisticated world burst other cultures. Although the usage of the term Scythian was often applied to any non-Greeks from Central and Eastern Europe, evidence of these distinctive people

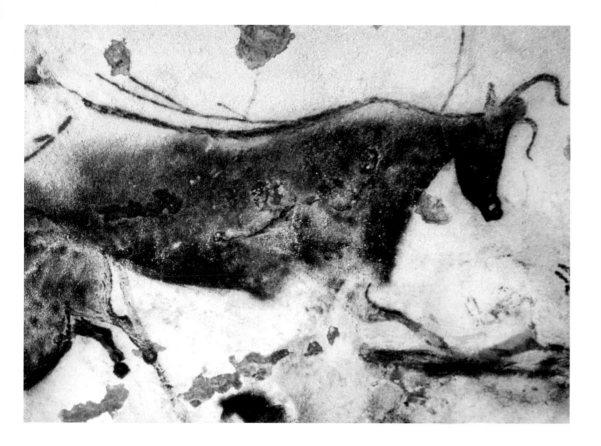

has come to light in excavations in the Crimea and elsewhere. The graves of their kings and aristocrats have revealed astonishing golden artefacts; "Scythian gold" has become synonymous with this still largely nomadic people who dominated large parts of what became the Ukraine and southern Russia from the 7th century BC onwards. To their west, Slavs and Teutons occupied much of what we know today as Eastern Europe and Germany. Western Europe was dominated by the "Celtic" peoples, whose distinctive cultures would be among the first to be recorded by literate observers from the more advanced civilizations of the Mediterranean, both Greek and Roman.

The Celts spanned the period from the close of the Bronze Age to the Iron Age, dominating an area from the west coast of Ireland to the Carpathians, eventually overlapping with the decline of the Greek city states and the expansion of the Roman Empire. Spreading south, they settled in northern Italy, sacked Rome in 386 BC, entered the Balkans, raiding as far south as Delphi in 279 BC. To the west they flooded into Gaul and the British Isles. Ruled by a warrior aristocracy, their hallmark was their taste for rich weapons and gaudy ornaments, left as grave goods, and the swirling, distinctive patterns of Celtic art. In

battle they were feared warriors, fighting virtually naked and displaying a reckless bravery. But they were also settled peoples, farming and animal ranching on a large scale, fortifying extensive citadels or hill-forts, protected by earth ramparts or more elaborate mud, stone and revetted walls.

Just as important was the development of lowland *oppida* (towns) occupied by a community where bronze-smiths, carpenters, furriers, and blacksmiths worked in long thatched buildings. Interaction with the Mediterranean world brought influences from classical art and culture: the leaders of Celtic society were consuming Mediterranean goods, such as wine, olive oil and fine pottery. Some petty kings were minting coins in imitation of Roman models. Although the Celts still dominated much of northern Europe into what we know as the Classical period, they belong to what we term "protohistory". Like the Scythians, the Celts are known not only through archaeology but also through the writings of the more advanced civilizations of the Mediterranean lands. For, in the Mediterranean, civilizations were in gestation that would produce the first history of Europe, through the art of writing and the development of literate, city-based civilizations.

The rich Palaeolithic paintings discovered in a small cave at Lascaux in south-west France are renowned for their naturalistic depiction of the animals hunted by the earliest Europeans c.15,000 BC. Cows, bulls, horses, bison, ibex, musk-ox, and reindeer illustrate the profusion of game that supported the first hunter-gatherer civilizations.

ANCIENT GREECE

2500–146 BC

3600 BC 2400 BC 1200 BC

POLITICS AND GOVERNMENT

*c.*3500 The beginning of urban settlements on the island of Crete, as permanent dwellings develop into village settlements.

1250 Traditional historical date of the Trojan War, narrated in Homer's *Iliad*.

*c.*1400 The palace at Knossos on Crete is destroyed.

1700–1200 Peak of Minoan and Mycenaean civilizations on Crete and mainland Greece. Agricultural and commercial societies thrive, directed towards providing for the royal palaces.

*c.*1200 The decline of Mycenaean civilization; the Dark Ages commence.

*c.*1125 Start of the Iron Age. Iron was used for the manufacture of weapons and tools. The use of iron gradually spread throughout Europe.

*c.*800 The era of the Greek coloniz of the Mediterranean be

*c.*1100 According to legend, Dorian tribes from northern Greece return to the Peloponnese.

3600 2400 1200

SOCIETY AND CULTURE

*c.*1600 The rulers of Mycenae begin elaborate burials with luxury goods from around the Mediterranean.

*c.*2600–2000 The development of Cycladic marble sculpture.

*c.*1700–1400 The peak of the Minoan civilization, which started to decline from *c.*1200 BC.

*c.*3500–3000 The manufacture of bronze begins in the Cycladic archipelago of the Aegean Sea. This led to the Bronze Age period, *c.*3500–1125 BC.

*c.*1500–1200 The Linear B system of writing Greek develops. Greek writing later spreads around the Mediterranean world.

*c.*1100 The development of the geometric style of vase painting.

*c.*800 The Greeks be establish ports of around the Mediterra

*c.*1200–800 The Phoenicians of the Levant dominate Mediterranean trade. It is through contact with them that the Greeks begin to develop their alphabet.

800 BC

400 BC

431–404 The Peloponnesian War. Athens survives the ravages of plague, but is defeated in the war. The historian Thucydides writes a history of the war.

490–479 The Persian Wars, concluding with Greek victory and the foundation of the Delian Confederacy. The Delian Confederacy develops over the course of the 5th century into an Athenian empire.

507 The democratic reforms of Kleisthenes herald the start of democracy at Athens.

594 Solon introduces social, political, and economic legislation in Athens.

358–276 The Macedonian Dynasty.

229/8 The beginnings of Roman intervention in Greece, as Rome defeats Queen Teuta in the First Illyrian War.

211–197 The First and Second Macedonian Wars. Rome is victorious, and Greece becomes a Roman province.

146 The sack of Corinth marks the completion of Rome's conquest of Greece.

400

0

c.600 The introduction of coinage in Lydia, in Asia Minor.

c.570 Birth of the natural philosopher Xenophanes of Colophon.

c.525 The development of the red figure style of vase painting in Athens.

499–406 The golden era of Athenian tragedy.

c.720 The development of the black figure style of vase painting in Corinth.

447 The Periclean building programme reaches its height with the construction of the Parthenon on the Acropolis.

c.750 Compilation of the Homeric poems to form the *Iliad* and *Odyssey*.

776 Traditional date of the first Olympic Games, at Olympia in the Peloponnese.

c.188–139 The construction of the Great Altar at Pergamum.

c.270 The poet Theocritus works in the court at Alexandria in Egypt, composing in the bucolic mode.

297 The creation of the library and the museum at Alexandria.

350–324 Athens undergoes an aesthetic revival with a building programme and scheme of religious, educational, and economic reforms.

387 Plato founds Academy in Athens.

399 Death of Socrates.

Much of the earliest Greek art preserved on vases consists of geometric patterns as well as illustrative scenes, as can be seen on this Attic vase of c.800 BC. Pottery finds not only provide a useful source for tracing the development of art, but can also be used to trace settlements and trade routes.

EARLY GREECE: 2500–750 BC

The period known as Early Greece covers a huge span of development, characterized by the rise and fall of the seafaring Cycladic civilization and the palace-based Minoan and Mycenaean cultures. These societies built networks of trade and artistic activity typical of later developed Greek civilizations.

Greek history can be divided into three periods: Early Greece (2500–750 BC), Archaic and Classical Greece (750–336 BC), and Hellenistic Greece (336–146 BC). They reflect the most historically significant events, as well as changes in the quantity and quality of available sources of data. The growth in the number and sophistication of sources means that Greek history is marked by an apparent acceleration in the succession of events.

The period known as Early Greece is essentially "prehistoric", accessible largely through archaeological discoveries. The evidence is patchy, however, so it is necessary to zoom in and out to look at developments that took place at different times in different areas of Greece. Today, our picture of Early Greece is more detailed than ever. As archaeological excavations took place over the 19th and 20th centuries, it became possible to trace the history of Early Greece further back and with more detail than was achieved by the Greek historians of the Classical and Hellenistic periods.

In about 3500–3300 BC, the inhabitants of islands in the Aegean Sea discovered how to make bronze from a mixture of copper and tin. Bronze became common at the end of the 3rd millennium BC, when trade connections ensured a supply of tin. The period c.3500–c.1125 BC has become known as the Bronze Age.

The earliest developed societies in Greece about which we have the most information are the Cycladic civilization (developed from c.3500 BC), the Minoan civilization of Crete (peaked 1700–1400 BC), and the Mycenaean civilizations located off mainland Greece (peaked 1600–1200 BC). In the last quarter of the 19th century, excavations at Knossos in Crete and Mycenae in the Argolid revealed significant remains of these prehistoric civilizations. These two cultures shared common elements in their systems of economy, government, and culture, and they provide some idea of the structure of early Greek communities.

Archaeological discoveries indicate that these societies centred on royal palaces, with groups of officials who supervised the labour of artisans and the flow of goods towards the palaces. These civilizations seem to have fallen into decline from about 1200 BC, as a result of dynastic rivalry and a breakdown in established lines of trade. The number of inhabited sites decreased, and those that remained in existence did so with a reduced population. It is reasonable to argue that the myths about the Trojan War in Homer's Iliad may reflect the upheavals that curtailed Mycenaean civilization. Greek myth tells also of migrations of populations after these upheavals. Myths such as these would form the basis for ideas about ethnic identity in the Classical period. A growth in the density of inhabited sites from the beginning of the 8th century BC may indicate a growth in population, coinciding with the formation of the Olympic Games, first held around 776 BC.

Environment and ecology are one part of the formative aspects of any society, and the civilizations of Early Greece are no exception. Mountains and the coast are the predominant features of the terrain, with only 20 per cent of the country consisting of flat land and the mainland having 4000 kilometres (2500 miles) of coastline. As the Greeks depended on agriculture and trade for survival, these features meant that Greek history was dominated by struggles for agricultural land and maritime supremacy.

Prehistoric Greece

The remains of Cycladic civilization and the Minoan and Mycenaean civilizations of Crete and mainland Greece provide some of the earliest and most spectacular traces of developed societies in Europe. Their civilizations were based on agriculture and trade; excavations of their settlements have brought to light impressive remains of palace-based societies.

Minoan Crete

Crete is the location of some of the earliest known populated sites in Greece, dating to around the beginning of the 7th millennium BC (*c.*7000 BC). They may have been established by settlers from South-West Anatolia. Evidence suggests that concentrated settlements arose from around 3500 BC. Some of these settlements developed into larger towns, which shared features with those in the Asian Near East, such as regular street planning and a focus upon a public square or an important building. As communities expanded and agricultural production grew, power in the villages and towns of Crete seems to have been concentrated in the hands of individual rulers. By the end of the third millennium BC (around 2000 BC), Crete was dominated by small city-kingdoms. At around this time, the construction of palaces began: the first was at Knossos in central Crete, three miles from the sea. Palaces at Phaistos, Mallia and Zakro followed soon after.

Over the course of the second millennium BC, Knossos became the largest and most important of the palaces. It is possible that a king ruled over a unified kingdom stretching across Crete. By the peak of its development *c.*1700–1400 BC, the population of Knossos may have reached around 12,000. In the early 15th century BC (*c.*1600 BC), all the palaces on Crete except at Knossos were destroyed by fire: this may have been related to power struggles with mainland Greeks. Knossos itself was ruined several times, but the final destruction of the palace took place around 1400 BC.

Greece in the Bronze Age
c.3500–1125 BC
This map illustrates some of the major Minoan and Mycenaean settlements in Greece during the Bronze Age, with a particular concentration of sites in the Argolid in the eastern Peloponnese. The very mountainous landscape of much of Greece meant that disputes over plains, which were especially valuable for agriculture, were a common cause of conflict.

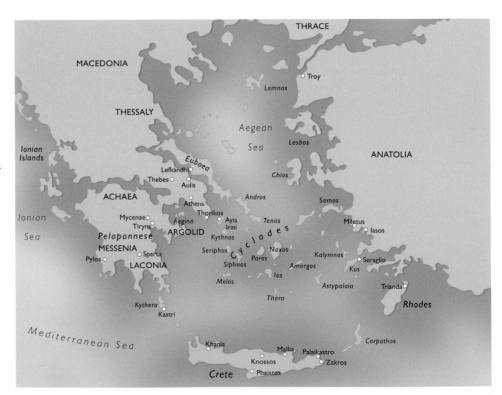

The burning of the palaces baked clay tablets containing text written in a script known as Linear B. Decipherment of these tablets in 1948 provided information about daily life in Knossos. They inform us that the herding of sheep was a major activity and that large numbers of women were employed in textile production. Rural farmers in the interior sent oil, wine, and grain as a tribute to the palaces of rulers who distributed or exchanged this produce as they pleased. Ideally positioned for participating in trade between Egypt, western Asia and the rest of the Mediterranean, Crete was blessed with natural harbours. Agricultural produce was traded for gold, bronze, ivory and other luxury goods from the east. A picture emerges of a society reliant on trade and agriculture, co-ordinated from a centre in which wealth was concentrated.

Wealth, however, was not evenly spread. While the finds at Knossos and other palaces indicate the existence of a wealthy nobility and upper class, these probably formed only a very small proportion of the population. They were reliant on the taxation and exploitation of farmers whose lives would not have changed for thousands of years, and who did not share in the luxuries of the palaces. Minoan Crete, like the Greek civilization that followed, was heavily reliant on the labour of men and women captured in war. Regarded as outsiders, they were enslaved, and would have carried out the most menial tasks in the palaces and lived without rights of any kind.

It is unlikely that Minoans ever exerted political influence beyond the island of Crete. However, the social and cultural influence of the Minoans was more widespread. Seventy miles to the north of Crete lay the archipelago of the Cyclades, home to an influential civilization from the start of the third millennium BC. They began to build cities in the second millennium BC, perhaps as a result of the influence of contact, through trade, with Minoans. Frescoes from the island of Thera in particular exhibit similarities of theme and technique to those from Knossos. A huge volcanic explosion, dated some time between 1600 and 1550 BC, caused widespread devastation; the volcanic ash that covered one important city has preserved it for modern archaeologists. It has been suggested that the resulting cloud of volcanic ash seriously damaged, or was a factor in the decline of, Minoan Civilization.

Mycenaean civilization

"Mycenaean civilization" refers not only to the society of prehistoric Mycenae, an important centre in the eastern Peloponnese, but also to a range of settlements in mainland Greece, which developed by about 1600 BC. The 16th to 12th centuries BC saw a division of Greece into small kingdoms governed

Cycladic sculpture

The archipelago of the Cyclades, in the southern Aegean, was the home of a seafaring and farming civilization influential across the Aegean in the 3rd millennium BC. During the Bronze Age, the inhabitants became experts at carving stone, using supplies of marble from the island of Paros to produce female figurines. The provenance and meaning of these objects is uncertain, but it is thought that examples were removed from tombs and might have represented deities placed there to protect the dead. Remains of paint on the figures suggest that they would have been more ornate than they now appear. Cycladic art reached Crete in its earliest period of civilization, c.2600–2000 BC.

from fortified citadels and royal palaces. With the decline of Knossos from the 14th century BC, the major rival to the Mycenaeans vanished, and Mycenaean civilization reached its zenith, dominating the southern Aegean. As warriors and traders, their power spread to Crete around 1450 BC, and it is probable that the form of writing known as Linear B developed because of interaction between these two civilizations. In the 14th and 13th centuries BC, their decorated ceramic vessels were exported throughout the Aegean and eastern and central Mediterranean, in exchange for copper from Cyprus and Sardinia, ivory from Syria, and other luxury items from Egypt.

Some of the most telling remains of Mycenaean civilization have come from the tombs of the ruling classes. The items found in these burials, such as weaponry or remains of horses, indicate that they were a civilization concerned with military kudos. After a breakdown in lines of trade and communication, dynastic unrest emerged during the 13th century BC, and Mycenaean civilization fell into decline.

The Dark Ages

For four centuries after the collapse of the Mycenaean civilization, writing seems to have vanished, and the changing nature of archaeological remains indicates that there was some hiatus in the development of communication between communities. This era is frequently known as the Dark Ages. However, archaeological excavations, such as those at Lefkandhi on the island of Euboea, central Greece, show evidence of considerable opulence and trade with Cyprus and the Levant in the 10th and 9th centuries BC. One innovation in this period was the use of iron as the primary metal for weapons and tools, leading to the use of the term Iron Age for the period after 1125 BC

Homer and the Trojan War

The *Iliad* and *Odyssey* are two great epic poems composed probably at some time in between 750 and 700 BC, and written down by 500 BC at the very latest. The culmination of a tradition of oral poetry stretching back over centuries, they are thought of as the oldest surviving literature of Europe.

This object was branded the "Mask of Agamemnon" by Heinrich Schliemann upon its discovery in 1876. The mask was found covering the face of a corpse, probably that of a leader, perhaps a king or other prominent individual, and has recently been dated to the 16th century BC: few now believe, as Schliemann did, that this covered the face of a hero of the Trojan War.

The Origin of the *Iliad* and *Odyssey*

According to the Greeks of the Classical and Hellenistic periods, Homer was the blind composer of ten epic poems that told the whole story of the Trojan War, which was thought to have taken place about 1250 BC. Of these poems, only two survive, the *Iliad* and the *Odyssey*. Modern scholars, for the most part, accept the Greek idea that the poems were the work of a single author and that the poems survive in their largely original form with some minor alterations and additions. But it is also generally accepted that Homer, if he existed at all, drew on a long tradition of the compositions recited by oral singer-poets for the purposes of entertainment. A favourite theme among these singers was the Trojan War and the deeds of its heroes. It was perhaps Homer who, at some point between 750 and 700 BC drew these stories together, and, making use of set phrases and lines, was able to recite the poems from memory. The length of the poems (the *Iliad* is almost 16,000 lines long; the *Odyssey* 12,000) meant that the exact content of the poems could have been stabilized only when they were written down. The Greeks began to use alphabetical writing in c.750 BC, employing a system based on one used by the Phoenician traders of the Lebanon, so the poems may have been written down shortly after their oral composition.

The Trojan War

In the *Iliad*, the Trojan War is portrayed as the conflict between the Achaeans (Greeks) and the Trojans. The Trojans were the inhabitants of Troy, a stronghold commanding the Dardanelles. According to Homer, the cause of the conflict was the abduction of Helen, wife of King Menelaus of the southern Greek city of Sparta, by Paris, the son of king Priam of Troy. The abduction was an insult to Greek pride, and with the purpose of recovering Helen, a Greek force gathered under King Agamemnon of Mycenae, the brother of the Spartan king, and sailed to Asia Minor. They besieged Troy for ten years. In the final year of the siege, Achilles, the greatest of the Greek heroes, withdrew from the fighting after an argument

with the Greek commander about the division of booty. As his share of the booty Agamemnon had been given Chryseis, the daughter of the Trojan priest of Apollo, but was forced to return her. He therefore took Briseis, Achilles' share of the booty, and whom Achilles had come to love. The *Iliad* opens with the line: "Sing, goddess, the wrath of Achilles", and is an account of action from the last 40 days of the war. The Trojans got the better of the Greeks until Achilles returned, when he killed the Trojan commander Hector and routed the Trojans. According to Homer, Troy was obliterated and its women and children sold into slavery. The *Odyssey* is the story of the return home of another Greek heroes, Odysseus, a hero famous not for his great strength or bravery, but for his ability to deceive and trick.

The Greeks regarded the Trojan War as a pivotal moment in their history, and the poems as a significant cultural achievement, but whether or not the war really took place is unknown. By the middle of the 19th century, historians had dismissed the Trojan War as a myth. But in 1870, a German businessman, Heinrich Schliemann, using Homer as a guide, undertook an excavation in northeast Asia Minor and uncovered the remains of a huge Bronze Age settlement. He declared that the city of Troy had been discovered. Modern historians are sceptical about the idea that the archaeological record can prove that the Trojan War really took place, and recognize that it is important not to confuse the legends of the *Iliad* and the *Odyssey* with historical fact. However, it is possible that a series of upheavals at the end of the Mycenean civilization or during the Dark Age may have inspired the story of the Trojan War. Indeed, the poems can also tell us a great deal about what the communities of 8th-century Greece thought about the customs and lifestyle that existed in an age that preceded them, and can perhaps be identified as those of Dark Age Greece.

Epic and history

Some of the customs that existed in epic poetry would have been relatively familiar not only to Greeks of the 8th century but also those of the city-based civilizations of the Archaic and Classical periods. Under this heading we can note the presence of slavery, and the lack of moral qualms about enslaving an enemy captured in battle or booty raids. The polytheistic nature of Greek religion, according to which several gods and goddesses were worshipped under different cult epithets, is common both to the Homeric epics and historical Greece. The means of honouring the gods was the same too, characterized by sacrifice, prayer, hymns, music and ritual processions; indeed, lacking a set of doctrines or a holy book, many beliefs central to Greek religion were influenced by the content of the epics.

The most important human, cultural, and moral values known to Greeks throughout their history are prominent in the epics: honour and virtue or greatness, and the reward for achieving them, fame. But other aspects of the Homeric epics were far removed from the day-to-day experiences of Greeks in the Classical period. Whereas the emphasis in later Greek warfare was on fighting in massed ranks known as phalanxes, the epics concentrate on the part in battle palyed by superhuman heroes such as the Trojan Hector, who casually brandishes as a missile a boulder, "which two men, the best of the land, could not easily life from the ground".

The political organization of the Greeks of epic poetry might also be contrasted with the political organization of the city-states of Classical Greece. The communities of the *Iliad* and *Odyssey* were dominated by basileis (chiefs or princes). Although power was passed from father to son, in order to establish his authority a chief would have to prove his skill in spear-throwing, fighting at close quarters, and also have the capacity to persuade and arbitrate in disputes that took place between senates of elders and assemblies of the people.

The epic poems can be appreciated as both a historical source and as a cultural achievement, but must also be reckoned for their influence on the Classical and Hellenistic Greek readers who regarded in particular the *Iliad* as the text by which all achievements, political, moral, military and cultural, were to be measured.

This Athenian red figure vase, dating to the late 6th or early 5th century BC portrays a scene from Homer's Odyssey. *Odysseus, listens to the songs of the Sirens, sea creatures who lure sailors to their death by singing seductive songs. He resists them by binding himself to the mast of his ship, while his companions row with their ears stuffed with beeswax.*

The Formation of Greek Identity

The ancient Greeks thought of themselves not only as Greeks, but also as members of ethnic groups, and as citizens of the *polis*, or "city-state". These interests were reflected in the mythology of the migrations of these ethnic groups during the so-called "Dark Ages", while *polis*-identity was a constant factor in the Archaic, Classical, and to a lesser extent, Hellenistic periods.

Greeks and non-Greeks

Writing in the 5th century BC, the Greek historian Herodotus of Halicarnassus had an Athenian speaker define Greek identity as "a community of blood and language, temples and ritual, and common customs." Indeed, the Greeks defined themselves as Greeks by claiming shared ethnicity, language, and religious rituals. Access to the most important inter-state religious sanctuaries and temple complexes in mainland Greece were reserved for Greeks alone. The Greeks shared the Eastern Mediterranean with non-Greek peoples such as the Egyptians and Libyans of north Africa, the Carians, Phrygians and Lydians of Western

Asia Minor, and the Phoenicians who were traders from the area of modern Lebanon. It was peoples such as these, who, along with the Persians and Medes of central Asia, that the Greeks regarded as "barbarians". These "barbarians" were characterized by their indulgence in luxury, their effeminacy, their subordination to absolute rulers, characteristics which made them suited to slavery. This stereotyped idea developed in tandem with the concept of what it was to be Greek. From the 8th century onwards, the Greeks developed an alphabet of their own, a development that reflected the emergence of a Greek identity.

According to mythology, the Dorians invaded from north-west Greece and settled the areas of Greece inhabited by populations who used the Ionian dialect, many of whom may have migrated to western Asia Minor and formed the Ionian League, which met at the Panionium.

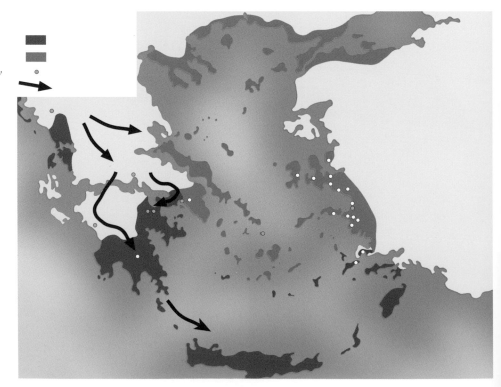

The city-states of Greece

At the same time, Greeks considered themselves to be citizens of one particular *polis*, or 'city-state': Athens, Sparta, Corinth are all examples. City-states were characterized by their territorial boundaries, political and military institutions, religious customs, walls and fortifications, coinage, laws, and a citizen body often restricted to those with two parents who were natives of that city. From the 8th century BC until the Macedonian invasion of the 4th century BC, the cities of Greece each took pride in their independence in domestic and foreign policy. It was as a result of this organization that, during the Classical period, the major city-states were almost constantly at war, as they vied for influence or domination over their neighbours.

Dorians and Ionians

The most socially and politically prominent ethnic identities in ancient Greece were those of the Dorians and the Ionians. Of the city-states in mainland Greece, the most famous to identify themselves as Ionian were Athens and the cities of Euboea. The most famous states to identify themselves as Dorian were Sparta and Corinth. The Greek-speaking cities of Asia Minor were divided between those who identified themselves as Ionians and Dorians. There existed Dorian and Ionian dialects of the Greek language, and the religious festivals of the two tribes were separate, but the division was most frequently enunciated in times of crisis. In the Classical and Hellenistic periods, when individual city-states faced a threat, they could appeal for help from other Greek cities on the grounds of these ethnic affinities. These appeals were based upon a series of legends that told of a migration of the tribe of Dorians into the Peloponnese. This so-called Dorian invasion of Greece was once believed to be the cause of the Mycenaean collapse, or the origin of historical Greece. More recently, given the lack of archaeological evidence, historians have cast doubt upon this.

The Dorian invasion

The myth of the invasion of the Dorians in the 11th century BC was closely connected to the stories surrounding the most popular and widely worshipped of the Greek heroes, Heracles, and his sons. According to this story, known as the "Return of the Heracleidai", the offspring of Heracles were expelled from the Peloponnese (the southernmost landmass of Greece) and fled north. Hyallus, the eldest son of Heracles, attempted to lead them back, but the effort ended in his death. Thereafter they remained in central Greece, until the Delphic oracle informed them that the time had come to return to their ancestral lands. Soon afterwards, they migrated south to the Peloponnese. The 5th-century BC historian Thucydides of Athens elaborated the myth, telling us that the Dorians took over the Peloponnese "together with the Heracleidai". Discounting the stories about Heracles, it is possible that the myth reflects migrations of peoples that took place in the Dark Ages. It is possible that a heavily depopulated Argolid was taken over by Dorians who came from northern Greece, perhaps Thessaly, around the start of the 11th century BC. The Dorians extended their conquests to populate a large part of the Peloponnese, and they reached as far as Crete and the south-west corner of Asia Minor, including Halicarnassus. In the Peloponnese, the residents of Messenia and Laconia were enslaved and, after the Dorian invasion, continued to inhabit their homeland as a subordinate race, known as the *helots* (serfs). Until 370 BC, they were subordinate to the citizens of Sparta, a city ruled by two kings from two separate families who both claimed to be the descendants of Heracles.

The Ionian migration

Some myths explain the presence of Ionian Greeks in western Asia Minor with reference to their expulsion from mainland Greece by the Dorians. One group of Ionians who were an exception to this rule were the Athenians, who appear to have remained steadfast in their homeland. Throughout their history, the Athenians took pride in being the indigenous inhabitants of their city, calling themselves *autochthons* – the "earth-born ones". In the 5th century BC, the Athenian playwright Euripides wrote a play called *Ion*, explaining the Athenian affinity with Ionian identity by reference to a myth about Ion, an ancient Athenian king. Ion, son of the god Apollo and the Athenian princess Creusa, became king of the Athenians at a time when the Athenians lacked a king of pure Athenian blood, and thus bequeathed Ionian identity to the Athenians.

This tiny cup was discovered in a grave in the Greek colony of Ischia, off the Bay of Naples. Dating to the late 8th century BC, it is one of the earliest examples of Greek writing. The graffito (writing) it bears has been translated as follows:"I am the cup of Nestor, good to drink from. Whoever drinks from be will be seized by fair-crowned Aphrodite" The cup jokes that it is the giant cup of Nestor mentioned in the Iliad.

Panhellenic Games

The Olympic Games in the ancient Greek world were given as much prominence in ancient times as their modern counterparts today. As an event reserved exclusively for Greek competitors, they became a gathering of great repute, sometimes taking on political overtones. Their foundation as a Panhellenic competition was highly significant in the formation of Greek identity as well as the city-state civilization of Greece.

Greek games

There were two kinds of Greek sporting contests in the Archaic and Classical periods: those contests held in city-states, which on the whole were restricted to contestants from an immediate locality; and those games at the Greek sanctuaries, which were open to contestants from any Greek city, and were known as Panhellenic Games. By the end of the 8th century BC, Panhellenic Games in honour of Zeus were being held every four years at Olympia during August and September, and attracted contestants and spectators from across Greece. In the first half of the 6th century BC, three other Panhellenic Games were founded: the Pythian Games at Delphi in honour of Apollo (which took place every four years), the Nemean Games in honour of Zeus, and the Isthmian Games in honour of Poseidon every two years. The games were so arranged that there would be at least one major games every year, and two in alternate years. The Olympic Games were recognized as the oldest and most prestigious event, and were celebrated until they were abolished as a Pagan rite by the Byzantine Emperor Theodosius I in 393 AD.

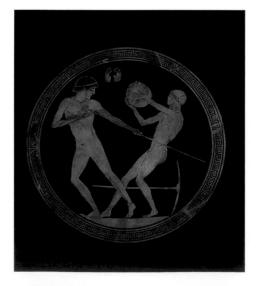

Many of the games practised in the modern Olympics have their roots in ancient games. This 5th-century cup depicts athletes with a javelin and discus.

The Olympic Games

Olympia was the site of the main sanctuary of Zeus in Greece, and was situated in the valley of the river Alpheus in Elis, in the western Peloponnese. It is likely that competitions for local contestants at Olympia began in the Dark Ages, perhaps around 1000 BC, and became Panhellenic in the 8th century, but the traditional interpretation was that they were founded in 776 BC by the hero Hercules in honour of his father Zeus.

For the first 50 years, the only athletic event was the stadion, a 210-foot sprint. The Olympic Games at their fullest development included a race in the full armour of a hoplite soldier, horse-racing, chariot races, the *pankration* (a combination of boxing and wrestling), javelin throwing, and the pentathlon (consisting of the javelin, discus, long-jump, running and wrestling). The long jump took place to a flute accompaniment, which helped the athletes to find rhythm while running.

The prize for victory was a wreath of wild olive, but the full consequence of victory was fame for the contestant and the glory that he bestowed upon on his city-state. On the return of an Olympic winner to his city, part of the city wall was demolished for his entry; in some cities, an Olympic winner was offered free meals for the rest of his life, or was rewarded with a lavish cash prize.

Greek politics and the Olympic Games

The fact that contestants from the Greek cities came together in these games meant that they were instrumental to the process by which artists and ideas moved quickly between city-states, and in turn to the development of a common Greek culture. Moreover, the games, by excluding non-Greek "barbarians" who, in the Greek imagination, were unable to compete physically with the Greeks, contributed to the Greek idea of themselves as civilized, heroic, and athletic. So important were the games to Greek identity that exclusion was an extreme insult. Control of the sanctuary at Olympia brought with it control of the games and the power to exclude contestants. This led to regular disputes between city-states about the control of the Sanctuary of Zeus at Olympia. In 668 BC, the inhabitants of a small town neighbouring Olympia, Pisa, asked the leader of the powerful city of Argos, to capture on their behalf the Sanctuary of Zeus from the city-state of Elis, 30 miles to the north-west of Olympia. Pheidon, the tyrant of Argos, with his army of well-trained hoplites (armed soldiers), marched across the Peloponnese, secured the sanctuary, and personally presided over the conduct of the Games. But Pisa's control of the Sanctuary was brief: by the next year Elis had regained control.

The Olympic Games were instrumental in highlighting or indeed perpetuating society's ranking at the time. Aristocrats and tyrants were heavily involved in the Games, and were able to establish or reinforce their positions through the acclaim of an Olympic victory. Cylon, an Olympic victor in the foot-race of 640 BC, attempted unsuccessfully to make himself tyrant in Athens in 632 BC. The Greek tyrants of early 5th-century Sicily, in a quest for fame, regularly commissioned the famous poet Pindar to celebrate their victories in Olympic chariot races. Even in democratic Athens of the late 5th century, where the assembly decided every aspect of the city's policy by popular decree, the power of Olympic victory held sway. The Athenian historian Thucydides records how, in an attempt to persuade the Athenians to adopt his policy, the wealthy politician Alcibiades boasted to the gathered audience that he had brought glory to the Athenians by entering seven chariots in the Olympic games and taking first, second and fourth prizes. The

acceptance of Roman competitors to the Isthmian Games in the early 220s BC and the other Panhellenic games shortly after was a reflection of their growing influence over Greek affairs.

The Olympics then and now

The Olympic games were revived in the 19th century and the first modern Olympics took place in Athens in 1896. The 2004 Athens Olympics tended to emphasise the similarities between the ancient and modern Olympics: the victors received wreaths of olive as well as metal medals. The political capital available to contestants and hosts of the Olympics is as alive today as it was in the ancient world. But it is worthwhile emphasising one vital difference between the modern and ancient Olympics: participation. The ancient Olympics were restricted to free male citizens who had never committed an act of murder or heresy. Women were not allowed to take part in the Games, though they were allowed to have an interest in them as owners of horses in the equestrian competitions. In fact, there was a separate festival in honour of Hera, the wife of Zeus, held every four years at the nearby Heraion, which included a foot race for unmarried girls. Finally, a modern myth needs to be exploded. It is commonly claimed that the ancient games were accompanied by a truce which put an end to fighting across the Greek world for the duration of the games. This was not the case: the ancient "Olympic truce" aimed only to prevent wars from disrupting the games or inhibiting the journey of those travelling to and from Olympia: the truce applied only in the immediate locality of the games.

The uncovering of the Stadium at Olympia is the result of excavations which have gone on since the 19th century. This view shows the race-track in the form that it took from the early 5th century BC onwards, with a length of 212.5 metres (619 ft) and a width of 28.5 metres (94 ft), with capacity on the surrounding banks for 45,000 spectators.

The Erechtheion was begun in 421
BC and finished in 407 BC. As the
most holy temple of the goddess
Athena on the Acropolis in Athens,
it housed a number of cults. The
temple's porch was supported by a
group of figures known as the
Caryatids. According to mythology,
they were named after the city of
Caryae in Laconia, which had
sided with the Persians in the
Persian Wars.

THE ARCHAIC AND CLASSICAL PERIODS: 750–336 BC

The Archaic and Classical periods constitute what is frequently described as the golden age of Greek city-state civilization. Thanks to the evidence of classical writers, inscriptions, and other archaeological material, we are able to build up a multifaceted picture of these city-states. The culture, history, and politics of the period have shaped and continue to influence our modern world.

"Archaic" and "Classical" are terms used to describe the periods of Greek history between c.750–479 BC and 478–336 BC, respectively. These dates correspond to political developments, but are useful in pinpointing cultural developments, too. The Archaic period reveals the origins of the most prominent form of Greek civilization in the Classical period, the city-state (*polis*). As states formed civic cults – religious practices – of their own, they began to build sanctuaries relating to these cults, both in their city centres and on the borders of their territories. The religious processions that connected these two types of sanctuary, in combination with natural boundaries, helped define the areas controlled by these city-states. The city-state consisted of a territory comprising a peripheral agricultural zone and a city centre with an area for holding civic activities such as trials and political meetings.

The city state was closely identified with its citizen community, which shared obligations, privileges of participation, and a form of government. The associations of the city-state formed the background for most of the political and cultural developments of these periods. During the Archaic period, Greek civilization reached towards Italy and Sicily for the purposes of trade and acquiring new resources, and settlements grew along the coast around the Black Sea. The Archaic period also saw the beginnings of democratic constitutions.

After the defeat of the Persians in the Persian Wars (490–479 BC), Greek identity became more consciously defined, as the differences between Greek and non-Greek ("barbarian") were emphasized. This period is frequently taken as the dividing point between the Archaic and Classical eras. The expulsion of the Persians from mainland Greece, the islands of the Aegean, and western Asia Minor opened the gates for Athenian expansionism. The Athenians formed the Delian Confederacy, which quickly developed into an empire. Throughout the 5th century BC, Athens became the focus of innovation in architecture, philosophy, and theatre. But this was also a time of conflict. The most important of these wars was the Peloponnesian War between Athens and its empire on one hand, and Sparta and its Peloponnesian and Dorian allies on the other.

After its defeat in the Peloponnesian War, Athens rebuilt its fortifications and political constitution, but was unable to re-create its empire. Over the course of the 4th century BC, as Athens, Thebes, and Sparta contended for ascendancy over Greece, the threat from the Macedonians in the north grew until their eventual defeat of the Athenians in 338 BC heralded the eclipse of "city-state" culture.

In the shadow of such events, the great historians Herodotus and Thucydides wrote their works, and Plato wrote the philosophical dialogues that raise questions still pertinent today. This period witnessed a golden age of the arts. Many plays of comic and tragic playwrights Aeschylus, Sophocles, Euripides, and Aristophanes survive to this day, and are still read and performed and interpreted by modern playwrights. Examples of sculpture and architecture still survive in the cities of the ancient world, while their legacy can be detected in modern architecture since the Renaissance.

Greeks on the Move

From the 8th century BC onwards, residents of the emerging city-states of mainland Greece formed communities in southern Italy and Sicily, and later, in the areas to the east of Greece. This process of colonization was linked to the development of trade across the Mediterranean and had an effect on the economic condition of the most important Greek cities.

The stories surrounding Solon the mythical lawgiver spread far beyond Greece. After passing his laws in 594 BC, he travelled to Egypt. One tradition preserved by Herodotus places him as a wise man journeying to the court of King Croesus of Lydia in Sardis. This 13th-century Turkish manuscript from Seljuk illustrates Solon in discussion with students of political science.

Greek mobility

As traders and seafarers, Greeks were always on the move, so it was likely there would be some dissemination of their communities and way of life away from mainland Greece. "Colonization" in Greek terms represents a different phenomenon from the modern European process of a state sending out a group of settlers. The Greek process of colonization was less formal and could take place whenever a group of Greeks, whether traders, soldiers, or reprobates from their home city, settled in a given area. For instance, at the end of the 6th century BC, the Athenian general Miltiades ruled an area of the Thracian Chersonese as a fiefdom with a group of Athenian settlers. This place gradually became known to the Athenians as a colony. Accordingly, in the 350s BC, when threatened by the growing power of Philip II of Macedon, the Athenian politician Demosthenes described the Chersonese as the property of Athens.

Cult ritual played an important part in the process of colonization. Colonists took with them fire from the sacred hearth of the mother city, in order to kindle a derivative flame in the colony. It was also usual for Greeks to consult the oracle at Delphi before beginning an expedition to found a colony, and a series of traditions relates the oracle's role in giving advice about the exact location and the population of such colonies. It is doubtful that these oracles were genuine: many of them were likely to have been inventions intended to justify the existence of the colony.

The colonists

The process of colonization frequently took place when disenfranchised groups of any one city-state moved to found a settlement or establish themselves in an existing settlement. Colonists could also be sent out by a community in order to rid itself of a surplus or undesirable population, as was the case with Taras in southern Italy at the end of the 8th century BC. A colonial settlement was founded there by a group of illegitimately born Spartans expelled from their home city after objecting to being deprived of their political rights. However, Sparta, the would-be mother city, retained close links with this settlement throughout the Classical period.

The colonies

Colonies arose most commonly at locations of commercial value. Thus the colonies at Taras and at the Chersonese were situated at points en route to supplies of grain. The same explanation could be applied to the Greek settlements on the Black Sea coast. In the second half of the 7th century BC, Milesians founded the first Greek settlements in this area. At the earliest point, these would have been trading settlements, with a population made up of both Greeks and indigenous residents.

Archaeological discoveries reveal the effects of colonization on both Greek and local culture, with Greek pottery discovered alongside local treasures in the graves of the local aristocracy. Greeks in the colonies did not forget their homeland, with settlers in Sicily continuing to make dedications at the pan-Hellenic sanctuary of Olympia. Greek gods such as Apollo were worshipped in the colonies alongside local deities.

The colonization of the Mediterranean coincided with and was related to the development of trading links between Greece and its neighbours. From the end of the 9th century BC, the Greeks supplanted the Phoenicians of the Levant as the most important trading partners of the Mediterranean, and trade became essential to the economies of both Archaic and Classical Greece.

The beginnings of trade

The Greeks of the Mycenaean civilizations were heavily reliant on trade as a means of survival. The most prominent group of merchants in the Mediterranean between the 11th and the 9th centuries BC was the Phoenicians. They built up trading stations and then colonies in Cyprus, western Sicily, Spain, and North Africa, and even reached as far as the tin mines of Cornwall in south-west England. Phoenician trade remained important throughout the Archaic period; however, from the 8th century BC,

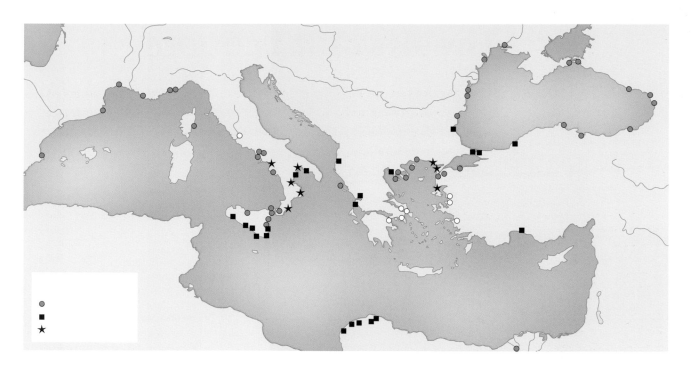

expansion ensured that the Greeks, and in particular the people of maritime cities such as Corinth and the cities of Euboea, gradually became the most important trading partners in the Mediterranean. Through trading contacts, the Greeks adapted the Phoenician alphabet for their own purposes, a development that contributed to the formation of the Greek alphabet as we know it today.

Trading posts

Trade and the search for valuable supplies of grain and metals were prime motivations of the Greek expansion from the 8th century BC onwards, and Greek colonies frequently served as trading posts (*emporia*). The first Greek colony in the West was on the Island of Pithekoussai off Campania. The discovery of Euboean pottery from around 770 BC, together with the discovery of iron-smelting works, suggests that the Greeks may have settled this area with the aim of gaining access to iron, which could be worked into weapons and armour. The Euboeans seem to have established trading posts at several other places, such as Al Mina ("The Port") on the Orontes Delta in northern Syria and Naukratis on the Nile Delta.

These societies differed from typical colonies in that they were entirely dedicated to the commercial exchange of goods. The Greeks brought materials to Al Mina for transfer deeper into Asia Minor, and the mouth of the Orontes river acted as the outlet for goods from inland Asia Minor, which were then traded around the Mediterranean or brought back to mainland Greece.

Trade and agricultural reform

In Athens, the emergence of the state as a regulator of economic transactions is attested to by the legislation of Solon, an Athenian politician and poet. In around 594 BC, Solon introduced a series of restrictions on commercial activity. These included measures affecting the export of goods, decreeing, for instance, that of all produce, olive oil was the only product allowed to be exported. Solon seems also to have introduced legislation that both unified and divided the citizen-body of Athens. One of his acts was to abolish the group of sharecroppers known as the *hektemoroi*, men who rented land on the basis of returning one-sixth of its produce to the owner, possibly in return for protection by the powerful.

Solon also abolished the custom of debt bondage, according to which citizens could fall into slavery if unable to pay debts. He also, however, introduced a four-stage class system that grouped men according to the amount of grain they produced each year. As political participation was based upon these class groups, political power thus became based on agricultural capacity.

In this way, Solon ensured that agricultural activity retained inextricable links with the class-system. This system reflected and perpetuated the idea that commercial activity was unsuitable for citizens. The stereotypical merchant of ancient Greece was a *metic*, a resident alien of a city who was liable to pay a tax in return for the privilege of residency. The Athenians preferred to think of themselves as farmers, rather than traders.

The locations of the Greek colonies founded across the Mediterranean in the Archaic period indicate the importance of the sea in the process of colonization. Most colonies were located on sea or trade routes and at places acting as ports.

The Ancient Economy

As trade developed in the Mediterranean over the 8th and 7th centuries BC, metal was introduced as a medium for exchange that would provide an accurate measure of value and a convenient means of storing wealth. Slavery was important in Mediterranean trade, and it played a significant role in the economies of ancient cities.

The origins of coinage

Archaeological and literary evidence indicates that coins were first utilized in western Anatolia. Measures of value pre-dated the existence of coinage: Homeric legends describe the use of cattle, slaves, and weapons as units of value. Over time, however, the Greeks, following the lead of the Egyptians and Mesopotamians, began to use metal as their predominant means of exchange. Initially, cumbersome iron spits were used as a means of transaction, and although the Spartans of the Peloponnese reputedly continued to use spits throughout the Classical period, the rest of the Greek world made use of coins.

In around 600 BC, coins came into use as a standard measure in western Anatolia, at the point where Greek cities of the Aegean coast and the inhabitants of the Lydian kingdoms of the interior of Asia Minor came into contact with each other. Electrum was used for this earliest coinage, an alloy of gold and silver that occurs naturally in tributaries of the river Hermus to the west of the Lydian capital, Sardis. Electrum was soon replaced by coins of either silver or gold. The introduction of coins of tiny fractional value suggests that states began to recognize the value of coinage not only for inter-community trade, but also for small transactions such as the payment of mercenary soldiers.

The characteristics of coinage

The earliest coins consisted of lumps of standard weight, marked with a square punch-mark on the

Our sources do not represent fully the kind of hardships that slaves or other manual labour who worked at mines must have undergone. On the contrary, this small clay plaque from Corinth illustrates a group of potters digging for clay while refreshment is lowered into the pit.

reverse. This form derived from the way the coins were minted. Molten metal was poured into moulds to make blank discs; the discs were then placed on an anvil and struck with a die made from either toughened bronze or iron. As time went on, different states introduced characteristic markings on the front (obverse) of the coin, using motifs associated with their city. The Phocaians of Asia Minor used a seal (*phoke* in Greek), punning on the name of the city. The most famous Athenian coins depicted a helmeted head of Athena on the obverse, with an owl on the reverse together with the abbreviated name of the city. In later times, coins could be used as an expression of political events. Coins of the 340s BC from Taras show a boy raising his arms in appeal to a seated god identified by his trident as the sea god Poseidon; Poseidon inclines his head in sympathy. This image represented the appeal of the Tarantines, symbolized by the child, to the Peloponnesians, represented by Poseidon, for aid against enemy cities in Italy.

Coinage and politics

The imposition of coinage also became a means of imperialism. In the 420s BC, the Athenians issued a decree enforcing Athenian silver coins, weights, and measures upon the subject states of their empire. While this decree signified the political and economic dominance of the Athenians, it is unlikely that they were able to prevent the allied states from issuing their own coins; indeed, the minting of electrum coins was not banned. The Athenians took a great deal of pride in their silver coinage, linking its authenticity to their production of silver in Attica and, on a more abstract level, to the survival of their constitution. After a period of crisis at the end of the 5th century BC, when bronze and gold issues were used, the Athenians returned to silver coinage in the 4th century and passed a law outlining procedures for the testing of the currency.

The overseas slave trade

Two types of slave population were common in Archaic and Classical Greece. Indigenous slave populations, whose native land was under a state of occupation, existed in the Peloponnese. However, the majority of slaves in the Greek world were victims of war or civil strife, or had been sold on by merchants as part of a trade in slaves.

Slave-holding formed an important part of Greek society from the earliest times: the Linear B tablets from the Mycenaean palaces of the 13th to 12th centuries BC mention the use of slave labour within the kingdoms. The Homeric poems refer to male herdsmen and female domestic slaves, usually owned by the aristocracy. But it was only after the emergence

of the city-state community that the division between citizen and slave became clearly defined. In the Archaic and Classical periods, slaves were more likely to be non-Greeks, and could take the name of their homelands. Hence "Carion" was a name for a slave of Carian origin. However, in the 5th and 4th centuries BC, the idea that non-Greeks were naturally subservient to Greeks exaggerated the divide between citizen and slave.

Enslavement

After Solon's reforms in Athens around 594 BC, citizens could no longer be sold into slavery in order to repay their debts, but there were other ways in which enslavement might take place. The first of these was through war: when the city of Melos was destroyed in the Peloponnesian War, its male inhabitants were killed and its women and children sold into slavery. Men captured by pirates were often enslaved. Another significant means of acquiring slaves was through the slave trade, either by direct contact with eastern neighbours whose surplus populations were often sold, or through unregulated and commercial activity. The historian Herodotus tells us the story of a certain Panionus of Chios, who made his living by procuring beautiful boys, castrating them, and taking them to Sardis and Ephesus, where he sold them at a high price. Panionus' activity was abruptly halted, however, when one of his eunuchs took revenge by forcing him to carry out castration on his own sons.

The uses of slaves

From the existing evidence, it is hard to tell whether slaves were an important source of agricultural labour. It is probable that hired labourers were used alongside slaves at the times of year that demanded the most intensive farm work. Slaves were just as likely to be employed in the cities as workers in the market place, while the city of Athens itself employed a group of Scythian archers who acted as a sort of police force. Probably the worst life for a slave was that of a labourer in the mines. In the late 5th century BC, it is known that some 20,000 slaves were employed in the Laurium silver mines in Attica, and these slaves escaped from the mines during the Spartan occupation of Decelea. Because of the racial mixture of much of the slave population of Greece, linguistic barriers hindered communication between slaves and consequently revolts were rare. However, this is not the case with the indigenous population of *helots* (serfs) in Lacedaimonia, whose rebellious activities were a constant worry for their Spartan rulers.

The silver didrachm *of the 4th century BC pictured here was worth 2* drachmai, *an amount that an architect was paid in Athens in the 330s BC for one day's work. A manual labourer may have earned just one quarter of the amount.*

Spartan Politics and Society

Greek politics in the period before the 7th century BC are thought to have been dominated by groups of nobles who obtained their positions through inheritance. From the 6th century BC, power-seeking individuals, known as tyrants, came to prominence. In Sparta, however, a unique political and social system appears to have emerged, in which the Spartans took great pride as a source of identity and stability.

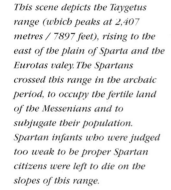

This scene depicts the Taygetus range (which peaks at 2,407 metres / 7897 feet), rising to the east of the plain of Sparta and the Eurotas valey. The Spartans crossed this range in the archaic period, to occupy the fertile land of the Messenians and to subjugate their population. Spartan infants who were judged too weak to be proper Spartan citizens were left to die on the slopes of this range.

Greek Tyranny

Modern historians have often approached the history of Greek politics as the history of progress from monarchy (the rule of a king), through aristocracy (the rule of the nobility) and tyranny (the rule of a usurper) to democracy (rule of the people). The development of Greek politics is now recognized as much less linear. While the political structures of Mycenaean Greece were in all likelihood dominated by a single ruler, the king or *wanax*, the true political structure of Greece in the period from the 12th to the 7th centuries BC is largely unknown. Tyrannies, meanwhile, are to be found in all periods of Greek history, but were perhaps most widespread in mainland Greece in the late 7th and 6th century BC.

In the southern Greek city of Argos in the early 7th century BC, the powers of the king (*basileus*) were severely restricted by the law. However, some time between 680 and 660 BC, King Pheidon appears to have used the Argive army to make himself an abso-

lute ruler. The city of Corinth in the middle of the 7th century BC was said to have been dominated by the Bakchiadai family for nearly 200 years. Their rule had become corrupt and harsh, and they were overthrown by Kypselos, a Bakchiad who was out of favour with the aristocracy. Kypselos won popularity by claiming to champion the popular interest. He made himself tyrant, and ruled for thirty years before passing power to his son Periander. Accounts of Periander portray him as a cruel tyrant who ruled by force and even murdered his own wife. The Athenians, so often associated with democracy, endured a period of tyranny, under the Pisistratid family from 546 through to 510 BC. For most of this period, the Pisistratids' rule was relatively lenient. Pisistratus, tyrant of Athens 546 to 527 BC, initiated a programme of public building, subsidized festivals and used cult practice to articulate the unity of Athens. He is said to have given loans to poor farmers and introduced travelling judges to the countryside around Athens. Only after the assassination of Hipparchus (Pisistratus' son and successor) in 514 BC did Pisistratid rule, under Hipparchus' brother Hippias, become harsh. The Pisistratids were overthrown by the Spartans, inspired by a command from the oracle at the sanctuary at Delphi.

Spartan politics

The Spartans seem to have avoided tyranny in the 7th and 6th centuries BC, and even claimed to have sanctioned the overthrow of tyranny across the Greek world in this period. However, our sources for this period of Spartan politics were written several hundred years later, from the 4th century BC onwards. The Spartans of the 5th and 4th centuries BC prided themselves on the stability and conservativism of their constitution, and so claimed continuity of its structures and ideologies from the time of their law-maker, Lycurgus. According to the Spartans, Lycurgus, whose life is dated alternately to the 8th and 7th centuries BC, brought an oracle from Delphi which revealed to him a set of directives for arranging their way of life and constitution.

The Spartan constitution divided power between two kings, a board of elders, and the people. The kings were from two families who, according to legend, derived from the sons of Heracles. The senior house, the Agiads, descended from the older son; the junior house, the Eurypontids, from the younger. The two kings were members of a senate, along with 28 elders, which decided the issues to be discussed by a popular assembly. All male citizens attended the assembly, which held the power to make decisions, although these could in practice be blocked by the kings and high-ranking officials (known as *ephors*). This form of government constituted a unique mix of democracy, monarchy and aristocracy. The Spartans' attachment to tradition prevented the evolution of their constitution, and from the end of the Archaic period, Sparta became an increasingly introspective society.

Spartan society

Sparta was famous not just for its political constitution, but for its way of life. The shape of Spartan society was directed by the existence of *helots*, or serfs. These were Messenians, enslaved by Spartans in the First and Second Messenian wars of the 8th and 7th centuries BC; some of them claimed to be the descendants of the inhabitants of Messenia and Laconia before the Dorian invasion. While the *helots* worked the land and provided food for their Spartan masters, the Spartan male citizens, known as the "equals", concentrated on developing military discipline within their own ranks. Spartan children embarked on a rigorous training programme, and, until the age of 30, a citizen lived in a military training camp. The aim of the system was to produce a body of citizens who would be able both to police the behaviour of the helots, and form the greatest fighting force in the Greek world.

This military ethos certainly contributed to Sparta becoming the most important city in Greece over the course of the 6th century BC, and a rival to Athens in the 5th century BC. This was reinforced by her dominance of the Peloponnesian League, an alliance of city-states that was a tool for Spartan influence over her neighbours. But her refusal to change or reform the qualifications for citizenship at Sparta contributed to the crisis of the Spartan citizen body. When Sparta was defeated by Thebes in 371 BC, the number of Spartan citizens had dwindled to 1500, from a figure of 8000 in 480 BC.

This oil on canvass, by Hilaire-Germaine-Edgar Degas (1834–1917), is an interpretation of the accounts that ancient sources give us of stout Spartan women. Here they are shown urging the Spartan men to fight. Spartans were said to exercise naked. Mount Taygetus looms in the background.

Democracy Established

Important political innovations took place in a number of Greek states in the 6th and 5th centuries BC. It was in Athens, however, that democracy reached its fullest stage of development, moving from the rule of the popular assembly in the 5th century BC to the rule of law and sovereignty of the lawcourts in the 4th century BC.

Ancient and modern democracy

Although modern democracy developed independently of the classical tradition, both forms of democracy as a political system and ideology lay emphasis on the values of liberty and equality. However, the two have different modes of participation. Ancient democracy placed stress upon the direct participation of a limited group of citizens, through the attendance of popular assemblies. Modern democracies, for the most part, feature a larger citizen body, with government functioning according to the legislation of a parliament representative of the people.

Democracy in Athens from the time of Solon

While the Spartan constitution appears to have been anchored in tradition, in Athens democracy found fertile ground and developed extensively between the sixth and fourth centuries BC. In the 7th century BC, Athens appears to have been ruled by a group of aristocrats, the *Eupatridai*, literally, "the well-fathered ones". Only gradually was their domination of Athenian politics reduced, and it never entirely vanished. The Athenians claimed that their earliest constitution was the work of the lawgiver Drakon in 620 BC. According to his lawcode, even the most minor offences were to be punished by the death penalty, and political activity was restricted to those who could afford to buy their own armour and spear. The most important part of the constitution was the aristocratic council of the Areopagus, a board of elders who met on the Areopagus hill in Athens, who possessed the power to guard and protect the laws of Athens.

The development of Athenian democracy begins with the reforms of Solon in 594 BC. What remains of Solon's poetry indicates that he took pride in having reduced social disorder in Athens by introducing laws for the benefit of both the rich and poor. It is vital to acknowledge that his reforms were instrumental in the development of an idea of citizenship. He introduced a four-stage citizen class system. Citizens qualified as such by virtue of birth and landownership. All citizens were allowed to take part in the popular assembly. The archonship, at that time the most important magistracy, was restricted to the two top classes. Solon also introduced a Council of 400, a senate that prepared the agenda for discussions which were to take place in the assembly. In this way, Solon located the focus of the political system upon the assembly and shifted the basis of qualification for office away from aristocratic lineage and towards agricultural production.

Kleisthenes' reforms

Many aristocratic aspects of Athenian politics were untouched by Solon's legislation. Periods of tyranny and civil war continued until 507 BC, when Kleisthenes mobilized popular support, seized power, and introduced a further series of democratic reforms. Kleisthenes was an Athenian politician from

Pericles, the Athenian statesman, was said by the biographer Plutarch to possess almost perfect physical features, "with the exception of his head, which was rather long and out of proportion. For this reason almost all portraits show him wearing a helmet." The comic poets of Athens could not resist nicknaming him "pointy-head".

the noble Alcmaeonid family. His main action was to reorganize the body of citizens. Formerly, the Athenian citizen body had been divided upon the basis of four tribes native to the Ionians, with 100 representatives drawn from each tribe to constitute the Council of 400 introduced by Solon. But Kleisthenes deprived the Ionian division of political significance and introduced instead 10 new tribes, of which each citizen was a member. It is possible that this reform aimed to disperse former spheres of aristocratic influence, although Kleisthenes' detractors argued that he aimed to augment the importance of his own Alcmaeonid clan through this new arrangement. Each citizen was also a member of one of the 140 *demes*, or villages, of Attica. Citizens were allocated to *demes* according to where they lived, and from 507 BC onwards their descendants retained identification with these *demes*. Many *demes* are known to have had an administration of their own: in this way, the Athenian democracy functioned on both city-state and local levels.

Ostracism

Kleisthenes is also believed to have introduced the institution of ostracism, first used in 487 BC. Each year, about halfway through the year, the question of the banishment of one citizen was raised in the assembly. If it were agreed that this should take place, an ostracism was held. Each citizen who wished to vote submitted to the assembly a piece of broken pottery (an *ostrakon*) inscribed with the name of the man he wanted banished. Providing that a total of 6000 votes were cast, the man whose name appeared on the largest number was banished for 10 years. This institution was initially intended as a safeguard against any man attempting to make himself tyrant; however, in practice, the institution was used as a means for powerful citizens to banish rivals. Evidence indicates that citizens were ostracized on the grounds of having collaborated with the Persians, religious offences, or, in one case, incestuous relations with his sister. The discovery of 190 ostraka dumped in a well, with the name of a prominent early 5th-century politician inscribed by only 14 different hands, has led to the theory that these ostraka had been prepared for circulation by conspiring opponents.

Athenian democracy after Kleisthenes

Democracy was far from secure in Athens after Kleisthenes. After his reforms, politics became divided upon ideological grounds, with one group of politicians appealing to popular support and offering further political reforms, and the other party appealing to the former aristocrats. While the leader of the aristocrats, Kimon, was on campaign outside Athens

The Athenian assembly

The regular Athenian assembly in the Classical period took place on the Pnyx hill. Excavation of the site has revealed three stages in its development. Assemblies, perhaps from the time of Kleisthenes, made use of the natural contours of the hill, with the speaker addressing the crowd from the bottom of a semicircular auditorium. The second stage of development coincided with the introduction of payment for attending the assembly at the beginning of the 4th century BC, and included filling in the surrounding land to flatten the natural slope of the hill. The orientation of the speaker's rostrum (bema) was reversed to face inland, while the people faced the sea. In the third stage in its development, in the 340s BC, the capacity was enlarged from 6500 to 13,800.

in 464 BC, the democrats seized the initiative. Under the leadership of Ephialtes, they curtailed the political powers of the board of former archons who met upon the hill of the Areopagus and who were drawn exclusively from the top two Solonic classes. Once this conservative body was rendered powerless (it now served only as a court to try cases of homicide), the floodgates were opened for more reforms, introduced during the period of Pericles' supremacy. The archonship was now opened up to the third class of citizens, while the introduction of payment for service on the council, the fulfilment of a magistracy, or jury service, meant that the poorer citizens of Attica were able to take a much more active role in democracy.

The development of Athenian democracy does not stop there. In the 5th century BC, sovereignty was possessed by the assembly. Democracy in the 4th century BC assumed a different shape, transferring sovereignty to the decisions of the lawcourts and written law. It is 5th-century BC democracy, however, that has most frequently captured the imagination of modern writers, as its development coincides with the most striking developments in other aspects of Greek civilization, such as architecture and drama.

Greek Warfare

While Sparta was the military city-state par excellence, every Greek city-state was to a large degree geared towards fighting in defence of its territory. Continual readiness for warfare influenced Greek concepts of citizenship, and the physical attributes of the *polis*. The typical mode of Greek warfare was the hoplite phalanx, but in the 5th century BC, battles at sea were regularly decisive factors in inter-state warfare.

This archaic black-figure case is decorated with a frieze illustrating hoplites fighting out of formation. The Corinthian helmet, with its crest, can be seen clearly, as can the shield, which the hoplite carried by passing his wrist through a central strap and clasping a handle at the edge of the shield.

Hoplite warfare

The most famous passages of Homer's *Iliad* describe combat between individual fighters or heroes, with men of superior social and physical prowess taking centre stage. But several times in the *Iliad*, we see heroes driven back by stones, spears and arrows thrown by unnamed fighters. The emphasis in the Archaic and Classical Greek warfare, however, was not on individual fighters, but the efforts of heavy infantry, who fought in massed ranks known as the phalanx. Hoplite warfare emerged in the 7th century BC as a means of defending agricultural resources, in particular fertile plains that were disputed by Greek city states.

The standard hoplite soldier was a citizen of at least moderate wealth, who could afford the requisite expensive equipment. Vital was the circular shield, 76 centimetres (30 in) in diameter, of wood or stiffened leather, its outer shell covered with bronze. Vital also was a thrusting-spear of 2.4–3 metres (8–10 ft) in length; a short sword was common but less important. The hoplite wore heavy bronze armour

consisting of a helmet, corslet, greaves and sometimes arm-guards. Hoplites typically went into battle in a closely arranged phalanx, usually eight or more deep. The phalanx advanced to face the enemy with the front ranks thrusting their spears at the enemy. The phalanx had a tendency to drift to the right as it moved forward, as each man sought protection from the shield held on his neighbour's left arm. Accordingly, when the opposing lines clashed, this was not usually head on, and the ranks soon broke. Despite the impediment of fighting with such heavy armour in the Mediterranean heat and the unwieldiness of the phalanx, Greek hoplites were responsible for the victories over the Persians at the plain of Marathon (490 BC) and at Plataea (479 BC).

Hoplite warfare was, in the Classical period, considered to be the kind of warfare most in tune with the ideologies of the city-state. It was fought by citizens on behalf of their city-state and was designed to defend or extend the agricultural land that those soldiers farmed. In Athens and other Greek city-states, those who had died in battle were rewarded with burial in a public tomb, and their names were inscribed on slabs of marble, some of which survive to this day. By the mid 5th century, Athenians held a public funeral for those who had died in that year's campaigns, and a speech praising the virtues of the city would be given by an eminent politician.

Training for military duties was not restricted to Sparta. The Athenians during the second half of the 4th century formalized a youth cadet scheme, or "ephebic" institution according to which, every year, a proportion of citizens who had reached the age of 18 were recruited. This training lasted for two years, and included training in barracks, training in handling weapons and guard duty on the frontiers of the city-state's territory.

While the *ephebes* went on to become hoplites, it is notable that in the 5th century BC, the Athenians and other city-states made use of a range of fighting methods. Light-armed troops were used as skirmishers, and their greater mobility must have made them particularly useful. The Athenian state also established a cavalry force, which, during the Peloponnesian War was employed in resisting hostile intruders intent on ruining crops, and to launch raids into enemy territory. But over the course of the 5th century BC, the Athenians became increasingly reliant on warfare at sea. After the discovery in the 480s of a rich vein of silver in the mines of Laurium within the territory of the city-state, the most persuasive Athenian politician of the day, Themistocles, persuaded the Athenians to spend the proceeds of this discovery on the construction of a fleet. This force was instrumental in the Greek victory in the Persian wars, and was also vital to Athenian tactics at the start of the Peloponnesian war.

The most important vessel for naval warfare in the Athenian navy was the trireme. Essentially, it was a slender 36.5 metres by 4.5 metres (120 ft by 15 ft) rowing ship, with a powerful bronze ram at its prow. Each was powered by 170 oarsmen who were arranged in three tiers, one on top of another. Poorer citizens, hired mercenaries and in times of crisis, slaves, were paid a small wage for this service. The ships would also have been manned by marines and archers, and a helmsman. The Athenians were the most important seafaring state of the 5th century BC, and sent out crews to practice rowing for months at a time. They perfected the skill of manoeuvring at speed to attack the vulnerable flanks of enemy warships. They developed a great harbour complex at Piraeus, to the south of the city of Athens. This port,

as the home of many of the poorer inhabitants of Athens, acquired a reputation as the heartland of Athenian democracy. It was connected to the city of Athens by a road protected by the Long Walls, which were to become essential to Athenian strategy at the outbreak of the Peloponnesian War.

Sea power and empire

Naval warfare was an expensive business. The Athenian state in the 5th and 4th centuries BC provided the ship, its rigging and oars, but relied on its richest citizens to command the ships and to bear the costs of maintenance, repair, as well as pay, sustenance and rewards for the crew. In the 5th century, Athens also supported her navy with contributions from her allies, and later her imperial states. In the aftermath of the Persian wars, the Athenians formed a league of allies known as the Delian Confederacy, with the ostensible purpose of ravaging the territory of the Persian king. At the foundation of the league in 478 BC, allies were given the choice of contributing a sum of money to the treasury of the league, or contributing in the form of triremes. But, after allied states had become unwilling to sustain the Delian Confederacy from 460 onwards, the Athenians used the strength of their navy to force allied states back into line, to impose garrisons, settlers and even forms of government on her subjects, and to extract a tribute from each city-state. For the Athenians in the 5th century, sea power and empire were intrinsically connected.

This marble relief depicts the top deck of rowers on a trireme taking the strain while pulling back their oars. It was found near the Erechtheion, the holiest temple on the Athenian Akropolis, and may have been a dedication, a gift to the gods, made by a rower or more likely, the commander of a trireme. As no wrecks of ancient ships have been discovered, this object has provided vital evidence in the reconstruction of the classical Athenian warship.

Warfare in the 5th Century BC

War raged continuously in Greece throughout the 5th century BC. Many of these wars were minor border disputes, but two conflicts stand out in importance. The Greek victory in the Persian Wars led to the crystallization of Greek identity, and was the origin of the Athenian imperial dominance of the Aegean Sea in the 5th century BC. The Peloponnesian War eventually curtailed the domination of the Athenian Empire.

The origins of the Persian Wars

The Ionian Greeks inhabited western Asia Minor, and had been subject to Persian rule since 546/5 BC. Further Persian expansion in the Black Sea area and Egypt led to increased taxation and conscription. Resenting this, in 499 BC, the Greek cities followed the Ionian revolt of the Milesian Aristagoras, deposing Persian governors and appealing to the Greeks of Europe for aid. Only the Athenians and Euboeans responded positively, sending an expedition that proceeded as far as Sardis, the headquarters of the Persian governorship, which they razed in 498 BC. The burning of the temple of Cybele inspired the Persian king Darius to swear revenge.

In 1955, the king of Greece uncovered a monument to Leonidas and the Three Hundred, who in 480 BC defended the pass of Thermopylae against the Persian invaders. This was located between the mountains and the sea, giving access to central Greece. The Persians, vastly superior in numbers, overcame the Greeks only after one Greek informed the Persians of an alternative route.

Having subjugated the Ionian Revolt in 494 BC, the Persians launched an attack on Greece in 490 BC. Having subdued many of the islands in the Aegean and forced the island of Euboea into surrender through a combination of force and treachery, the Persians landed at Marathon, on the north-east coast of Attica. But before they could advance to Athens, 10,000 Athenians and their Plataean allies advanced against the 20,000-strong Persian force. After widening their line of attack, the Greeks ran towards the firing bows of the Persians. After success on their strong wings, the Greeks turned inwards to encircle the victorious Persian troops at the centre. The Persians fled to their ships, pursued by the Greeks.

Despite this defeat, the Persians were not deterred. The next Persian attempt of 480 BC was on a much bigger scale, led by King Xerxes, son of Darius. Xerxes advanced across to Europe with some 100,000 men and up to 1200 triremes. Early Greek attempts at resistance were unsuccessful: the attempt to hold the pass between the mountains and the sea at Thermopylae in central Greece ended in the heroic death of the Spartan king Leonidas. The Athenian commander Themistocles, interpreting the cryptic advice of the Delphic oracle to rely on "wooden walls" as a reference to their wooden ships, commanded the Athenians to evacuate the city and fight the Persians at sea. After the defeat of the Persian fleet at the battle of Salamis to the south of Attica, and the defeat of the Persian infantry and cavalry at Plataea, the Persians began to retreat.

The aftermath of the Greek victory

After the battle of Plataea, the Spartans assisted the revolts against Persian rule of Chios and Samos, and helped defeat the Persian fleet off Cape Mycale in 479 BC. The Ionian Greeks of the west coast of Asia Minor appealed to the Spartans, then Athenians to liberate them from Persian rule. In a repetition of the events of 499 BC, only the Athenians responded positively. This response contributed to the emergence of the so-called Delian Confederacy, a league of states led by Athens. This alliance, initially consisting of Greek cities on the west coast of Asia Minor and the islands of the Aegean Sea, was based at the religiously significant island of Delos. The pretext of the organization was to take revenge upon the Persian king in return for wrongs suffered by the Greeks. The Athenians went on to liberate cities of Asia Minor from Persian rule until the mid-460s BC. At some point in the middle of the 5th century BC, a peace agreement between the Persians and Greeks was made, but the rivalry for control of the Greek cities of Asia Minor was revived at the start of the 4th century BC. The continuing presence of the Persian threat served as a reminder to Greeks that their strength lay in pan-Hellenic unity.

The Peloponnesian War

The Peloponnesian War is the name given to a series of struggles between Athens and its allies on the one hand and Sparta and its allies of the Peloponnesian League on the other, in the period from 431 to 405 BC. The war saw some innovation in the techniques of warfare, but also coincided with a golden age of comedy and tragedy in Athens.

Rivalry between Athens and Sparta had been growing since the formation of the Delian Confederacy by Athens and her allies. Athenian interventionism in the affairs of the Greek states is in striking contrast to Spartan introspection in the aftermath of the Persian Wars. From the period up to around 460 BC, the Spartans suffered trouble at home from their servile population, the *helots*, and disunity in their own organization of allies, the Peloponnesian League.

The historian Thucydides claims that the truest explanation for the outbreak of the Peloponnesian War was the Spartan fear of the growth of Athenian power. Athens' control of its allies grew between the end of the 460s BC and the outbreak of the Peloponnesian War. The treasury of the Delian confederacy was transferred from Delos to Athens in 454 BC, and by the start of the war its allies had become imperial subjects paying contributions to Athens. Thucydides describes complaints from the people of Aegina, Corinth, Megara, and Potidaea about Athenian intervention in their political affairs, adding further possible reasons for the outbreak of war.

The course of the war

At the outbreak of the war, when it became clear that the Spartans were about to invade Attic territory, Pericles advised the Athenians to withdraw within the Long Walls connecting the city to its port at Piraeus.

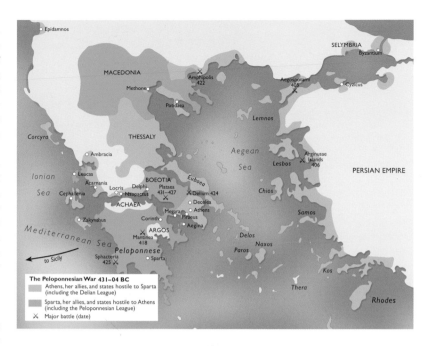

The Peloponnesian War 431–04 BC
- Athens, her allies, and states hostile to Sparta (including the Delian League)
- Sparta, her allies, and states hostile to Athens (including the Peloponnesian League)
- ✗ Major battle (date)

The Athenians relied on their fleet of at least 200 triremes to secure the importation of grain to the city. Partly as a consequence of the crowded conditions in the centre of Athens, a great plague broke out, which, at its peak in 430 BC, damaged support for Pericles' policy. Spartan attempts to invade Attica continued for the first five years of the war, until the Athenians captured some Spartan hostages on the island of Sphacteria in 425 BC.

After his death in 429 BC, Pericles' successors followed a more offensive war policy. However, after the death of the most belligerent leaders on both sides, Cleon the Athenian and Brasidas the Spartan, the Peace of Nicias was agreed in 421 BC. The Athenians became involved in hostilities again after launching the overambitious Sicilian expedition in 415 BC. This ended in failure, following the Spartan response to requests for aid from their Dorian kinsmen in Sicily. Between 413 and 404 BC, the Spartans placed a garrison within Attica at Decelea, making much of the Attic farmland inaccessible to the Athenians. The focus then shifted to strategic points on the Athenian grain-supply route from the Black Sea. The Peloponnesians built a fleet that blockaded Athens and caused its surrender after the battle of Aegospotami in 405 BC.

Thucydides' account of the Peloponnesian War appears at first glance to be a military narrative of the war, but a closer reading reveals many socio-political factors which were important in fifth-century Greece. Control of agricultural land and sea power; leadership, military tactics, and finances; ambition and the desire for revenge all were essential to the course of events during the war.

The Athenian policy in the Peloponnesian War was initially defensive, but also included a biannual invasion of the territory of Megara and raids on the Peloponnesian coast. The focus at the end of the war shifted towards the east, as the Peloponnesians attempted to cut off the grain supply of the Athenians, succeeding in their goal with their final victory at Aegospotami.

Greek Poetry

Greek poetry was used in several contexts: on grave monuments, as prize inscriptions on vases, on dedications to the gods, and on victory commemorations. Poetry also played a didactic role in recording laws or even delineating ethics. The plays of the Classical period were written in verse and provided a publicly accessible medium for poetry.

This Roman portrait of Euripides may have derived from a Greek version. Around 330 BC, the Athenian orator and statesman Lycurgus had statues of the three famous poets Aeschylus, Euripides, and Sophocles erected in Athens, and persuaded the Athenians that official proof copies of the texts of their plays be made and stored in the city's archives.

Epic poetry

The term "epic poetry" describes verses that narrate stories about the deeds of heroes, men, and gods. Perhaps the best-known examples of epic poetry are Homer's *Iliad* and *Odyssey*. Epic poetry derived from an oral tradition of verse. Professional reciters, known as *rhapsodes*, were responsible for communicating this verse to the public. These men would recite the verses from memory at public festivals, where they would compete for prizes.

The subject of epic was often the horror and glory of warfare. A few lines describing King Menelaus of Sparta killing a Trojan, Scamandrios, communicate the bloodiness of an epic battle and the powerlessness of the goddess Artemis to intervene:

> *As Idomeneus' henchman stripped the corpse*
> *Meneslaus took Scamandrios down with a sharp spear –*
> *Strophios' son, a crack marksman skilled at the hunt.*
> *Artemis taught the man herself to track and kill*
> *Wild beasts, whatever breeds in the mountain woods,*
> *But the Huntress showering arrows could not save him now*
> *Nor the archer's long shots, his forte in days gone by.*
> *No, now Menelaus the great spearman ran him through*
> *Square between the blades as he fled and raced ahead,*
> *Tearing into his flesh, drilling out through his chest –*
> *He crashed face down, his armour clanged against him.*

Lyric poetry

While some poets continued the tradition of Homer by composing epic narratives, others in the 7th and 6th centuries BC turned their attention to alternative forms of poetry, collectively known as lyric poetry. This was recited at harvests and wedding festivals, as *paeans* (songs of praise addressed to Apollo or Asclepius) and as *dirges* (lamentations), and at drinking parties.

Lyric poetry is usually classified as either monodic (solo) or choral. Monodic lyric poetry is believed to have originated in eastern Greece. Its subjects could include love, politics, war, and wine. Choral poetry was performed by a singing and dancing choir. This collective voice represented the community, and consequently most choral song was associated with worship. One particular type of lyric poetry was known as *dithyramb*, a choral song in honour of the god of wine, Dionysus. During the Classical period, *dithyramb* was performed at several Athenian festivals.

Lyric poets held widely differing social attitudes. Some express a reaction against the aristocratic ideal of the epic poets. The poetry of the Ionian philosopher Xenophanes poked fun at the ostentatious dress sense of his contemporaries, while the poet Hesiod, a shepherd, wrote about the harsh life of farming in central Greece in a 7th century composition, *Works and Days*, offering his contemporaries wise advice:

> *I suggest you reflect on the clearing of your debts and the avoidance of famine. First, a household, a woman, and a ploughing ox – a chattel woman, not wedded, one who could follow the herds. The utilities in the house must all be got ready, lest you ask another, and be refuse, and you be lacking, and the right time go past, and your cultivation suffer. Do not put off things till tomorrow*

*and the next day. A man of ineffectual
labour, a postponer, does not fill his
granary: it is application that promotes
your cultivation, whereas a postponer
of labour is constantly wrestling
with blights.*

In contrast, during the 6th century BC, tyrants of Greek cities attracted poets to their courts, seeking to take advantage of the heroic ideal sometimes represented even in lyric poetry. The work of Pindar, reciting the achievements and strengths of aristocrats, falls into this category. Some time after 476 BC, Pindar wrote an ode to celebrate the victory of Chromios, a general of the tyrant of Syracuse (a Greek city in Sicily), and praised his famous hospitality which won him many friends:

*And I have taken my stand at the court-
yard gates
Of a man who loves to entertain strangers,
singing of noble deeds,
Where for me a fitting
Feast has been set, for frequently
This house has experience of men from
overseas;
And he has been fated to bring good men
against his detractors like water
against smoke. Various men have various skills;
We must walk on straight roads and strive
with all our natural powers.*

Poetry and politics

Throughout the Classical period, poetry was established as the medium through which sages could express models of heroic or ethical conduct. The Athenian law-giver Solon was thought to have inscribed his laws in prose, but many of the aims of his legislation, including the appeasement of strife between rich and poor, are outlined in his poetry:

*I gave the common people as much
privilege as they needed
Neither taking honour from them nor
enhancing it.
But as for those who had power and were
admired for their wealth,
I arranged for them to suffer nothing
unseemly.*

*I stood with a mighty shield cast round
both sides and did not allow either
To have an unjust victory.*

The ideals of the community could be couched in poetry. In about 330 BC, the Athenian orator Lycurgus, finding that the law provided insufficient guidelines for good citizenship, quoted poetry in the prosecution of a citizen who had fled Athens during wartime. Drawing a contrast between the readiness of the accused to flee his city and the heroism of the Greeks who sacrificed themselves during the Persian wars, Lycurgus quoted the 5th-century poet Simonides, whose verses were inscribed on a funeral monument for the Athenians:

*Fighting for the Greeks, the Athenians at
Marathon
Brought low the might of the gold-
apparelled Medes.*

The most famous Spartan poet was Tyrtaeus, who composed in the mid-7th century, at the time of the Second Messenian War, urging the Spartans to fight to the death for their city:

*With feet set well apart, firmly planted on
the ground, endure biting your lip and
covering thighs and legs below and
chest and shoulders above in the hollow
of your broad shield.
Let each shake the mighty spear in
his right hand and the frightening
crest upon his head.
Let each learn by practice to do the mighty
deeds of war and not stand outside
the range of the missiles with shield
in hand.
Rather everyone should close up to his
man with his great spear or sword and
wound and kill his enemy.
Standing leg to leg, resting shield against
shield, crest beside crest, and helmet
to helmet having drawn near, let him
fight his man with his sword or
great spear.
And you, O light-armed fighters, crouching
behind the shields on either side, hurl
your great boulders.*

Athenian Drama

Greek drama was first and foremost a public art, and it is crucial to consider the context of its performance to understand its relevance to the community. Plays were performed in a public place, and served to explore the role of the gods, to express, reinforce, and question certain moral values, as well as draw attention to the shortcomings of human morality.

Comic actors wore outrageous or monstrous masks, and their attire was designed to emphasize misshapen bellies or make room for outsize phalli. As demand for Attic comedy and tragedy spread across the Greek world in the Hellenistic period, Greek actors, from the 3rd century BC organized themselves into guilds, basing themselves in Greek cities, and performing at a fee for Hellenistic monarchs.

The origins of drama

Every year, at the festival of Dionysus in March, groups of male actors gave dramatic performances composed by three tragic poets and five comic poets. Afterwards the spectators would vote on which play they thought best, and the victorious poets would be declared in public. The festival of Dionysus was a religious occasion, but also celebrated the city of Athens and its values. The names of manumitted slaves and men being honoured by the state were announced at the festival, the city paraded the tribute which had been sent by the imperial subjects of the 5th century, and war-orphans, granted maintenance by the city, were paraded in hoplite armour and their fathers' names were announced in the theatre. The assembly convened immediately after the festival met at the theatre.

Today over 30 tragedies and 12 comedies dating from the 5th and 4th centuries survive complete, and there survive fragments of other lost plays. The origins of Greek drama are obscure, but depictions of performers on vases from the 6th century BC suggest that it may stem from a tradition of entertainment at festivals, in particular those in honour of Dionysus the god of wine. Greek drama owed many of its themes to Homer: the gods, warfare, the family, the nature of life and death, mythology, and the question of fame and honour were all reconsidered in tragedy, and even mocked in comedy.

Early tragedy

Most surviving comedy and tragedy derives from Athens in the period after the Persian Wars. Among the earliest surviving examples is the *Oresteia* trilogy of Aeschylus (458 BC), which reworked the myths about the accursed House of Atreus whilst giving them contemporary resonance to 5th-century Athens. In this series, Orestes, the son of Agamemnon and Clytemnestra, avenges his mother's murder of his father by killing her. Orestes is pursued by the Erinyes, deities of the underworld, until Athena intervenes, and tries Orestes on the Areopagus hill in Athens, thus instituting the first ever homicide court.

Plays sometimes addressed subjects of particular relevance to their audience, but rarely referred explicitly to specific events. Two exceptions to this rule are *The Capture of Miletus* by Phrynichus and *The Persians* by Aeschylus. Phrynichus' play was performed soon after the city of Miletus, supported by the Athenians in the Ionian revolt, had been captured and destroyed by the Persians in 494. This sensitive subject matter so upset the Athenians that they fined the playwright.

In 472 BC, *The Persians* by Aeschylus (the earliest of the three famous tragedians, followed by Sophocles and Euripides) had a more appealing subject for the Athenians: the naval victory at Salamis in 479 BC. The theme of the tragedy is the defeat of the Persians; the battle is described by a Persian messenger from the viewpoint of the Persians and their Phoenician allies, thus placing the tragic focus on the defeated enemy of the Greeks. This passage gives us vivid insight into the nature of naval warfare:

A Greek vessel began the ramming, and smashed off the entire stern of a Phoenician ship; each captain steered his ship against another. At first the flood of the Persian force put up a resistance; but when the mass of their ships was crowded together in a narrow strait, and they could not bring any assistance to one another, they struck each other with their bronze-mouthed beaks, and shattered all the rowing equipment; the Greek ships judiciously encircled them and made their strike, and ships' hulls were turned upside down, and it was no longer possible to glimpse the sea, which was brimming with wrecked ships and dead men. The shores and reefs were brimming with corpses. Every ship was being rowed in disorderly flight – every ship, that is, in the barbarian fleet. But they kept on striking and splicing us with broken oars and fragments of the wreckage as if we were tunny or a catch of

*fish. At the same time groaning and shriek-
ing filled the sea, until black-eyed night
brought it to an en.*

Sophocles, Euripides, and Aristophanes

Over the course of the 5th century BC, tragedy
addressed ethical matters more and more frequently,
in particular examining the relationship between the
citizen and the state, most famously in Sophocles'
Antigone (441 BC). In this play, following a civil war
between the nobility of Thebes, Antigone, simultaneously the sister and daughter of the incestuous King
Oedipus of Thebes (he had unknowingly married his
own mother), insists that the corpse of Polyneices,
her defeated brother, be buried in the customary
way. Her uncle Creon, the tyrant of Thebes, objects
to this most strongly, and claims that Polyneices was
a traitor unworthy of burial. Antigone's defiance of
Creon's absolute authority leads the audience – or
modern reader – to dwell upon the position of
women in Athens, and the clash of family interests
with the demands of the state. Sophocles offered no
explicit solutions, and asks more questions than he
gives answers.

The poet Euripides also sought to question traditional Greek values by reinterpreting mythology. His
Hecuba, performed in 425 BC explored the notions
of cruelty and revenge. Hecuba, the Queen of Troy,
suffers a double misfortune as her daughter is sacrificed at the tomb of Achilles by the victorious Greeks
at Troy; meanwhile she realizes that her son,
Polydorus, has been murdered by King Polymestor
for his money. She takes revenge on Polymestor by
luring him and his sons into the women's tent with
the promise of more Trojan treasure, then blinding
Polymestor and killing his sons. Hecuba justifies her
behaviour in a legal hearing over which Agamemnon
presides; Agamemnon declares Polymestor guilty
for his unjustified murder of Polydorus. The play
ends with Polydorus' prophesying that Hecuba
will be transformed into a dog. Given that the
Peloponnesian War was raging in Greece in the year
that the play was first performed, it is possible to
interpret the play as a comment on the cruelty of
the kind of atrocities carried out on a regular basis
in wartime.

Aristophanes is the best-preserved writer of comedies in Greek antiquity. His comedies address themes
of conflict between the young and old or the rich
and poor, the impediment of war, and the customs of
the city which are found to be strange compared to
those of the countryside. His whimsical humour
barely conceals the serious agenda that lies behind
his plays: in *The Acharnians* (426 BC) and *Lysistrata*
(411 BC) his leading characters were heavily critical
of Athens' involvement in the Peloponnesian War. In

The Theatre of Dionysus at Athens

Theatres in Classical Greece were frequently located on the sides of hills, taking advantage
of the naturally sloping sides for terraced banks of seating. The most important theatre of
Classical Athens was situated at the base of the south slope of the Acropolis. As was
common throughout the Greek world, the theatre was enclosed within a sanctuary of
Dionysus. The processions forming part of the festival known as the Great Dionysia
terminated here, transporting to the sanctuary the statue of Dionysus as well as loaves,
phalli, bowls, and animals for slaughter.

The Acharnians, Aristophanes both highlighted the
preposterousness of war and parodied the myth of
the abduction of Helen in Homer's *Iliad*, by claiming
that the Peloponnesian War arose after a dispute
between the Athenians and the Megarian allies of the
Spartans over the abduction of prostitutes.

*Lysicrates, an Athenian citizen,
was the victorious sponsor
(choregos) of the boys, chorus of
the Athenian Akamantid tribe in
the dithyrambic contests of 335/4
BC. Awarded the prize of a bronze
tripod, he placed this on a
spectacular purpose-built
monument, originally sheltering a
statue of the God Dionysos: this
provided an ostentatious display
of his prize and emphasized his
generosity to the city and piety to
the gods.*

Greek Art

Greek art includes sculpture and vase painting, but also decorative bronzeware and funerary decoration. A large proportion of artwork and sculpture was created by itinerant craftsmen or groups of workers, making it possible to outline trends that enveloped the whole Greek world, although, particularly in the sphere of vase painting, more local fashions can also be identified.

Illustrations on cups would sometimes reflect the contexts in which that vessel was used. This cup of c.450 BC shows a flute girl entertaining the aristocratic partakers in a symposium, or drinking party.

The Greeks developed more sophisticated methods of making bronze sculpture in the 8th century BC, using methods established in the Near East. Bronze statues created an entirely different effect to that of marble statues. Bronze reflects rather than absorbs light, and therefore a wider range of surface textures is possible. This is demonstrated particularly well in the sculpting of hair.

Greek vases

One of the most distinctive kinds of artefact from ancient Greece is the vase. Produced in Greece from the Neolithic period and for the duration of the historical period in which ancient Greece thrived, they provide insight into popular art, domestic life and trading routes. Modern scholars today classify vases according to their shape, of which there are more than 100 varieties. Their shape, together with their decoration, helps to identify their age and purpose. Vases were used for storage and other practical purposes such as drawing or carrying water, the export of wine or oil, drinking and mixing wine. Specific kinds of vases were used to keep cosmetics or carry oil to the gymnasium, as offerings in tombs of the deceased, and even as containers for the bones or ashes of the deceased. Greek vases were exported all over the Mediterranean, and many of the Greek vases on display in modern museums were found in Italy, where, during antiquity, there was a large market for Greek vases.

Amphoras containing up to 10 gallons of olive oil were given as prizes in the Panathenaic Games held every four years in the city of Athens from the 6th century BC onwards. These were decorated with a depiction of Athena, the patron goddess of Athens on one side, and a scene depicting the sporting event for which the prize was given on the other. To ensure that the viewer would appreciate the generosity of the Athenians and their readiness to recognize sporting prowess by awarding such an expensive prize, the vases carried a painted inscription, "One of the Prizes from Athens".

Decorative pottery was also used by aristocratic drinking groups, forming part of the extravagant show of wealth, wit and wisdom that went on in parties, known as *symposia* (literally meaning "a drinking together"). One such vase, a black-glazed, red-figured wine-jug dating from the 460s BC, known as the Eurymedon vase, contains a particularly topical message. It depicts two figures: one of them, a Greek male, unclothed, and holding his penis in his hand, strides towards another figure, bent over and clothed in a speckled bodysuit. An inscription on the vase states, "I am Eurymedon. I stand bent over." The Athenians had inflicted a crushing defeat on the Persians at a battle by the Eurymedon river in Asia Minor in the 460s, and it is plausible that this vase is a light-hearted reference to that victory.

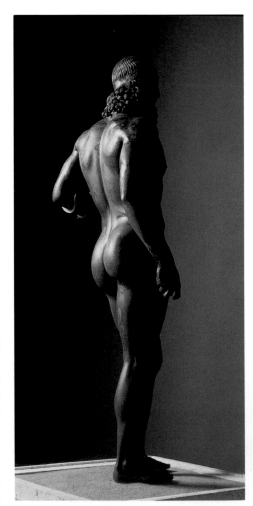

Vase painting

The prehistoric Mycenaean and Minoan civilizations painted vases, and it is thought that the Mycenaeans imitated the natural motifs favoured by Minoan artists. Many of the skills in vase painting developed during the Bronze Age were lost after the breakdown of Mycenaean civilization; however, the skill of pot making was never lost, and decorations that emerged at the end of the Dark Ages rivalled those of the Bronze Age in sophistication.

Between the 10th and 9th centuries BC, geometric designs were the most popular type of decoration, usually consisting of bands around the vase, which were elaborated with other patterns. From around 725 BC, the orientalizing style of Greek pottery began in Corinth. Geometric patterns were replaced by a whole range of patterns including rosettes, lotus flowers. Images of animals, real and imaginary, became popular too. The increased complexity of decoration was made possible by a new technique known as "black figure". The pot was made of naturally red clay. A black glaze matter was added where a figure was desired. Before firing, details could be scratched into the black glaze, then coloured with white or purple paint. By c.525 BC, Athenian potters, having imitated the Corinthian techniques, began to develop a method of their own, known as "red figure". In this style of decoration, the painter would decorate the pot with the black glaze solution in the places where a black background was required. After firing, red figures would appear in the areas where the black glaze had not been applied. The resulting red figure would then be decorated. This technique allowed for more ornate decorations than the black-figure method. Athenian vases from the 6th and 5th centuries often depicted scenes from mythology and have been used to date the popularity of certain myths. From the mid-6th century BC, a cycle of Theseus' adventures appear on Athenian vases, suggesting that the fame of this mythical king of Athens was promoted by the Pisistratid tyrants.

Greek bronze

Bronze was a highly valued material because its use on shields and in making weaponry meant that it was closely associated with warfare. Unlike pottery, it could be easily melted down and cast and shaped, and was often considered a material worthy for dedication to the gods. In the 8th century BC, small bronze horses were commonly dedicated at sanctuaries across Greece, while at Olympia larger objects such as bronze tripod cauldrons, up to 91cm (3ft) in height, start to appear, dedicated by victors to commemorate their piety to the gods. Cauldrons became highly decorated, often featuring the heads of griffins, mythical winged birds that appear also on

orientalizing pottery. There were two principal ways of decorating bronze: beating and casting. The Greeks imitated the "lost wax" technique for casting bronze in the 8th century BC. This was carried out by the creation of an original sculpture etched onto wax, moulded over a clay dummy. This in turn was covered in clay; the wax was melted away and bronze was poured in to replace the "lost wax". If the procedure was carried out properly the resulting sculpture could be of very high quality, and had great potential to highlight anatomical details.

Sculpture

The other most prominent decorative art form was sculpture. From some time after 650 BC, the stone sculptures depicting skirted, striding male figures that were common in Egypt were imitated in Greece, and became known as *kouros* figures. Such figures, with their sleek, muscular forms, were not intended to represent individuals, but were an idealized type. They were used as offerings to the gods and as grave-markers. At the same time, a female version of these sculptures developed, known as the *kore* figure. These figures are more ornately decorated and sometimes hold out an offering.

In the Classical period, the standard *kouros* type vanished, and a new style of representation emerged. Characteristic features such as swinging hips, decorated hair, and turning heads all appeared on figurative sculpture in the period immediately after the Persian Wars. During the 4th century BC, sculpture is prominent in the adornment of grave-markers. These decorations no longer represent a generic human type, but illustrate personal achievements or interests, or civic virtues. One grave-marker depicts a little girl holding her pet doves, while another, for an aristocratic horseman, depicts him victorious on horseback. Greek sculpture reached its zenith in the Hellenistic period (336–146 BC), as sculptors developed more sophisticated means of decoration.

Detail of early Greek fresco of diving man from Tomb of the Diver at Paestum. While the 2nd-century AD traveller Pausanias reported seeing paintings at numerous sites around Greece, today the best-preserved examples of Greek 5th-century wall painting come from the Tomb of the Diver from Paestum in Italy. This scene suggests that the arts of wall-painting and vase-painting were closely related, but shows the effects of the space that the former form allowed the artist.

Greek Architecture

Greek cities can be considered as both communities and territories. The territory of a typical city-state was made up of an outerlying region (*chora*) and a city centre (*asty*). City centres featured monumental buildings which served secular and religious purposes, and displayed the wealth and piety of the city to visitors. Some of the most striking images of ancient Greece derive from the sacred and secular buildings which were erected in the Classical period.

Building materials

Mud-brick, stone and wood were all important building materials in Greece for temples in the 7th century, and houses throughout Greek history. However, the Greeks knew that wood was flammable and prone to decay, and that mud-brick was not stable. From the 6th century BC, and increasingly over the course of the 5th century, limestone and decorative marbles were used as a primary building material for the most important public buildings of the Greek city-states. A ready supply of fine white marble was available from quarries in Athens and around the Greek world. As a result, a good deal of ancient Greek monumental architecture survives to this day in the shape of temples, sacred treasuries, theatres, and military storehouses. Many of these were decorated with architectural refinements and painted sculpture

Religious buildings and the Periclean building program

A significant proportion of the ancient Greek monumental buildings that remain today had some sort of religious function as sacred treasuries – storehouses of dedications to the gods – or as temples. From the 6th century BC onwards, there emerged two clearly distinct styles of architecture for temples: the Doric and the Ionic. In the Doric style, columns were placed directly on the upper foundations of the building; Doric columns tapered upwards, with a convex curve. In the Ionic style, the columns were placed on bases which were then placed on the upper foundations. The columns were straight and more slender than the Doric, with more ornate bases and capitals.

The peak of the Doric style was reached in the mid-5th century BC. The Parthenon, a temple to Athena and a sacred treasury, was built upon the Acropolis in Athens in this style. In 447 BC, work on this building, which had originally begun before the Persian Wars, was resumed as part of Pericles' plan to embellish the city with architecture which would serve to impress the Athenian citizen body, intimidate her imperial subjects and rival city states, and demonstrate to the gods the piety of the Athenians. The building was constructed from marble drawn from the quarries of Mount Pentelicon to the northeast of Athens.

The decorative panels (*metopes*) on the front of the Parthenon illustrated well-known scenes of Greek mythology, the battles of heroes and humans against Amazons, centaurs, giants, and Trojans. They represented the victory of the Greek forces and human reason over non-Greeks and monsters, and perhaps alluded to the Greek victory in the Persian Wars. The pediment illustrated divine scenes centring on Athena, representing her birth and her struggle with Poseidon for the control of Attica. The friezes illustrated scenes believed to be from the pan-Athenaic procession, which formed part of the four-yearly festival in honour of Athena, and which culminated with the handing over on the Acropolis of the sacred robe (*peplos*) to adorn the statue of Athena Polias (Athena of the City). Viewed in their original position, around the top of the inner building (*ante*) of the Parthenon, they directed the viewer's attention to the central scene representing the delivery of the *peplos*. All of the sculptural dedication of the Parthenon was painted in vivid colours. The innermost room of the building contained the gold and ivory cult statue of Athena Parthenos, upon which rested the reputation of Phidias, the most famous sculptor of 5th-century Athens. Standing 12 metres (40 ft) high, and decorated with over a ton of gold, it took nine years to complete.

The Parthenon was just one part of the work that was undertaken on the Acropolis during the stewardship of Pericles. Constructed at around the same time was the monumental gateway (*Propylaion*) to the Acropolis. After Pericles' death a smaller Ionic temple known as the Erechtheion was constructed. Like the Parthenon, it was built with Pentelic marble but was

decorated with friezes of black stone. Begun in 421 and completed in 407 BC, it was regarded as the spiritual home of the Athenians because it was built on the spot where the deities Athena and Poseidon were said to have contested for control of the city, and it was here that Athena allowed her sacred olive tree to grow.

A further striking feature of the Acropolis in the 5th and 4th centuries BC would have been the number of public inscriptions that stood as a monument to Athenian power and democracy. The Athenians recorded on slabs of white marble on the Acropolis their laws and honorific decrees awarded by the assembly. Most impressive would have been the 3.6 metre- (12 ft-) high slab of marble, erected in 454 BC, which recorded the 1/60th portion set aside for the goddess Athena of the tribute paid to Athens by her imperial subjects.

The 4th century BC

It was a common complaint of 4th-century Athenian orators and politicians such as Demosthenes that the Athenians of his generation had failed to emulate the great architectural achievements of Periclean Athens, and instead paid too much attention to the construction of elaborate private dwellings, or monuments which flaunted the private wealth of individuals. Demosthenes' complaints reflected the fact that with-

out a tribute-paying empire, the Athenians were, in the first half of the 4th century BC, unable to afford a monumental building project to match that of Pericles. However, in the second half of the 4th century BC, after financial restructuring under the politicians Eubulus and Lycurgus, a new building programme was pursued in Athens. During this period, work was carried out on temples and other religious buildings, but attention was also paid to the enlargement of the Theatre of Dionysus and the Pnyx (assembly place).

Another innovation in the buildings of the city was the construction of a huge warehouse for the storage of rigging, sails, and ropes for ships in Piraeus, known as Philon's Arsenal. Built between 337 and 330 BC, it was no ordinary warehouse, featuring provision for the maintenance of an air supply so that the nautical equipment would not moulder. In the same era, the walls of the city were renewed; and a series of fortifications were constructed to the north of Athens, perhaps as a response to the emerging threat from Philip of Macedon.

There is no doubt that innovation in Greek architecture advanced for practical as well as aesthetic reasons. However, it was for aesthetic reasons that Greek sculpture and the Greek principles of proportion in architecture were to be highly influential during the Renaissance and beyond.

At the time of the Pisistratid tyranny in the late 6th century BC, the Athenians commenced work on a massive temple which was not completed because of the collapse of the tyranny. In 174 BC, Antiochus IV Epiphanes, Seleucid monarch of Syria recommenced work on the temple, but it was completed only in the period of massive public works undertaken in Athens by Hadrian, Roman emperor in 124/5 AD. The largest temple in Athens, it measured 110 metres by 43 metres (361 by 141 ft), and was supported by 104 columns.

Philosophy and Religion

Over the course of the 5th century BC, owing to its cultural and political prominence, Athens became an important location on the circuit of the itinerant teachers of rhetoric, known as the Sophists. Socrates became famous for his conversations with these men, and his pupil Plato founded the Academy in Athens. While philosophy challenged many conventional beliefs, it did not undermine the vivacity of Greek religion.

Aristotle is best known as a philosopher who has been highly influential on Western thought. He started his career, however, as a member of the medical practice of the followers of Asclepius. His early interest in biology was reflected in his writings.

Philosophy in Archaic Greece

Philosophy is a Greek word, translated best as "devotion to knowledge". In its earliest stages of development, it did not require a specialized knowledge of any subject. Culture in the Archaic period had not undergone the process of specialization familiar to the modern world, where specific subjects become the domain of experts. The earliest Greek philosophers were poets simultaneously concerned with natural phenomena, cosmology, and theology. Philosophers of the Archaic period, known as the Pre-Socratics, attempted to explain natural phenomena and the world around them in comprehensible terms. Many of these philosophers came from the Ionian Greek towns of the west coast of Asia Minor, where Greek culture mingled with Near Eastern influences.

Exposure to different cultural influences encouraged a more cosmopolitan outlook and a philosophical, relativistic approach to thinking. Perhaps the most radical of the Pre-Socratics was Xenophanes of Colophon. He lived in the 6th century BC and migrated to Sicily, where another centre of Greek philosophy was emerging. His relativistic approach to theology was novel. Stressing that human customs were based upon convention, he postulated that each culture recognized gods that reflected themselves, and so Thracians represented their gods as Thracians, Ethiopians their gods as Ethiopians, and so on. Xenophanes left a legacy of understanding that paved the way for the development of relativism, and made important distinctions about the difference between belief and knowledge, a central tenet of Plato's *Republic*.

Philosophy in the 5th century and beyond

The skills of the Sophists were highly prized in the nascent democracy, where oratory and skilled debate were valued as tools for political participation. The most famous of the Sophists was Protagoras of Abdera, who was associated with the politician Pericles. Plato describes his contribution to the development of ethical theory, arguing that humans need institutions to survive in the world and

Zeus was the chief of the gods and is illustrated on the right of this plaque reclining with a sceptre. In Homer, Zeus was represented as a "father" and as a "king", but never as a tyrant.

that justice and temperance are necessary if these institutions are to survive.

Socrates' ethical system stressed the development of thought through discussion, and therefore he refused to write down any of his philosophy. The writings of Plato, Athens' most famous 4th-century philosopher, are based upon conversations supposed to have taken place between Socrates, Sophists, and other philosophers. Plato portrays Socrates as someone interested in discovering the usually flawed origins of others' beliefs. His investigations were based on the *elenchus*, a system of eliciting opinions and then proving these opinions to be flawed. Plato used this method as a springboard for his own ethical systems, including the ideal society described in his *Republic*. The work of Plato paved the way for the more empirical investigations of Aristotle, whose method had significance for much of Western philosophy.

Religion

Religion was part of everyday life in Greece. Each house had its own shrine, and sacrifices were made at important moments, such as just before a battle. These rituals and religious conventions played an essential role in the relationship between individuals and their city-state.

The Greeks lacked any kind of sacred text or bible, there was no official religion that everyone had to follow, nor was there an idea of sin or redemption. Instead, Greek religion was embedded in the individual's consciousness through the myths concerning the "Pantheon" of 12 gods. The legends in the *Iliad* and *Odyssey* contributed to the formation of every Greek's idea of religion, portraying gods living in a society much like a human community. The list of these gods would sometimes vary, but usually included Aphrodite, Apollo, Ares, Artemis, Athena, Demeter, Dionysus, Hephaestus, Hera, Hermes, Poseidon, and Zeus. In addition to these, there were local deities who varied from state to state, and groups of heroes who were even more specific to individual localities. These deities were associated with different aspects of daily life. Hephaestus, for instance, was the god of fire, blacksmiths, and artisans, while Demeter was the goddess of corn. Many of the festivals associated with her were celebrated at times of the year associated with agricultural activity: the *Thesmophoria*, a festival in her honour, took place in autumn before sowing time.

The relationship between individuals and the gods was important on both private and public levels. The most important part of Greek worship was sacrifice. Calendars of sacrifices were inscribed on stone, and could include details of the time of year of sacrifice and the value of the animal to be sacrificed. After a

Socrates
An Athenian citizen, Socrates was famous for questioning everything. Plato describes how his conversation and endless questions upset others' systems of belief. His encouragement of free thought annoyed many Athenians, and, in 399 BC, he was charged by three citizens with introducing new gods and corrupting the youth of Athens. In his trial, Socrates argued that his conversations were a blessing for the city, persuading people to perfect their wisdom. Although found guilty, he proposed that he be rewarded with free meals in the public building known as the prytaneion. Instead, his contemporaries condemned him to death by drinking hemlock.

sacrifice, the meat would be shared among those present. Another important form of piety was expressed through cult oracles. Individuals would visit an oracle, such as the one at Delphi, for guidance on all kinds of issues. While many inquiries concerned religion or changes in cult practice, others were related to matters such as whether a wife might conceive a child on a journey or about health problems. Alternatively, city-states could claim the support of an oracle for a particular action, such as the foundation of a colony.

The Greeks used different cult names for their gods, which defined the nature or location of the worship. Hence Zeus Agoraios presided over the commercial life of the community, in particular that which took place in the *agora*, or market place. Greek religion was highly sensitive to social and political change: names such as *Eleutherios* (liberator) or *Soter* (saviour) were applied to the cult of Zeus to mark Athens' victory in the Persian Wars and survival after its defeat in the Peloponnesian War. Greek religion was dependent upon the human interpretation of responses and was associated with every aspect of life. For this reason, it remained a prominent part of daily life as it developed alongside the emergence of rational thought.

Science and Medicine

Greek science and medicine relied on the empirical method, forming rules on the basis of observation. This meant that scientific theories often arose in opposition to one another. Medical practitioners, too, were competitive and keen to promote their own theories.

Blood-letting and cupping was a form of treatment used up to the 19th century. This Greek plaque illustrates the blades, used to make the incisions for bleeding, and the cups, which were heated, and placed over the wound. As the air in the cup cooled, it drew blood from the wound as a result of the vacuum. The bleeding created would stop when the cup was removed.

The nature of Greek science

Greece in the Classical period for the most part lacked public libraries or laboratories, so the fundamentals of scientific thought were based on conversation and observation. Because of this, in its earliest stages science was inseparable from related disciplines such as philosophy, theology, and rhetoric. In his play *The Clouds*, Aristophanes illustrated one example of the fusion, or confusion, of the study of science and philosophy by parodying Socrates as a natural scientist, expert in "the air theory", who spent his time talking to the clouds. A more serious assessment of Greek scientists in this period recognizes their progress in theories of natural causality and rational proof, as well as scepticism about religious explanations of phenomena.

The natural sciences

One of the most important spheres of scientific progress in this period was in the field of explaining natural phenomena. In the 4th century BC, while doctors advanced rationalizing explanations about the causes of disease, Theophrastus, who was a colleague of Aristotle, developed theories about the nature of plants. His work included classifications of plants depending on their parts, their qualities, the habitats in which they grew, and the course of their life. His work was based upon observation, and he was often critical of the ritual practices of "root cutters" and "drug sellers", who attributed the medicinal qualities of plants to magical powers. Although his work may have had some practical use, he was more concerned with rationalizing, observing, and defining phenomena than improving agriculture.

Mathematics and geometry

Architectural developments in the 5th and 4th centuries BC were heavily reliant on the progress of mathematics and geometry. One of the earliest thinkers to make important headway in the

This cup depicts a scene from Homer's Iliad, *showing Achilles bandaging his wounded comrade Patroclus. It expresses not only the tenderness in the relationship of the couple, but also the care that might be taken in dressing wounds received in battle.*

exploration of mathematics and geometry was the 6th-century BC Samian, Pythagoras. Tradition describes him as a philosopher, magician, and priest, who dressed in a white robe, golden crown, and trousers. Through his mystical interest in numbers and music, he devised the geometric theory that bears his name to this day. He also contributed to the development of theories about musical harmony, and his school of successors, known as the Pythagoreans, continued his work.

Other developments took place in the 5th century, with, for instance, the mathematician Zeno of Elea posing the "Achilles Paradox". This proposed that a quicker runner can never overtake a slower runner who starts ahead of him, as he must always first arrive at the place that the slower one has already occupied. His method of theorizing was based on attempting to contradict his contemporaries and illustrates well the competitive nature of the developing Greek sciences.

Medicine

Working along the same lines as the scientists and philosophers, Greek medical practitioners attempted to understand illnesses through reasoned explanation and observation, sometimes with an element of theology. Descriptions for the treatment of wounds sustained in combat are included in the Homeric epics, while the medical texts known as the *Hippocratic Corpus* provide evidence for the development of Greek medicine from the 5th century BC onwards.

While the Greeks may have learnt medical practice from the Egyptians, over time they outstripped them in skill. As early as the 6th century BC, Greek doctors were acclaimed throughout the Mediterranean. The historian Herodotus relates a story in which the Persian king, Darius I, in the late 520s BC, dislocated his ankle while dismounting a horse. The king immediately turned to Egyptian doctors; however, when these failed to cure his injury, he sought out a Greek doctor, Democedes, who was kept as a slave in his court. After curing the king, Democedes became highly esteemed at the court and renowned throughout the Greek world; he was even hired by the state of Athens.

Medical practitioners

In the 5th century BC, groups of medical practitioners became more common, the most famous of which was headed by Hippocrates of Kos. By the late 5th century BC, Hippocrates was well known as both a teacher and practitioner of medicine. The *Hippocratic Corpus* reveals the development of medical thought based on scientific enquiry, and an interest in separating medical enquiry from the activ-

Asclepius, the healing god

Although many of the writings of Hippocrates ruled out supernatural causes of particular diseases, Greek medical practice was inseparable from religion. The most famous healing cult in the Greek world was that of Asclepius, who had a sanctuary on the south slope of the Acropolis in Athens. Treatment was offered for all kinds of conditions, such as hair loss, blindness, lameness, parasitic afflictions, and snakebite. The patient would be sent to the shrine and would purify him or herself. Then, wearing a white robe and olive wreath, the patient would go to sleep on a bed of twigs or the hide of a sacrificial animal. He or she would receive dreams from the deity concerning healing. Frequently, medical treatment would follow the advice communicated in the dream.

ities of faith-healers and other quacks. These works place a great emphasis on diet and exercise, and recognize the importance of external environment in causing disease. The ancient interest in the ethics of medical teaching and practice is detailed in the Hippocratic Oath, which was used as a code of conduct by practising doctors and is one of the origins of the ethics of modern medical practitioners.

The Hippocratic approach is well illustrated in the treatise known as *The Sacred Disease*. This work is a critique of popular superstitions about the causes of epilepsy. The author is keen to stress that the disease is no more "divine" than any other disease, and he argues this by pointing to the fact that it is treatable. His argument does not preclude belief in the divine nature of disease: rather, he argues that no other disease has less claim to be divine than this one. The author's own explanation for the "Sacred Disease" is the flooding of the brain with phlegm – one of the four humours believed to affect health.

An interest in observation, causation, and diagnosis is evident in the theories of historians as well as those of the scientists of the 5th century BC, with Thucydides showing specific interest in medicine. He described in detail symptoms of the plague and various aspects of contagion. Medical practice, we can deduce from his interest, was a well-respected practical and intellectual pursuit by the end of the 5th century BC.

Histories

The development of Greek historical writing is hard to trace, as most texts by Greek historians survive only in fragmentary form. Yet it is clear from the surviving works that the Greeks employed several important elements of historical inquiry. Research was carried out through conversation or through examination of written documents.

The origins of history

The first Greek historian was Hecataeus of Miletus, who played a part in the Ionian revolt. The celebrated opening words of his work reveal a great deal about the nature of his history: "I write these things, as they seem to me to be true. For the stories of the Greeks are many and ridiculous, it seems to me." Herodotus, writing in perhaps the 440s BC, described his work as *historia*, referring to the processes of questioning, enquiry, and research that he had gone through in order to reach his conclusions.

Herodotus' subject matter

Herodotus continued and extended interest in *historia*. Aiming to correct, update, and surpass the work of Hecataeus, Herodotus made the subject of his work the growth of the Persian Empire and the curtailment of its expansion by the Greeks. He takes as his starting point the causes of the conflicts between Greeks and non-Greeks. After surveying the traditional explanations of a series of mutual kidnappings, Herodotus goes on to give an account of the growth of Persian control of the Greek cities and the Ionian revolt. Herodotus' readiness to discuss the part played by women in social and political affairs is unique among ancient Greek historians.

While Herodotus' book is essentially an historical narrative, his interest in cause and consequence frequently leads his work into digressions in the form of fantastic tales. Sometimes Herodotus expresses his opinion on the truth of these stories, but more often he implies that they are important not because they were necessarily true, but because they were used as explanations of phenomena. For example, when relating the suicide of the Spartan king Cleomenes, Herodotus reports three alternative explanations for its cause, each representing some aspect of divine retribution. He reports that most Greeks thought it was punishment for his bribery of the Delphic oracle concerning the succession to the Spartan throne; that Athenians believed it was because he laid waste to some sacred ground at Eleusis in Attica; and that the Argives blamed it on his sacrilege in Argos. For Herodotus, therefore, the recording of beliefs and customs was essential to the recording and interpretation of actual historical events.

Greek depictions of Orientals show them dressed in flapped headdresses, patterned tunics, beards, and trousers, the latter of which was thought to be particularly un-Greek. This depiction was continued in Roman art, seen here in a Roman mosaic of the 2nd to 1st century BC. It illustrates the Battle of Issus between Alexander and Darius III, and is from the House of the Faun at Pompeii.

Herodotus the anthropologist

At other times, Herodotus provides anthropological insights, narrating the habits of the people central to the events he describes. The fourth book of his history is concerned with the Persian king Darius' attempt to subdue the nomadic Scythian tribes who lived to the north and east of the Danube and across southern Russia to the north of the Black Sea. Much of that book is spent describing the life and ways of the tribes resident in the lands beyond Scythia. He reports the existence of a race of peace-loving, bald-headed men, the Argippaians. These, he informs us, live from the produce of a particular fruit tree, which bears a fruit the size of a bean, containing a stone. This race also used the tree as a dwelling place. While ready to believe the authenticity of the lifestyle of the Argippaians, Herodotus was reluctant to give credit to the Argippaians' own stories of the existence of a race of men with the feet of goats or of others who hibernated. Herodotus' rejection of such stories provides the basis for the rationalizing scepticism of the next Greek historian whose work survives, Thucydides.

Thucydides

Thucydides was an Athenian general, exiled in 424 BC, who wrote a history of the Peloponnesian War. He left an unfinished work that went up to 410 BC. The history was intended as an "eternal possession", which would communicate Thucydides' belief about the human race: that it was reluctant to learn from its mistakes.

Thucydides is said to have burst into tears at a recitation of Herodotus' history. Whether out of pleasure or despair it is not known, but the great impact that Herodotus' work had upon him is clear. Thucydides retained the theme of Herodotus' work – the accumulation of power and its eventual destruction – but, unlike Herodotus, he largely excluded women from his narrative. The most striking difference between the two historians is that Thucydides aimed to remove the religious and mythological context of history and was more interested in the way that political beliefs or traits in human nature explained human action and the course of events. While this allowed for a more reasoned account of events, it led him to ignore the importance of cult practice as a motivating cause.

The content of the work

Thucydides' history begins with an account of early Greek history and introduces to the reader the importance of sea power, which was so vital for the growth of the Athenian Empire in the 5th century BC. The mixture of politics and war in the introductory section is representative of the contents of the rest of

Thucydides' legacy

It is believed that Thucydides' history was read by later Greek and Roman historians, perhaps by the philosophers Plato and Aristotle, and also by later rhetoricians and critics. One later commentator of the 1st century BC, Dionysius of Halikarnassus even goes so far as to criticize Thucydides' style of writing as poetic, convoluted, and compact. Such comments are fair, but these very attributes allowed Thucydides to construct a history that analysed in depth the causes not only of the Peloponnesian War, but also of war in general, and the desire for power latent in human nature.

the work, and it continues with his in-depth and two-layered analysis of the causes of the Peloponnesian War.

Much of the history consists of military narratives of the Peloponnesian War. These narratives are arranged in independent but related sections. For instance, the story of the disastrous Sicilian expedition of 415–413 BC seems independent from much of the rest of the history, but it stresses the usual themes of the work: the importance of naval technology, human greed, expansionism, and a failure to learn from the past. The gravity of Thucydides' writing reflected the very serious nature of his subject – war. His uses of documentary evidence and his focus on methodical theories of causation, human nature, inevitability, and the value of historical writing itself influenced the themes chosen by later historians such as Polybius.

The speeches

One of the most important elements of Thucydides' history is its speeches; their value cannot be overestimated. He states at the beginning of his history that the speeches reported "the necessary things" for the speakers to say, while adhering as closely as possible to what was actually said. He took the opportunity to adapt the content of the speeches for his own purposes, so if he wanted to paint a favourable picture of a character, he gave the impression that that character possessed foresight by ensuring his predictions turned out to be true. Pericles' funeral speech, a version of which was given at the funeral of those who had died in the first year of the Peloponnesian War, is frequently cited as one of the defining orations of Athenian democracy. In this speech, Pericles outlines his notion of the ideal community as one inspired by a combination of individual freedom and heartfelt duty to serve the State, an ideal shared and adapted by many modern Western liberal thinkers.

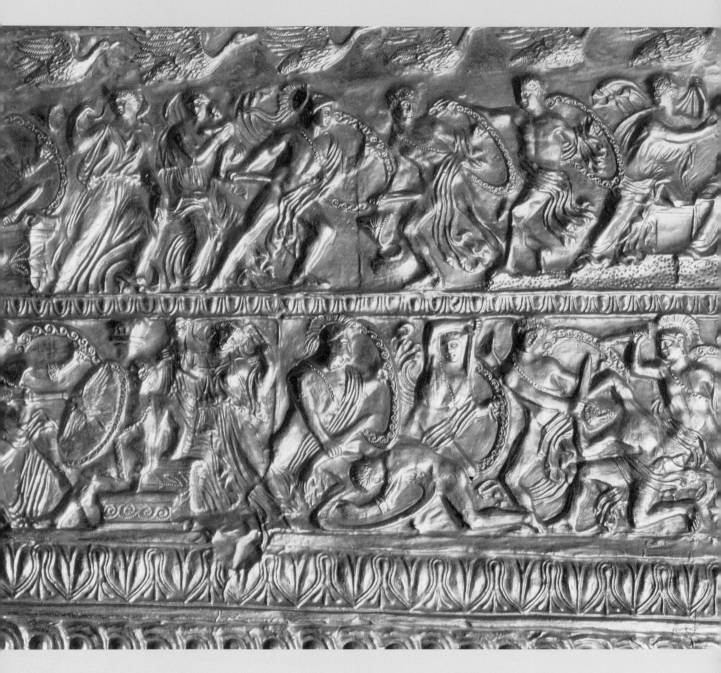

In 1977, three 4th-century tombs
were excavated at Aegae, the
burial place of the kings of
Macedonia. The frescos and
offerings in gold were of the
highest quality, and they
encapsulate the spirit of conquest
which contributed to the
Macedonian subjugation of
central Greece in the 330s BC.

THE HELLENISTIC PERIOD: 336–146 BC

The conquests of Philip II of Macedon had far-reaching consequences. By imposing Macedonian power over all Greece, Philip belittled the importance of the inter-state relations of the city-states of Greece. Thus his conquests marked the beginning of the eclipse of the city-state system which had been the most important method of political organization in Greece since the start of the 8th century BC.

The Hellenistic period is generally said to begin in 336 BC with the death of Philip II, king of Macedonia. From the 350s BC, Philip led Macedonia to a position of supremacy. Philip had taken advantage of Greek disunity to establish a hegemony over Greece that reached new peaks with his defeat of the Athenians at Chaironea in 338 BC. Alexander the Great, Philip's successor, strengthened the Macedonian grip over Greece and embarked upon a conquest of the Persian Empire. When he died in 323 BC, Alexander left an empire that stretched from Albania to India. Over the next 50 years, a struggle to win control of as much of this empire as possible ensued between Alexander's successors. By 276 BC, the Mediterranean was divided into three territorial states, each with a dynastic monarch. The Antigonids had control of the area known as Macedonia now including Greece; the Ptolemies held Egypt, and the Seleucids held the area that included Syria, Iraq, and Iran. Macedonia was the last of the areas to settle under a dynasty, that of Antigonus II Gonatas, who took control in 277/6 BC.

After the death of Philip, much of mainland Greece was subject to the rule of the Macedonian monarchy, and Greek inter-state diplomacy was no longer determined by relations between individual city-states. But another type of political organization now rose to prominence: the inter-state confederation. Of these, the Aetolian League grew in importance after the Aetolians of west-central Greece had been instrumental in the defeat of a Gaulish invasion in 280/79 BC. Another rival to the Macedonian control of Greece was the Achaean League, which became powerful in the 240s and 230s BC. However, after receiving Macedonian aid against the Aetolian League in the 210s BC, it allied with Macedonia, although under pressure it joined the Romans against Macedonia in 196 BC. Despite their evacuation of Greece in 194 BC, the Romans returned to make Macedonia a Roman province by 149/8 BC.

The Hellenistic period is often perceived as the story of the decline of Greek civilization to make way for Roman expansion. However, as interest in the period grew during the 19th and 20th centuries, it became clear that the era was significant not only as a link in the development of the ancient world, but also as a period of cultural innovation and the dispersion of Greek culture outwards from the Mediterranean basin. Some historians have seen the period as the time when Greek and Near Eastern cultures intertwined to form the background from which Christianity would arise. Although the military power of the Greek city-states contracted, the Greek way of life extended its geographical limits: a mark of this cultural expansion was the fact that Greek became the language of government from the shores of the Mediterranean to the borders of India.

The period saw intense activity in art, architecture, philosophy, and science. Alexandria became the centre of the scholarly world with the creation of its museum and library. Athens also remained important as a home of scholars and philosophers, and hundreds of small religious, professional, and social organizations developed there. Innovations in sculpture and technology took place in the wider Greek world. The Hellenistic period featured development, rather than decline, of lifestyles and political organizations, as the city-state was eclipsed rather than destroyed.

Philip and the Rise of Macedon

Macedonia, a kingdom to the north of Greece, was inhabited continuously from early Neolithic times, but played only a peripheral role in Greek history until the mid-4th century BC. Under the leadership of King Philip II, it rose to become the most important power in the Greek world by 338 BC.

Demosthenes, was an Athenian orator and politician, of whom some 60 speeches are preserved today. These speeches, made in the lawcourts and Athenian assembly, indicate Demosthenes' role in attempting to persuade the Athenians to resist the Macedonian threat. His rival Aeschines, however, claimed that it was Demosthenes,' policy that led the Greeks to disaster on the battlefield of Chaironea in 338 BC.

Greece in the 4th century BC

When the Athenians surrendered at the end of the Peloponnesian War, they accepted the Spartan terms, forcing them to surrender all but 12 ships of their fleet, to pull down the walls of their city, and to join the Peloponnesian League. The Spartans imposed an undemocratic government on the Athenians, known as the regime of the Thirty Tyrants. By the end of 404 BC, this regime was overthrown, and the Athenians re-established their democracy, and made a concerted effort to found a government based on the rule of law. Athenian democracy remained relatively stable throughout the 4th century, and Athenian domestic politics were dominated by orators such as Demosthenes and Lycurgus.

The inter-state politics of 4th-century BC Greece, however, were chaotic. The 5th-century division between Athens as a sea power and Sparta and her Peloponnesian allies as the land power gave way to a succession of short hegemonies. For 10 years after the Peloponnesian War, Sparta was the most powerful Greek state, expanding her sphere of influence into the Greek cities of Asia Minor. However, Spartan rule was harsh, and this led to a coalition of Greek states disputing Spartan leadership of Greece in the Corinthian War. Only the intervention of the Persian King Artaxerxes put an end to this war: the King's Peace was a treaty between Artaxerxes and the Greeks of 386 BC that guaranteed the autonomy of Greece in return for the recognition that the Greek cities of Asia Minor should belong to Persia. This marked a Greek retreat from the east which lasted until the time of Alexander the Great. Spartan strength withered in Greece, and her position was further eroded by a crisis of the citizen population in Sparta, which had fallen to 1500 by 371 BC. Meanwhile, the Athenians founded a new naval league in 378 BC, which has become known as the Second Athenian Confederacy. This aimed to secure Athens' influence in the Aegean Sea and beyond, but the Athenians promised not to repeat the exploitation of their allies which had been a feature of her 5th-century empire. However, Athenian power was undermined: first, by the Thebans of central Greece, who, after their defeat of the Spartans at the battle of Leuctra in 371 BC, became the most important city in Greece for the duration of the 360s; then by the Social War of 357–5 BC, essentially a revolt by some members of the Confederacy led by Rhodes, Cos, and Chios, with the support of the Carian monarch of Halicarnassus, Mausolus. This instability in Greek inter-state politics opened the way for a new player: Macedonia, under the leadership of King Philip.

Macedonia

In the Archaic and Classical period, most of central and southern Greece was dominated by the city-state system, according to which city-states of varying size were independent and had their own territory and community of citizens. However, to the north of Thessaly, Macedonia was a large kingdom whose inhabitants identified themselves as members of the

Macedonian tribe or nationality; there was probably little urbanization in Macedonia before the 4th century BC. Ruled by a king who consented to the law, this form of organization was strange but not entirely unknown to the Athenians: in the 5th century BC, the historian Thucydides remarked that the Aetolians of north-western Greece lived by tribe in unwalled villages.

Macedonia was relatively unimportant in the 5th century. During the Persian Wars, the Macedonians had allowed the Persians to occupy their territory from 512–479 BC, in return for which their territory was extended. In 479 BC, the Persians sent King Alexander I of Macedon to Athens to try to persuade the Athenians to end their resistance to the Persians, but his speech made little impact on the Greeks. As Athenian influence expanded across the Aegean region in the 5th century, the Athenians, attempting to set up a colony at Amphipolis in northern Greece, came up against the Macedonians. The Athenians succeeding in establishing a colony there in the 430s BC, but the settlement was to remain a bone of contention between the Athenians and Macedonians for another 80 years.

The Macedonian kings, from the 5th century BC, appear to have claimed Greek heritage. But, whether and in what way the inhabitants of ancient Macedonia were Greeks remains uncertain, and is a dispute that will never be resolved. However, it is likely that under King Archelaus (413–399 BC), the Macedonians began to adopt many Greek customs, inviting the Athenian playwright Euripides to stay at the new capital, Pella. In addition, Archelaus built fortifications and straight roads, and reorganized the Macedonian army. In many ways, he pre-empted many of the efforts of Philip II.

Philip II of Macedon

The Macedonian kingdom almost disintegrated as it faced dynastic upheaval between 399 and 360, and threats from the neighbouring tribes, the Paeonians and the Illyrians. The education of Philip, born in 382 BC was curtailed by these upheavals in the 370s, and he spent the years 369 to 367 as a hostage in Thebes. However, his residence in that city at the time when it became the most powerful in Greece gave him valuable experience of Greek politics and military tactics. Philip came to power in 360 BC, after his brother Perdiccas was killed in the war with the Illyrians. Quickly, Philip assumed control of Macedonian forces and regained control of western and north-western Macedonia by suppressing the Illyrians and Paeonians. Next, Philip turned his attention southwards. In 357 he captured the Athenian colony of Amphipolis, and he occupied the area around Mount Pangaeus (in Thrace, northern Greece), famous for its gold mines. These mines provided the finances required for conquest and the reorganization of Macedonian society.

Philip encouraged the urbanization of Macedonia, and the movement of populations from the mountains to the plains and coastal cities. Of vital importance for understanding the Macedonian conquest of Greece are Philip's military innovations. He developed a new system of phalanx fighting that exploited the shortcomings of Greek hoplite warfare. The soldiers of the new Macedonian phalanx had lighter armour and were more mobile, but their main advantage was the *sarissa*, a pike of 5.4 metres (18 ft) in length, which allowed the Macedonian phalanx to strike a pre-emptive blow against the regular hoplite phalanx. By reorganizing the Macedonian army, he attempted to secure the loyalty of his soldiers, bestowing the title "Foot Companions" upon his regular fighters. He also improved the strength of catapults by introducing more powerful torsion ropes.

Philip spent the period from 357 to 346 asserting Macedonian power over the tribes of Thessaly, immediately to the south of Macedonia, and intervening in central Greece under the pretext of punishing the Phocians for having cultivated land sacred to Apollo. Further Macedonian expansion was stalled by a peace treaty with the Athenians in 346 BC. However, in 340 war became inevitable as the Macedonians interfered with the Athenian grain supply from the Black Sea area. A reorganization of public finances in Athens and the revival of the Athenian navy in the aftermath of the Social War was not enough to resist Philip. In 338 BC, Philip inflicted a massive defeat on combined Greek forces at Chaironea in central Greece. Philip forcibly enrolled the Greek states into a new organization, the League of Corinth, ostensibly an organization founded to make war against the Persians, but which served as an instrument of Macedonian supremacy.

The image of Philip of Macedon had become famous throughout the Greek world by the end of the 4th century BC. His image appeared on Macedonian coinage, but also in portraits and statues. The proliferation of his image set the standard for his son and successor Alexander and the Hellenistic monarchs, who commissioned ever-increasingly individualistic images of themselves.

Alexander the Great

King Philip II of Macedon, under whom Macedonian power expanded into central Greece, was assassinated in the autumn of 336 BC by a slighted former lover. His son Alexander was proclaimed king, and he consolidated his position through a policy of military expansionism and by undermining potential threats.

Early life and the securing of Greece

Alexander III of Macedon was educated by the great philosopher Aristotle, and in his youth emerged as a precocious military talent. His father was assassinated when he was 20 years old. Despite the fact that Alexander had been groomed for the throne, it was only through the intervention of Antipater, one of Philip's generals, that the succession was secured for Alexander.

After the murder of Philip, the Athenian assembly voted the privilege of a gold crown for Philip's assassin and entered into negotiations with one of Philip's former generals, Attalus, about overthrowing Alexander. Thus Alexander's first task on the international front was to secure recognition of his succession throughout Greece. He marched south against the Thessalians, who soon admitted defeat and proclaimed Alexander their leader (*tagos*), as they had done earlier for Philip. He was also proclaimed leader of the League of Corinth, an organization of Greek states founded by Philip for the purpose of waging war against the Persians. In 335 BC, the Thebans rebelled against Macedonian leadership, but

Alexander oppressed them by destroying their city and enslaving the population. Having established his supremacy over Greece, Alexander turned his attention to the war against Persia.

Alexander's Persian expedition

The idea of a pan-Hellenic expedition against Persia was not a new one. In the 4th century BC, the Athenian intellectual Isocrates had urged the Greeks to proclaim Philip of Macedon leader of such an expedition. Philip made plans, seeing a conquest of Asia Minor as a potential source of wealth; when he died in 336 BC, a force of 10,000 men had already crossed the Hellespont. In 334 BC, Alexander led his force in the same direction. Consisting of over 30,000 infantry and 5500 horsemen, it was probably the largest expedition ever to depart from Greece. On landing at Elaious, he began by paying sacrifice at the tomb of Protesilaus, the first of the Greek heroes in the Trojan war to set foot in Asia Minor. By offering this sacrifice, Alexander proclaimed his ambition to avenge the former misfortunes of the Greeks in Asia Minor.

Alexander's conquests were met with a mixture of resignation and fierce resistance. While Egypt surrendered peacefully, he moved through Mesapotamia and won a decisive victory against the Persians at Gaugamela. This opened the gateway to the East and the conquest of Bactria by 329 BC. In 326 BC, Alexander reached Taxilia, east of the Indus. In 325 BC, he returned west and reached the Persepolis and Susa in 324 BC.

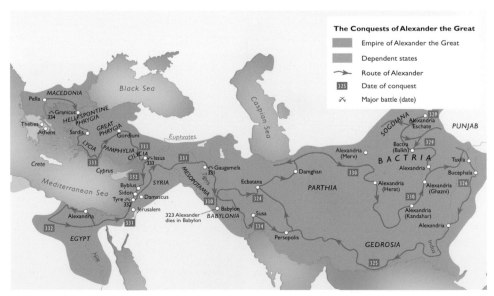

Alexander first met the Persians in 334 BC in a pitched battle at the river Granicus in north-west Asia Minor. After routing the Persian cavalry, the Macedonian horsemen surrounded the foot soldiers of the Persians and their mercenaries.

In Alexander's march across Asia Minor, Greek and non-Greek cities were treated in the same way: new governments were installed, and cities retained independence as long as they remained loyal to Alexander. By emphasizing its pan-Hellenic nature, he attempted to secure unanimous Greek support for the expedition.

Alexander in the East

Alexander's expansion into Asia continued after the battle at Granicus, as he moved inland south towards Phrygia, Pamphylia, and Lycia. Having made Cilicia his base of campaign in 333 BC, he lured the Persian army to Issus, the town north of the coastal plain on the way to Syria. Alexander was able to reverse early losses, making use of the narrowness of the plain by instigating a cavalry charge from the right, prompting panic in the Persian lines.

After victory at Issus, the cities of the eastern Mediterranean, Sidon and Byblus, surrendered to Alexander. The ancient Phoenician port of Tyre on the Levant refused to capitulate, but was eventually captured by siege. Egypt, a restless possession of the Persians, surrendered peacefully to Alexander's forces in 332 BC. After the conquest of Egypt, Alexander visited, in the desert at Siwah, the oracle of the god Ammon, whom he equated with the Greek god Zeus, and proclaimed himself to be "the son of Zeus-Ammon".

Whilst in Egypt, he also founded the city of Alexandria, after which Alexander's forces returned to the East. They marched on Mesopotamia, and after defeating the Persian King Darius in a great battle at Gaugamela in 330 BC, took Babylon and Persepolis, the native residence of the Persian kings in Persis. This city was destroyed in a fire allegedly started at a great drinking feast.

But Persian resistance was not yet stamped out: a provincial governor, Bessus, murdered the Persian king Darius, proclaimed himself king of kings, and instigated a revolt against the Macedonians. Alexander responded to this threat by appointing provincial governors of his own.

He then turned his attention to a march through Asia, crossing the mountains of the Hindu Kush by 327 BC, reaching the Punjab by 326, and making offerings to the gods at the mouth of the river Indus in the summer of 325 BC.

Forced to turn back by a revolt of his troops, Alexander left India for Persia in August 325 BC. On his return, he went ahead with a purge of his gener-

als, venting his anger at the curtailment of the Indian expedition on those around him. Despite failing health, he planned an expedition against the Arabians who had refused to honour him as a god. His hopes were dashed when he fell ill at a party hosted by one of his generals on 10 June 323 BC. His body, wounded and exhausted by years of continual warfare, was unable to ward off malaria.

Alexander's monarchy

Macedonia was an absolute monarchy under Alexander. Although the king was the traditional head of the Macedonian state, Alexander added refinements to the position. For instance, Alexander included the Persian tunic, diadem, and girdle in the dress of the king. By fusing Macedonian and Persian elements of royal government, and making his monarchy acceptable to East and West alike, Alexander set a trend for the monarchs of the Hellenistic period.

By exaggerating the greatness of his victories over Indian tribes, and by founding a substantial number of Greek-style cities across Asia, Alexander made himself the object of cult worship throughout his empire. The worship of Alexander was long lasting, and left a legacy in the shape of the stories now known as the "Alexander Romance". These probably derived from a Greek source, and exist in a range of traditions, from Hebrew to Hungarian. The longevity of these myths is evidence of the success of Alexander's self-mythologizing.

Detail from the Roman mosaic from the house of the Faun at Pompeii from 2nd–1st century BC. It shows the battle of Issus between Alexander the Great and Darius III of Persia. Alexander is supposed to have located Darius with the intention of killing him. Darius turned to flee, and the Persians followed him.

Greece between Alexander and the Romans

Alexander's campaigns had the twin consequences of putting an end to the dominance of the Achaemenid clan in Persia, which had ruled the Near and Middle East for two centuries, and curtailing the importance of the Greek city-states in politics. Their replacement, however, was far from stable.

The Empire after Alexander

The period after Alexander's death to 276 BC saw a constant struggle between his successors to grab what pieces they could of his vast empire. Soon after his death, a settlement at Babylon confirmed Perdiccas, head of Alexander's cavalry, as regent. The heirs to the throne were the mentally impaired and physically weak Philip Arrhidaeus, son of Philip II, and Alexander IV, Alexander's son by his Bactrian wife Roxane. By virtue of his Macedonian mother, Philip Arrhidaeus was the popular choice as heir among the Macedonian army. But for now, political power was not in the hands of the royal successors.

Perdiccas the regent offered to revive Alexander's policy of expansion, but his soldiers rejected this proposal. From this point, the age of Macedonian expansion was over. Perdiccas set about distributing areas of the Empire for the governorship of Alexander's former generals. Antipater was allocated the generalship of Greece, Ptolemy was given Egypt, Antigonus the One-Eyed was given western Asia Minor, and Lysimachus received Thrace. These four, along with Eumenes, sent to establish Macedonian control in Cappadocia and Paphlagonia in Asia Minor, became the most important men in the struggle for power.

The conflicts that began with the disputed succession of Alexander led to the division of his former empire between successor monarchs. This map shows the strongholds of the first generation of monarchs: Lysimachus (died 281 BC), Antigonus the One-Eyed (died 301 BC), Ptolemy (died 282 BC), Seleucus (died 281 BC), and Cassander (died 297 BC). Greece changed hands but witnessed the rise and fall of the Achaean and Aetolian Leagues before the Roman domination.

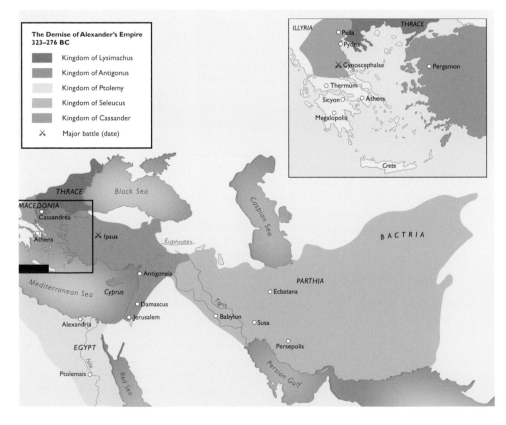

The Demise of Alexander's Empire
323–276 BC

- Kingdom of Lysimachus
- Kingdom of Antigonus
- Kingdom of Ptolemy
- Kingdom of Seleucus
- Kingdom of Cassander
- ✕ Major battle (date)

The Wars of the Successors

The spark that began the Wars of the Successors naturally concerned Alexander. Ptolemy diverted Alexander's funeral cortege towards Egypt, claiming that Alexander had expressed a desire to be buried at his father's shrine. After resisting an invasion by Perdiccas, Ptolemy formed an alliance of generals against the regent. Soon afterwards, Perdiccas was murdered by his demoralized officers.

By 316 BC, Antigonus the One-Eyed emerged as the dominant general, while his son, Demetrius the Beseiger, conquered the Greek states through siege warfare. Their success in conquering Greece, however, served to divide rather than unite. In 306 BC, after Antigonus had declared himself king, he was followed by Ptolemy, Seleucus, Lysimachus, and Cassander (the son of Antipater). In 301 BC, Antigonus' death at the battle of Ipsus in central Phrygia ended his dreams of succession. Between 301 BC and his death in 283 BC, Demetrius the Beseiger attempted to re-establish his father's position, but with little success. Only Antigonus Gonatas, Demetrius' son, established Antigonid power over Macedonia. With the Ptolemies holding power over Egypt and Seleucus over the area covered by Syria, Mesopotamia, and Iran, monarchy was established across the Mediterranean.

The Aetolian and Achaean Leagues

As the Hellenistic monarchies grew in power, Athens and Sparta formed an anti-Macedonian alliance which lasted until their defeat in the Chremonidean War by the Macedonians in 262/1 BC. But other states came together in unions made up of various city-states or tribal communities.

The Aetolian League was based on the tribal organization of the Aetolians centred at Thermum in west-central Greece. The Aetolian defeat of the invading Gauls at Delphi in 280/79 BC gave them prestige, and it also helped them to establish control over the Delphic Amphictyony, the organization devoted to the upkeep of the sanctuary of Apollo at Delphi. The festival of Zeus Soteria was reorganized into a pan-Hellenic, four-yearly festival, as a commemoration of their victory and in order to publicize their control of Delphi. Attracted by this success, distant states such as Chios and Vaxos in Crete joined the League. This increased membership enabled the organization to become an important player in the political development of Greece in the 3rd century BC.

Always rivals of the Aetolians, the Macedonians declared the Social War of 220–217 BC on behalf of their so-called Hellenic League, accusing the Aetolians of plundering sites in Greece. The Macedonians shocked the Aetolians by ravaging their

federal sanctuary at Thermum. Never devoted to Greek independence for its own sake, the Aetolians became allies of the Romans in 212/11 BC. However, as a reaction against the restraint of their independence after the Second Macedonian War in 196 BC, they joined the Seleucids against Rome; they were never prominent again.

The original Achaean League, an organization based in the Peloponnese, was dissolved by the Macedonians in the early 3rd century BC, but was revived in 281/80 BC. The League became important in the mid 3rd century BC, after the Sicyonian Aratus brought his home city into the League. From 245 BC, he led the Achaean Confederacy in opposing Macedonian control, liberating Corinth and Athens. However, he joined with Philip V of Macedon for the Social War of the Hellenic League against the Aetolians. After the Romans began to appear in force in Greece, the Achaeans transferred their support to Rome. The Romans helped the Achaeans extend their control over the Peloponnese, but the alliance fell apart after the Spartans were dissolved into the League: their secession in 149/8 BC led to the Achaean War and the destruction of the League by Rome.

The Confederacies of the Greeks showed that they were capable of innovative political organization that resisted monarchy. The members of the Achaean League shared coinage and laws, as well as an assembly, common councils, and judges. An annually elected general served as commander in the battlefield. Thus, while the Hellenistic world saw a great expansion of Hellenism, the land mass of Greece itself remained an energetic centre of activity and political innovation.

Greece as a Roman Province

The coming of Rome happened in stages, by means of both diplomacy and warfare. Taking advantage of internal and external pressures on the Ptolemaic and Seleucid kingdoms, and the occasional readiness of the Greek cities and federal states to form alliances with it, Rome was able to establish absolute domination over Greece by 146 BC.

The Tower of Winds was built in the 1st century BC in the Athenian market place of the Roman period. It served as a waterclock. Its octagonal tower carried reliefs illustrating the eight winds, which, at the time of creation, would have been painted in bright colours. This detail shows Boreas, the north wind.

Early contacts

Military expansion was not the first contact that the Romans had with the Greeks. The presence of Greeks in Campania (west-central Italy) and the flourishing of trade routes meant that the Romans were exposed to Greek civilization from an early date. It was in defence of these trade routes that Roman intervention began in Greece.

Roman intervention in Greece began in the 280s BC, when Rome began to place colonies near the western shore of the Adriatic, thus opening the way for more Roman trade links with Epirus and Greece. From 280 BC, the Romans suppressed the rebellious movements of the city of Taras in southern Italy. With the fall of Taras in 272 BC, the Roman conquest of Italy was complete. The first direct Roman military intervention east of the Adriatic Sea was in the First Illyrian War (229/8 BC). This came as a response to the growth in power of the Illyrian kingdom under Queen Teuta, whose expansion became a threat to the stability of Roman communication and trade in the Adriatic Sea. A successful campaign left the Romans with a group of friendly states in the Adriatic area, and soon the Romans began to make defensive alliances with Greek cities on the east coast of the Adriatic. Their admission into the Isthmian Games of 228 BC indicated that Greek states accepted the Romans as honorary Greeks.

The First and Second Macedonian Wars

The next major Roman involvement on the Greek stage was in the First Macedonian War (211–205 BC). At a conference in Naupactus in 217 BC called to end the so-called Social War, the Aetolians expressed concern that the power in control of Italy posed a threat to Greece. From this point, according to the historian Polybius, Rome entered into diplomatic considerations whenever Greek leaders made war or peace with each other.

Philip V put an end to the Social War, and in 215 BC turned his attention west by making a pact with Rome's enemy Hannibal. In turn, in 211 BC, the Romans allied with the Aetolians. In the ensuing war against Philip V, the Romans showed their readiness to plunder and to enslave populations. The war ended after the Aetolians withdrew their support; in the ensuing Peace of Phoenice, Athens and other Greek states were listed in a treaty as allies of Rome. It was the establishment of this relationship that gave Rome a reason to make demands in relation to the Macedonians' behaviour in Greece.

In late September 201 BC, two uninitiated Acarnanians wandered into the temple of Demeter at Athens at the time of the religious ceremonies known as the Eleusinian Mysteries, and the Athenians promptly put them to death for their sacrilege. The Acarnanians, allies of Philip V, appealed to the Macedonians, who in turn ravaged Attica. By this time, the Romans had already demanded that Philip not make war on the Greek cities, a demand made either from fear of Philip V or through covert expansionist aims. Philip had ignored the demand, and Rome intervened in the Second Macedonian War (200–197 BC). Throughout this conflict, the Romans maintained that they were fighting for the "Freedom of the Greeks" from Macedonian rule. After the defeat of Philip in a pitched battle at Cynoscephelae in 197 BC, the Romans proclaimed the freedom of the Greeks at the Isthmian games of 196 BC. While this freedom was subject to the constraints of Rome, and the declaration itself a piece of theatrical propaganda, the defeat of Macedonia did put an end to absolute Macedonian domination of the states of central Greece.

As the Romans asserted their power over the Aegean, the Seleucid monarch Antiochus III established dominance of coastal Asia Minor. Antiochus' crossing of the Hellespont and his contact with the Aetolians, combined with a rumour that he harboured ambitions to invade Italy, led to a renewal of the Roman presence in Greece from 192 BC. Between 191 and 188 BC, the Romans reconstituted the Delphic Amphictyony, under their own leadership. The defeat of the Seleucid king and his Aetolian allies by 189 BC served to reinforce Roman authority over Greece. From this time, the Romans subjected the Greek states to their ally King Eumenes of Pergamum, and the Romans were now able to deal with all Greek political problems in the service of their own interests.

The Romans in Greece

The efforts of Perseus, Philip V's successor to the Macedonian throne, to revive Macedonia's power in Greece, combined with unrest in Greece, led to the outbreak of the Third Macedonian War in 171 BC. By 168 BC, at the battle at Pydna, Perseus was defeated, the Macedonian monarchy was abolished, and Macedonia was split into four republics. In 149 BC, a pretender to the throne led a revolt against Roman rule. However, this was quickly crushed and Macedonia was reduced to the status of a Roman province in 149 BC. Similarly in 146 BC, after the repression of the Achaean League, the Roman general Mummius razed Corinth, killed most of the men in the city, and sold the women and children into slavery. Democracies were abolished, and wealth became the requisite to qualify for government. Greece was placed under the rule of a Macedonian governor from Corinth, and it was made a separate province known as Achaia in 27 BC.

When Flamininus, the Roman general who defeated Philip V at Cynoscephelae, evacuated Greece in 194 BC, he took with him many works of art and treasure to mark his triumph. Similarly, the Roman defeat of the Macedonians in the

Polybius

Vienna's neoclassical parliament building is flanked by statues of the great historians of antiquity. Polybius, from Megalopolis in the Peloponnese (*c.*200–118 BC), wrote a history of Rome's rise to power. He was active in the Achaean League as an envoy, and was later involved in installing the Roman settlement of Greece in 146 BC. While his history shared with Thucydides' work a focus upon politics and war, he also included clear distinctions between "causes" and "beginnings", and observed the importance of chance on historic events. His legacy includes an image of Greek decline in the 2nd century BC and the power that the mixed constitution gave to Rome.

Third Macedonian War brought the contents of the Macedonian Royal Library to Rome. As a result of such plundering, many portray Greece as a desolate place in the 2nd century BC. The historian Polybius describes this period as a time of depopulation and abandoned cities. In some ways this reflects a true picture; however, it did usher in the tremendous popularity of Greek culture with the Romans.

Carthage fell to the Romans and was razed at the same time as Corinth. In 1817, the painter J. M. W. Turner captured his impression of the destruction of Carthage in a scene bathed in the light of the setting sun.

Hellenistic Society and Politics

The Hellenistic period was characterized by remarkable social and political changes. The city-state organization of Greece survived, but the territorial kingdom became the most important political unit, and the king the most important individual, with significant consequences for Greek religion.

The altar of Zeus found at Pergamum contains this scene of Gigantomachy, the fight against giants. This theme was a familiar one, appearing also on the metopes of the 5th-century Parthenon on the Acropolis, and might be interpreted as the visualization of the struggle of the known and reasonable against the unknown and irrational.

Greek City-States in the Hellenistic World

As 2000 Greeks lay dead on the battlefield of Chaironea, it became clear that the Greek city-states, even united, were unable to resist the power of the Macedonian state. This was reiterated in 335 BC, when, after an unsuccessful revolt, the city of Thebes was destroyed by the forces of Alexander. In 323 BC, the Athenians, disturbed by the excessive interference by the Macedonians in the affairs of the Greek states, and inspired by the death of Alexander in Babylon, led another revolt against Macedonian rule. However, the Athenians lacked manpower, and the revolt was suppressed by the Macedonian general Antipater.

In 268 BC, the Athenians made an alliance with Ptolemy II, King of Egypt, against the Antigonid monarchy of Macedonia. It inspired an Athenian politician called Chremonides, using rhetoric which recalled the Greek success in the Persian wars, to manufacture a confederacy which linked Sparta, Athens and other Greek states. The confederacy was heavily reliant on the sea power of the Ptolemies and the confederacy of Greek island states, the Islanders' League. The Athenians, hoping to regain full control over their historic territory as well as reasserting control over the domestic and foreign policy of the city, led a revolt against the Antigonids. The revolt led to the so-called Chremonidean War which lasted until the Athenians surrendered in 262, when the Antigonids installed garrisons in the city of Athens and fortresses in the surrounding countryside. While the Greek city-states expressed their identity through revolt, the Hellenistic monarchs expressed their power by their capacity to put down revolts and to expand their "spear-won" territory.

Their loss of independence notwithstanding, the city-states of Greece were still autonomous in the

sense that they possessed political institutions which determined the domestic policy of the city, and, for the most part, they retained a contiguous territory, and a community of citizens that identified itself with that city. Old institutions evolved to suit the political climate. In Athens, for instance, the *ephebic* institution continued in the 3rd century BC as an educational organization reserved for citizens, providing training in philosophy, oratory, music and athletics as well as an induction to civic religion. The assembly and council continued to meet regularly, but the implementation of their decisions was frequently subject to the cooperation of a monarch. In public finances, the Greek city-states became more reliant on wealthy benefactors to finance the celebration of festivals, and would offer prestigious rewards of crowns and statues to those who gave generously.

Monarchy in the Hellenistic world

In the Classical period, with the exception of Sparta, the Greek states considered monarchy to be a form of government suitable for non-Greeks, such as Persians or as a backdrop for legends. Their main exposure to monarchies was with areas considered peripheral to the Greek world, such as Cyprus, Thessaly, and Macedonia. In the Hellenistic period, monarchy, or kingship, was the prevailing form of government across the Greek-speaking world. The earliest Hellenistic monarchs were keen to emphasize their identities as successors of Alexander, and as Macedonian monarchs. Increased exposure to non-Greek peoples of north Africa and central Asia meant that Hellenistic monarchy developed in diverse ways.

The Seleucids

The Seleucid empire, founded by Seleucus (a general who had served under Alexander), at its greatest extent, stretched from western Asia Minor as far east as Syria, Babylonia and Iran. It included many of the cities founded in Asia by Alexander, and exploited the vast resources of central Asia. It adapted many of the institutions of the now defunct Persian monarchy, imitating its taxation system and allocation of regional administration to local rulers who worked in native languages. It was the most diverse of the successor empires, and recruited its fighting force from diverse regions. The sixth Seleucid king, Antiochus III, declared himself a living god. The final Seleucid king, Antiochus XIII, was deposed by the Roman commander Pompey in 64 BC.

The Ptolemies

Ptolemy was a Macedonian nobleman and general who accompanied Alexander on his conquest of Asia. He established himself as ruler of Egypt, having hijacked the funeral cortege of Alexander. In 305 BC he declared himself king, established a Greek-speaking bureaucracy in Egypt, and shifted the capital of his kingdom to Alexandria, which became one of the most culturally important cities in the Hellenistic Mediterranean. Its population was diverse, consisting of Greeks, Egyptians and Jews. Alexandria became famous as a cultural centre with a famous library and museum; it was known as the location of the tomb of Alexander; it was guarded by the Pharos, a lighthouse at the entrance to its artificial harbours. When Ptolemy II came to the throne in 285 BC, he celebrated his accession by a huge procession and celebration, featuring a fountain that flowed with wine, a four-wheeled wagon pulled by 180 men, and a procession of 57,000 infantrymen and 23,000 cavalry. The same king also promoted the worship of his dead father, and attempted to elevate the status of the games held in honour of him, the Ptolemaia, to equal that of the Olympic Games. Ptolemaic rule of Egypt lasted until the Roman conquest of Egypt and the suicide of Queen Cleopatra VII, a descendant of the Ptolemies, in 30 BC.

Religion

The Hellenistic period saw the emergence of new religious cults across the Greek world. In Egypt, a Hellenized form of Egyptian religion developed when Ptolemy I called upon an Egyptian priest and an Athenian religious expert to fashion a new god as Alexandria's patron deity. The result was a god named Sarapis, who was identified by Hellenistic writers with the Greek gods Dionysus, Pluto, Zeus, and others. In Greece itself, deities adopted from elsewhere were also transformed: the Egyptian goddess Isis, for example, became identified with Greek goddesses and assumed the Greek identity as a creator of the universe. Innovation coincided with preservation: in Athens, in the last third of the 4th century BC, there was a movement to preserve the traditional city deities, manifested in the building-works at important sanctuaries. However, the practice, unfamiliar to the Greeks of the classical period, of worshipping the king or his family became common throughout the Hellenistic world and took hold in Greece too, to the disgust of some. Even in Athens, during the early third century BC, the Antigonid monarch Demetrius the Besieger was proclaimed a living god in a hymn composed in his honour, in the hope that he would treat the city kindly:

> *For the other Gods either are far away*
> *Or they have no ears*
> *Or they are not, or they do not heed us,*
> *   not even one,*
> *But we see you present,*
> *Not wood, nor stone, but real.*

Hellenistic Culture

Alexander's conquest of central Asia spread city-state civilization to the east and exposed the Greek ways of life and thinking to Persian, Egyptian and Mesopotamian influences. Combined with the imposition of one-man rule across most of the Greek world, the result was the emergence of a diverse Hellenistic culture, which displayed both Greek and non-Greek elements.

Technology

The expansion of the Greek world in the Hellenistic period brought new problems that demanded new solutions. Alexander, for instance, was particularly interested in canals for drainage after encountering them in Mesopotamia, and in the use of dams to prevent silting. Irrigation became more common, and important innovations in agricultural equipment took place. The screw developed by Archimedes, an inventor and mathematician of the 3rd century BC, facilitated the workings of water-pumping devices for drainage and was also used in olive and grape presses. However, the application and availability of new goods and scientific innotations varied from city to city. Most of the city-states of Greece remained reliant on commercial imports and the donations of foreign benefactors for their food supply.

Sculpture

While standards of living varied across the Hellenistic world, the cultural development of the Hellenistic world does show some uniformity. As sculptors would travel to centres where there was employment, it is difficult to establish regional trends in architecture or sculpture. There was a move away from the idealized forms of earlier sculpture, as Alexander commissioned busts of himself with life-like features. A more individual style of portraiture developed as Alexander's successors followed his lead, commissioning portraits of themselves as rulers in order to show aspects of their personalities as well as to reflect their positions of power. More life-like representation is also seen in everyday contexts. Small terracotta figurines, depicting ordinary people such as craftsmen, children, and the elderly were common throughout this period, commonly used as dedications to the gods.

Some of the most striking sculpture derives from the building projects initiated by kings to decorate their royal capitals. The famous 2nd-century BC frieze on the Great Altar at Pergamum, the capital of the Attalid kingdom, is an exceptional example of Hellenistic sculpture. This features scenes of war between giants and the gods, a theme encountered in the 5th century BC on the *metopes* of the Parthenon. However, the frieze at Pergamum sur-

The lighthouse at Alexandria was one of the Seven Wonders of the Ancient World. Located on the island of Pharos, off the coast of Egypt near to the city of Alexandria, it was constructed in the early 3rd century BC under Ptolemy I of Egypt, who made use of the experts attracted to his kingdom to build the world's first lighthouse and what was said to be the tallest building of the Mediterranean world.

passes classical sculpture in its painstaking detail. The decorative detail on the figures and the variety of intricate surface textures depicting fur and feathers contribute to the power of the narrative. They also illustrate the height of stylistic virtuosity reached in Hellenistic sculpture.

Poetry

Other disciplines combined revival with innovation. The poet Theocritus drew inspiration from the epic poetry of the *Iliad*, as well as from lyric poetry, but also invented a new genre known as *bucolic*, which refers to his rural sketches sometimes written in the Doric dialect. A Syracusan who worked at the royal court of the Ptolemies from the 270s BC, he also composed poems praising the king. His *Idyll 17* is an example of this, reckoning King Ptolemy to be the first of mortals – in the same way that Zeus was first of immortals – boasting of his vast, "spear-won" territory, his immense power on land and sea, and the productivity of Egypt:

Zeus son of Cronos cares for august kings, but pre-eminent is the one who attends him in abundance, and vast is the territory he rules, and vast the sea. Countless countries, ... helped by the rain of Zeus, cause their crops to grow, but none is as productive as the lowlands of Egypt when the Nile in flood waters and breaks up the soil, nor does any have as many towns of men skilled in work. Three hundred cities are built there, then three thousand in addition to thirty thousand, and twice three and three times nine besides; over all these mighty Ptolemy rules as king. ... he cuts off for himself a part of Phoenicia, Arabia, Syria, Libya, and of the dark-skinned Ethiopians. He gives orders to the Pamphylians, to the Cilician spearmen, to the Lycians and to the warlike Carians, and to the islands of the Cyclades, since his are the finest ships that sail the seas. All the sea and land and the roaring rivers are ruled by Ptolemy, and about him gather a host of horsemen and a host of shielded warriors, equipped with glittering bronze.

Books and libraries

The first books in Greece were probably written on sheets of animal skin or panels of wood in the Archaic period, which were succeeded by the introduction of papyrus from Egypt towards the end of the 5th century BC. A major development was made in Pergamum in the 2nd century BC, when parchment was made from animal skins. The Hellenistic period also saw the creation of large buildings to be used as libraries. The two major libraries of the period were based at Alexandria and Pergamum, but there were also important libraries at Athens. Founded and funded by the Ptolemaic monarchy, the library at Alexandria held some 700,000 books by the 2nd century BC. At this time, a real interest in the preservation of classical culture can be seen: Ptolemy III, for example, borrowed manuscripts of the tragedies from Athens on deposit. However, he was more interested in keeping the texts than retrieving his money and refused to return them.

Philosophy

Philosophy underwent considerable development in this period, and there was a move away from the focus on purely political idealism classical period. One group of philosophers, known as the Cynics ("the dog-like") for their shamelessness were the followers of Diogenes. Diogenes believed that wisdom lay in action rather than thought. He spent his life as primitively as possible, eschewing possessions, living in a barrel, and surviving by begging. He was renowned for his belief in freedom of speech and actions, and he rejected traditional sexual customs. The philosophers known as the Stoics were not so far removed from the Cynics in their idea of liberty as the ability to live as one pleases. The founder of Stoicism, Zeno, agreed with the Cynics that general education was useless. The Stoics were interested in logic, physics, and ethics, and argued that virtue is happiness, nothing except virtue is good, and that emotions are always bad. Some Stoics such as Epictetus created a literary form of the *diatribe*, the address exhorting morality given to a large outdoor audience.

Greek culture and Rome

The history of ancient Greece and its culture does not end with the Roman conquest. A visitor today to the ruins of any Greek city will see a large number of ruins of the Roman period, such as the 20,000-capacity theatre at Argos or the Tower of the Winds in Athens. The munificence of wealthy Roman individuals often financed these buildings, illustrating Greece's economic reliance on Rome. Levels of prosperity varied throughout Greece, and the population moved away from isolated rural settlements towards larger villages and cities. Although Rome controlled Greece through the governors of Macedonia, Greece continued to be an area of self-administering communities, self-regulating with regard to their domestic affairs. Greece, and in particular Athens, remained a place of education and a haven for philosophers, where statesmen such as Cicero were educated in philosophy, and exiles went to muse over the injustices of life at Rome.

The Rosetta Stone is a decree written up in 196 BC by Egyptian priests in honour of the cult of the 13 year-old Ptolemy V, ruler of Egypt. It is inscribed in two languages (Egyptian and Greek) and uses three scripts: hieroglyphic (used for religious documents), demotic (the common script of Egypt), and Greek (the language of the Hellenistic rulers of Egypt). The texts are thought to be parallel, and therefore this stone was the key to the decipherment of Egyptian hieroglyphics by 1822.

ANCIENT ROME

753 BC–476 AD

800 BC

475 BC

754/3 Traditional founding of Rome by Romulus.

c.490–338 Wars with Latin League lead to Roman control of central Italy.

264–146 Punic between Rome Carthage: In 241 Romans takes Sic 218, they defeat Han and take much of S

509–287 The Struggle of the Orders: the plebeians gradually wrest political and economic concessions from the patrician aristocracy.

192–189 War against Antiochus III of Syria.

218–167 Macedonian Wars: Rome defeats Philip V and Perseus, and the Roman General Flamininus declares the freedom of Greece at Corinth's Isthmian Games in 196, 50 years before the Romans raze Corinth to the ground.

754–509 Legendary kings rule Rome and conquer Latium.

509 Traditional date of founding of the Republic by Brutus.

390 The Gauls sack Rome.

800 BC	700 BC	600 BC	500 BC	400 BC	300 BC	200 BC

451–50 The Twelve Tables are the first publication of Roman laws.

c.600 The Forum valley is drained and laid out, beginning the urbanization of Rome.

200–160 Plautus and Terence write the classic Roman comedies.

312 Via Appia built from Rome to Campania.

150 BC

AD 175

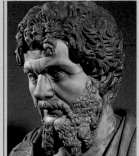

Spartacus
s a massive
slave revolt
ainst Rome.

–78 The
of Sulla,
e march
ome sets
years of
civil war.

88 The
Italian
ubjects
olt and
are
ntually
given
Roman
enship.

70–57 Ascendency of Pompey, who serves as consul in 70, breaks the pirates in 67, defeats Mithridates in 63, and secures the corn supply for Rome in 57.

49–46 Civil War between Caesar and Pompey; when Caesar wins he assumes dictatorial power at Rome. He is assassinated in 44 and the state descends into civil war.

31 BC Octavian finally defeats Antony and Cleopatra at Actium, and they commit suicide. He takes the name Augustus and becomes the first Roman Emperor.

14–68 Julio-Claudian Dynasty: Tiberius, Gaius "Caligula", Claudius, and Nero.

98–192 Antonine Dynasty, including Trajan (r.98–117), the first emperor from the provinces, and the one who takes the empire to its greatest extent.

476 Last Western Emperor Romulus Augustulus driven out by Goths and abdicates. The Greek-speaking, Eastern Empire survives as Byzantium until 1453.

193–235 Severan Dynasty; Septimius Severus (193–211) is the first African emperor. In 212, his son Caracalla grants Roman citizenship to almost all the free men in the empire.

293 Empire divided into two halves – east and west – each with an emperor (an Augustus) and a deputy (a Caesar).

312 Constantine unites the Roman Empire, and makes Constantinople the capital in 330.

395 Empire again split into eastern and western halves.

410 Sack of Rome by Alaric the Goth.

100 BC   0   AD 100   AD 200   AD 300   AD 400   AD 500

31 Augustus and Agrippa begin a building programme that transforms Rome, including the Augustan Mausoleum, the Pantheon, and the Ara Pacis.

123 Hadrian's Wall is built. It is the only permanent defensive border in the empire.

324 Christianity becomes a recognized state religion.

250–310 Climax of the persecution of Christians.

80–140 The Age of the Satirists: the corruscating Juvenal (58–140) and exuberant Martial (40–102).

0–43 Career of cero: politician, ter, rhetorician, nd philosopher.

87–8 The heyday of Roman poetry, culminating with Virgil (70–19), who wrote the Roman epic *The Aeneid*.

79 Eruption of Vesuvius destroys Pompeii and Herculaneum.

35–65 Seneca publishes Stoic philosophy and political drama.

64 Great Fire of Rome. Execution of Christian apostles Peter and Paul at Rome.

*A view across the Roman Forum
towards the Colosseum, past the
round temple of Vesta, and the
surviving columns of the temple of
Castor and Pollux. The Forum was
the political and social centre of
Rome for the seven centuries from
the Period of the Kings to the
death of Julius Caesar.*

THE ROMAN REPUBLIC: 509–44 BC

During its first seven centuries, Rome grew from a set of hilltop villages to the largest city in the Mediterranean, commanding the obedience and fear of almost all the known world. This growth took place amidst continuing conflict – both external conflict with other powers and internal conflict at the heart of the state itself.

In the centre of the new city lay the Roman Forum. This provided the stage on which the political dramas of the period were played out, and to tell the story of this urban space is to relate the history of Rome itself.

When the first settlers arrived on the hills that would later become Rome, they buried their dead in the swampy valley. It was drained during the Period of the Kings c.600 BC and quickly began to fill with temples, precincts, sanctuaries, and shrines, as the new city acquired both citizens and territory through war.

The last king of Rome was expelled in c.509 BC with the help of the army and the people, and two consuls were elected to lead the state. An integrated complex of political institutions grew up in the Forum. The new Republic required a Senate House, public assembly area, and a rostrum, from which magistrates could address the people. After a long struggle between the plebeians and patricians, there was also a bench for the plebeian tribunes, who had won the right, and the duty, to protect the people from the excesses of their rulers.

The Forum also became a showplace for the noble families of Rome, whose funeral processions wended their way there. The funerals would end with addresses from the rostrum by relatives of the deceased on the history and glory of the family and sometimes with great gladiatorial contests in the middle of the Forum.

As Rome's power in Italy grew, its citizens were in a constant state of military alert. The temple of Janus in the Forum was a reminder of war at home: by tradition, its gates were closed only in peacetime, and they remained open (with one brief respite) throughout the entire Republican period. Roman troops ventured further and further afield in the Mediterranean, and the wealth and glory of empire were brought right into the heart of the city. Statues of victors, collections of spoils, and foreign art jostled for space amid the monumental new buildings erected by generals along the route of their triumphal processions.

But empire also brought popular discontent to Rome, and the plebeian tribunes played a central role in battles in the Senate, and with the people, over land, political rights, debt, and food shortages. From the mid-130s BC, Tiberius and Gaius Gracchus fought for their radical reforms from the rostrum, before their deaths at the hands of senators.

The dictator Sulla increased the power of the Senate at the expense of the people, but his attempt to silence the tribunes failed. During the last decades of the Republic, the Forum witnessed rioting, occupations, and barricades. Pompey and Caesar vied for the support of the people and the army. In the fevered revolutionary atmosphere of the 50s BC, the last great popular tribune, Clodius Pulcher, was murdered; in a parody of an aristocratic funeral in more peaceful times, his supporters displayed his body on the rostrum before cremating him in the Senate House, burning it to the ground.

These battles between great men for individual power foretold a new era in Rome. Caesar built a new Senate House, obliterating the public assembly space, and then began work on an entirely new Forum. His funeral in the old Forum in 44 BC marked the very end of its glory: his successors in power, including Mark Antony and the future emperor Augustus, would later use its rostrum to display the remains of hundreds of victims of their persecutions.

The Foundation of Rome and the Period of the Kings

Traditionally, the rise of Rome begins with the fall of Troy. Aeneas, a Trojan prince, escaped the burning city, holding his infant son by the hand and carrying his father on his back. They set off on an odyssey through the Mediterranean which eventually led to the shores of Italy and the kingdom of the Latins, where Aeneas married a local princess.

The Etruscans were Rome's most powerful neighbours. A wealthy, cosmopolitan federation of towns grew up north of the Tiber, flourishing from the 8th to 6th centuries BC, with an artistic tradition that rivalled their military reputation.

Legends of early Rome

The historical origins of Rome are shrouded in legends such as the one narrated in *The Aeneid*. They are found in versions told almost a millennium after the first archaeological traces of settlement on those hills around 1000 BC. These tales were retold and reshaped over the years by Greek scholars and by Italy's travelling story-tellers and performers.

Romulus and Remus, it is said, were descendants of Aeneas, twin brothers of mixed Trojan and Latin blood. They were born to Rhea Silvia, a princess of Alba Longa condemned to life as a virgin priestess when her uncle usurped her father's throne. Despite this precaution, she became pregnant, apparently by the god Mars. After their birth, her uncle threw her into prison, and the infants were placed in the Tiber to drown. There they were discovered by a she-wolf, who suckled them until they were found by the king's shepherd. He and his wife raised the boys as herdsmen. When Remus, now a young man, was jailed on a charge of cattle-rustling, he was recognized by his grandfather Numitor, the rightful king. The truth out, the brothers reinstalled Numitor on the throne before leaving to found a city at the place they had once been left to drown, where seven hills surrounded a crossing of the Tiber. There they quarrelled over the right to govern the new city, and in the fight Remus was killed. Romulus fortified the Palatine hill and became the first king of Rome. The traditional date for the city's foundation is 753 BC.

The beginnings of Rome

In order to amass a population for his fledgling city, Romulus opened the gates to the homeless, the poor, the criminals, and the slaves of nearby communities. This marked the beginning of Rome's traditional openness to outsiders. He organized the population into tribes and chose 100 senators to form a council of advisers.

The new city and its unsavoury inhabitants were viewed with deep suspicion by the Latin communities in the area and the Sabines to the north-east, and they refused to intermarry with the Romans. In need of wives for his citizens, Romulus invited these neighbours to a festival. They came, curious to see the new town, and they brought their families. On a pre-arranged signal, young Romans seized the women and carried them off. This act of treachery led to war. Romulus gradually defeated the surrounding communities and invited the inhabitants to move to Rome, reuniting many of the women with their families and increasing the extent of Roman territory. The Sabines were the last to attack Rome; the Sabine women threw themselves between their husbands and fathers on the battlefield and begged them to make peace. The two populations merged, and the Sabine king Tatius ruled jointly with Romulus. By the time Romulus died, Rome was a thriving local power.

Rome's early territory in the immediate vicinity of the city expanded during the Period of the Kings to fill the prosperous and productive lowlands of Latium between the Sabine Mountains to the north and the Alban Hills to the south. Despite skirmishes, the hill towns and tribes of central Italy were not yet threatened by the fast-growing city in the plain.

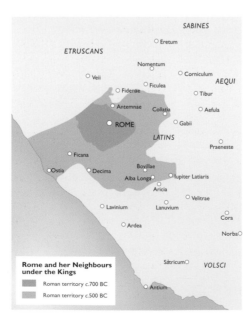

Rome and her Neighbours under the Kings

- Roman territory c.700 BC
- Roman territory c.500 BC

SABINES
Eretum
ETRUSCANS
Nomentum
Veii
Corniculum
Ficulea
AEQUI
Fidenae
Tibur
Antemnae
Collatia
Aefula
ROME
Gabii
LATINS
Praeneste
Ficana
Bovillae
Ostia
Decima
Iupiter Latiaris
Alba Longa
Aricia
Velitrae
Lavinium
Lanuvium
Cora
Ardea
Norba
Satricum
VOLSCI
Antium

Perhaps the most famous statue from Roman antiquity, the "Capitoline Wolf" is actually an Etruscan bronze sculpture dating from around 500 BC. It stands almost a metre (3 ft) tall. The she-wolf was the symbol of Rome from an early stage, athough this statue may not have been intended to recall the myth of Romulus and Remus: no doubt because the story of Romulus and Remus was so central to Roman mythology, the twin boys were added to the sculpture during the Renaissance.

The legendary kings

The legends of the regal period tell us little about what actually happened in early Rome, but they do reveal a great deal about Roman self-identity and self-understanding as a military and religious community. The Roman character, at least as it was later understood, was based on centuries of military glory, collective piety, and a curious combination of aggression towards neighbouring peoples and generosity to defeated foes. The stories of Romulus' reign reflected and perpetuated an image of Rome as an inclusive city, where initiative and courage counted for more than racial or tribal origins, and enemies were incorporated into the Roman population, rather than wiped out.

The kings who were supposedly elected to follow Romulus are also ciphers, fictions with which the Romans explained the origins of their political and religious institutions. Priesthoods, rituals, and the sacred calendar are ascribed to Romulus' peace-loving successor Numa Pompilius, who was, like Tatius, a Sabine; political institutions such as the Senate House are attributed to Tullus Hostilius. In the same spirit, the religious regulations governing declarations of war and treaties are said to be the work of Ancus Marcius. Archaeologists in Rome have found evidence of trade with the rest of Italy and with Greece, of craft production, and of increasing prosperity in Rome from this period (*c.*750–600 BC).

The Etruscan kings

The last kings of Rome, the household of an Etruscan immigrant of Greek descent, presided over the urbanization of the city until 509 BC. Although we do not

know if the Tarquins really ruled at Rome, the military and engineering projects attributed to them are genuine. Monumental building, trade, contacts abroad, and the influence of the Greeks and the Etruscans increased dramatically in this period. The stories of these kings are also full of the boldness and ingenuity of the women around them, a reflection of the high standing that women had in Etruscan society.

As the story goes, Tarquin the Elder came to Rome with his wife Tanaquil to seek his fortune, befriended the king Ancus Marcius, and was elected to succeed him on his death in 616 BC. He waged war on the Latins, drained the marshy valley to create the Forum, and laid the foundations for the great temple on the Capitol to Jupiter, Juno, and Minerva, before the old king's sons assassinated him. Tanaquil's cunning saw to it that they would not succeed him. She told the people that her husband was merely wounded and that their son-in-law, Servius Tullius, would act as regent while he recovered. By the time the truth was known, the young man had entrenched his position.

Trying to avoid the fate of his father-in-law, Servius had his own daughters, both named Tullia, married to two of Tarquin's descendants. Another Tarquin, an arrogant man, married a dutiful daughter; his milder brother Arruns married an ambitious one. Both matches were unhappy, and the bolder pair arranged the murders of their respective spouses and married. Tarquin began canvassing the support of the aristocrats, who felt that Servius was too generous in distributing land to the citizens, and staged a coup. He ruled from 534–510 BC, retaining the throne through fear, and came to be known as Tarquin the Proud.

The Early Republic and the Struggle of the Orders

Tarquin the Proud was a successful general, but he ruled without reference to the people or the Senate. He operated at home through a mixture of murder, exile, and confiscation of property from the rich and forced labour for the poor. The nobles rebelled against him, and a republic was established on the banks of the Tiber.

A typically salacious 16th-century painting of the legend of the Rape of Lucretia. This Roman myth, like its Renaissance re-interpreters, explored the political and social upheavals of the age through the metaphor of women's bodies and sexuality.

The end of the monarchy

The constitutional revolution at Rome may have been sparked by palace or aristocratic intrigue, or the intervention of an Etruscan leader, but the Romans themselves told the story of the rape of Lucretia, whose husband Collatinus was a relative of the king. Lucretia was famed for her virtue. One night, when the king and all the nobles were away on campaign, the king's son Sextus visited her house in Collatia, near Rome, and raped her at knife point. She summoned her father and husband, and made them promise to avenge her. They proclaimed her innocence, but she insisted that she should not be an example of unchastity and killed herself. Collatinus had brought with him the king's nephew Brutus, who until that moment had feigned stupidity to avoid assassination. Brutus took charge of the situation and marched on Rome. Moved by Lucretia's plight and reminded of their own suffering, the people rallied to him. When Tarquin returned to Rome, he found the gates barred against him. Inside the city, two consuls were elected to replace the king: Brutus and Collatinus. Tradition dates the founding of the Republic to 509 BC.

The early Republic

The early years of aristocratic rule in Rome were lean ones for the new Republic. A treaty with Carthage traditionally dated to the first year of the Republic in 509 BC recognized Roman suzerainty in Latium, but within a decade Rome was once again at war with the Latins. With aid from the gods Castor and Pollux, according to legend, the Romans triumphed at the battle of Lake Regillus in 493 BC, and the Romans and the Latin towns made a treaty granting their citizens the right to intermarry, conduct business, and transfer their citizenship. Peace with the Latins lasted for at least a century, but the surrounding mountain peoples went on the offensive and took much of the territory the kings had won. Rome soon lost the southern half of Latium to the Volscians and was harassed by raids from the Sabines in the north and the Aequi, a highland tribe to the east. On occasion, the enemy threatened Rome itself. There was also ongoing conflict between Rome and the Etruscan city of Veii, just 16 kilometres (10 miles) to the north.

Alongside the loss of power in central Italy came trouble at home. Foreign contacts and trade dried up by the second quarter of the 5th century BC. There is no evidence of monumental building for about 75 years, with few temple dedications and a decline in the quantity and quality of artistic production. This is probably not due to the political changes; the same phenomena is also apparent in the cities of Etruria, Latium, and southern Italy, and the incursions from the mountains are related to migrations of peoples causing havoc all through Italy.

The "Struggle of the Orders"

In these difficult times, the Roman aristocracy was split between a patrician minority supposedly descended from Romulus' first 100 senators, and a larger group of plebeians of more recent wealth and status. The patricians controlled religious offices and had the power of veto over decisions taken by the people. In the first years of the Republic, the consulship could be held by plebeians, but the patricians monopolized it from the 480s BC. The first Roman law code, published c.450 BC, confirms the schism: among the provisions was a ban on intermarriage between plebeians and patricians.

The plebeian families fought this inequality by refusing on occasion to fight on Rome's behalf. They withdrew to hills outside the city on a regular basis, only returning when their demands were met. There were small victories for the plebeians, including the right to elect tribunes to represent them. At some point these tribunes acquired the power of veto over any magistrate or law. It was not until 367 BC, however, that a law was passed re-opening the consulship to the plebeians. In 300 BC, the priestly colleges were divided between the two orders; in 287 BC, the decrees of the plebeian tribal assembly became binding.

Although the "Struggle of the Orders" was a dispute among the elite, the plebeian assembly and tribunes also represented the city's lower classes. These peasants and artisans must have suffered during the troubles of the 5th century BC. They would have gained little material advantage from the political concessions made in that century, but in 367 BC there is credible evidence of laws passed to relieve debt and protect the access of the peasants to land. Most importantly, debt bondage was abolished in 326 BC, which meant that Roman citizens could no longer be enslaved for falling into debt. This flurry of legislation suggests either that the woes of the poor worsened in the 4th century BC, or that they had learnt to voice their discontent in such a way as to elicit some response. In any case, a more lasting solution to their problems was sought in the establishment of colonies throughout Italy.

Was Rome democratic?

Only free male citizens could vote, and their votes were not equal. The junior magistracies were elected in the Tribal Assembly, where each tribe had one vote. There were 15 tribes for rural voters and only four for city dwellers, so the system was weighted towards the more conservative rural population. The consul and the other senior magistrates were elected by the Centuriate Assembly. Here voters were allotted to "centuries" within five property classes, and each century had one vote. The wealthiest class had an overall majority of centuries and began the voting. The election ended once a majority was reached, so the votes of the lower classes were rarely needed. With the introduction of the secret ballot in the late 2nd century (depicted on the coin above), the average citizen could cast his vote in greater safety.

This depiction of a census comes from an altar dedicated on the Campus Martius in Rome by the consul Domitius Ahenobarbus in 122 BC. The citizens are being registered on lists by the official on the left. The census took place every five years, and was followed by a ritual purification ceremony.

Rome in Italy

Military fortunes began to improve at the end of the 5th century BC for the Romans and their Latin allies. They clawed back southern Latium from the Volsci, founded a number of colonies there, and introduced pay for soldiers. In 396 BC, Veii fell to Rome after a long siege and was destroyed.

Annexation and colonization

With the fall of Veii, the Romans adopted a new strategy. They annexed its territory and divided it among the Roman people. By settling citizen-farmers on new land, they not only quieted discontent among the rural population, but also ensured that these peasants could meet the property qualification to serve in the army. Around this time, Rome imposed a property tax on its citizens to fund military operations and instituted indemnities for defeated enemies. These changes put the army on a more secure footing; however, things would get worse before they got better. The Gauls attacked and sacked Rome in 390 BC, almost capturing the Capitol itself – and this time it was the Romans who had to pay a large indemnity in order to persuade them to leave.

Rome recovered quickly from the Gallic sack, and military policy became more aggressive. The city continued to make war on the mountain peoples, annexed more land, and began to found colonies in Etruria. This added to the difficulties of the Etruscans, who had lost their holdings in southern Italy in the 5th century BC and were now trapped between the newly powerful Romans in the south and the Gauls in the north. Roman activity was gaining notice outside Italy, too: in 348 BC, another treaty with Carthage viewed Rome as a military, colonial, and trading power, and as a potential threat to Carthaginian interests in all these areas.

Citizenship and expansion

The rapid expansion of Rome alarmed its allies, and the Latins sometimes sided with the mountain peoples against the city. In 341 BC, the Latins united against Rome, but they were comprehensively defeated in 338 BC. Many Latin communities were directly incorporated into Roman citizenship, much of their land was annexed, and the ancient League of the Latins was broken forever.

Rome now turned its attention south, where the Samnites had been attacking and occupying Greek and Etruscan cities, also weakened by class conflict, for almost a century. Roman progress was rapid. Their first intervention in the region had come in 343 BC, when the besieged city of Capua appealed for help against the Samnites. Roman armies lifted the siege, and in 340 BC the Capuan aristocracy were granted Roman citizenship. The remainder of the Campanians received a form of the citizenship in 338 BC. They did not receive the right to vote, but they did incur the responsibilities of taxation and military service. Rome made further strategic alliances: in 326 BC, for instance, the Romans came to the aid of the aristocratic faction at Naples against the Samnites, who were supported by the Neapolitan masses. The first Roman colonies south of Latium were established in 334 and 328 BC, and many more were to follow.

These local conflicts escalated into several full-scale wars between the Romans and the Samnites. The final battle occurred in 295 BC, when the Samnites, having formed an alliance with the Gauls, Etruscans, and Umbrians against Rome, made one last effort to resist Roman hegemony. After defeating this coalition, Rome was unquestionably the greatest power in Italy. Some of the Greek cities in the south held out a little longer, and democratic Tarentum (the Roman name for Taras) the longest of all. The Tarentines summoned the Greek war hero Pyrrhus of

By the middle of the 3rd century Italy was a patchwork of communities of Roman citizens and "allies". Although all were effectively subject to the government at Rome, the different classifications and privileges given to the various towns and peoples were one of the reasons why they developed little solidarity against their common overlord.

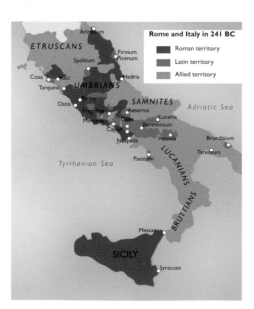

Rome and Italy in 241 BC

- Roman territory
- Latin territory
- Allied territory

ETRUSCANS
Ariminum
Firmum
Picenum
Spoletium
Cosa · Vulci
Tarquinii · Hadria
UMBRIANS
Ostia · Rome
Fregellae
Minturnae · Cales · SAMNITES
Capua · Aesernia
Neapolis · Luceria
Beneventum
Venusia · Brundisium
Paestum · Tarentum
Tyrrhenian Sea
LUCANIANS
Adriatic Sea
BRUTTIANS
Messana
SICILY
Syracuse

The Roman amphitheatre at Capua in Campania. Capua was one of the first cities in southern Italy to ally itself with the Romans, in 343 BC. The alliance was valuable to both sides, and the first major Roman road in Italy, the Via Appia, was built from Rome to Capua in 312 BC. It was a major blow to Rome when the city defected to Hannibal in 216 BC.

Epirus to their aid – the first foreign general to fight on Italian soil – but he, too, was defeated by a Roman army in 275 BC.

Roman hegemony

The Romans conquered Italy in several different ways. They annexed land to the city, incorporated communities into different forms of Roman citizenship, and established colonies throughout the peninsula. They appeased their own lower classes with land, booty, and the benefits of civic prosperity such as aqueducts and roads, and they forged alliances with aristocratic factions in other cities. Most Italians, on their defeat or surrender, became allies of Rome, rather than citizens. They were liable for military services – and shared in the profits of war. As in the incorporated towns, the aristocracies of these allied communities could rely on Roman help if they experienced domestic troubles. Italy became a patchwork of Roman citizens, colonies, and allies, and soon Sicily beckoned.

The First Punic War

Sicily was divided between Greek cities in the east of the island and Carthaginian foundations in the west. In 288 BC, the Mamertines, a rogue band of mercenaries from Campania, had taken control of the Sicilian city of Messana just across the straits from Italy. They caused a great deal of trouble for the Greeks and Carthaginians on the island, and in the end the Syracusans besieged them in their city. One faction at Messana appealed to Carthage for help, while the other appealed to Rome. The Carthaginians arrived first and installed a garrison. At Rome, the consuls put the question of intervention to a vote of the people (dwelling, it is said, on the material gains of war). The Romans voted to send an army to Messana in 264 BC, and the conflict escalated. With the troubles of Messana soon forgotten, Rome and Carthage were at war with one another in the first of the conflicts known as the Punic Wars.

This war for Sicily was long and fought largely at sea. The Romans were not seafarers, which initially put them at a disadvantage. It was only when they captured a Carthaginian war ship that they were able to build their own warships on the same model. Three times they lost an entire fleet at sea. Eventually, the Romans forced a truce in 241 BC. The Carthaginians were to pay a large indemnity, and to withdraw from Sicily entirely, leaving Rome with its first province outside the mainland. Carthage was immediately confronted with a bitter rebellion by its own mercenaries and African subjects. The Romans took advantage of the city's distress to demand that they also cede the island of Sardinia. The Carthaginians could not refuse, but never forgot the injustice. With the coming of Hannibal, the Romans would regret their greed.

ROME IN ITALY   77

The Conquest of the Mediterranean

The First Punic War brought the Romans into the Mediterranean; victory in the Second Punic War against the might of Hannibal led to their domination of the entire region. Their rise was rapid. The Greek politician and scholar Polybius claimed that in less than 53 years (220–167 BC), they brought almost the whole of the inhabited world under their rule.

The Hannibalic War

Deprived of Sicily and Sardinia, the Carthaginians turned their attention towards Spain. By the time Hannibal became leader of the Carthaginian forces in Spain in 221 BC, a large portion of the peninsula was already under Punic (Carthaginian) control. For their part, the Romans went to war against Queen Teuta of Illyria, claiming that she sponsored piracy in the Adriatic, and took steps to pacify the Gauls who were threatening their northern frontier.

The two states came to blows again over Hannibal's siege of Saguntum, a city on Spain's eastern coast. The Romans claimed this city as an ally, and further claimed that Hannibal was breaking previous treaties both by attacking this city and by advancing so far north in Spain. The Carthaginians disputed these claims, and the city fell to Hannibal after eight months. Rome sent envoys to Carthage, demanding that they surrender their champion. When the Carthaginians refused, the envoys declared war. The Romans assumed that they would fight this war in Spain and sent one consular army there, with another to Carthage itself. To their astonishment, Hannibal set out overland for Italy.

After a difficult march over the Pyrenees and the Alps, during which many of his soldiers, horses, and elephants perished, Hannibal defeated the hastily recalled Roman armies at Trebbia and Trasimene in northern Italy. He moved through the peninsula, bypassing Rome, and in 216 BC he won a devastating victory at Cannae in the south: the Romans lost more than 70,000 men in a single day of fighting.

Hannibal found many allies, both among the Gauls in the north of Italy who had been resisting Rome for several years, and among the Greek and Italian cities in the south who now rebelled against their overlord. Hannibal's boldest alliance was with King Philip V of Macedon in 215 BC. Philip was also interfering with Roman interests in the Adriatic, and when a treaty between the two was discovered by the Romans, they declared war on Macedonia as well. As they were fully occupied with the war with Hannibal, this war was fought largely by Greek allies on their behalf and reached an impasse in the last years of the 3rd century BC.

After their comprehensive defeats on the battlefield, the Romans pursued a policy of avoiding direct confrontation, on the advice of the general Fabius Cunctator, who was known as the "Delayer" because of his military tactics. They harried the Carthaginian troops, recovered cities in the absence of Hannibal's army, and gradually clawed back control of Italy. At the same time, they captured Carthaginian strongholds in Sicily and Spain. With Hannibal eventually confined to the far south of the peninsula, the Romans went on the offensive

Elephants were first used in war against the Romans by Pyrrhus of Epirus in 280 BC, who brought twenty of these "Lucanian Cows" with him to Italy. They were also used by the Carthaginians in the First Punic War, and Hannibal led a troop over the Alps. The Romans used them only occasionally in war, from the 2nd century onwards. Elephants were more prized at Rome for ceremonial purposes.

and took the war to Africa, with Hannibal hard on their heels. The great Roman general Scipio eventually defeated Hannibal's forces there at the battle of Zama in 202 BC, earning himself the nickname "Africanus".

Now that the Carthaginians had been forced out of Spain, the Romans took some areas of the peninsula under their direct control. From 197 BC, they made a permanent military and administrative commitment, sending out annual praetors to two separate regions, Nearer Spain and Hither Spain. As in Sicily and Sardinia, the presence of Roman troops and officials enabled the Romans to exploit the area's mineral and agricultural resources, as well as to claim tribute from its inhabitants. Although formal Roman colonies were not established, the new opportunities attracted Italian merchants and businessmen to the areas.

Wars in the East

With victory over Carthage secured, hostilities were now resumed with Macedonia, and Philip was defeated at Cynoscephalae in 197 BC. At first, instead of creating provinces in the eastern Mediterranean, the Romans consolidated their hegemony through alliances and political intervention. Building on the diplomatic success of their earlier victory over Illyria, whose pirates had threatened Greeks in the Adriatic as well as Italians, they now posed as liberators of the Greeks from Macedonia. At the conclusion of the war with Philip, the Roman general Flamininus appeared at the Isthmian Games at Corinth in 196 BC, and declared that the Greek cities henceforth would be free of garrisons and tribute,

and subject to their own laws. It was said that the Greeks' jubilation was so loud that birds fell out of the sky.

The Romans returned to the East in 192 BC to take on the Syrian king, Antiochus III, after he defied their order to free the Greek cities in Asia. That war ended in defeat for Antiochus, but the freedom of the Greeks was to be conditional. Rome established oligarchic governments in some cities, and encouraged them in others. The Senate expected all disputes in the East to be referred to them for settlement, and all Roman commands to be obeyed, even by the Hellenistic kings. Philip V's son Perseus tried to reinvigorate Macedonian influence in Greece and received a great deal of popular support, but was defeated by Rome in 167 BC. Roman hegemony was complete: when Antiochus IV of Syria invaded Egypt in the same year, he was met by a Roman envoy who handed him instructions from the Senate to leave the country. Antiochus said that he would consider the request, whereupon the Roman drew a circle around him with a stick and ordered him to remain inside the circle until he had made a decision. Antiochus agreed to leave.

The Romans made another military intervention in the East in the early 140s BC, when a revolt in Greece brought about a war with the Achaeans, leading to the Roman destruction of Corinth in 146 BC, the same year that Carthage was finally destroyed. Over the next decades, the Romans gradually formalized their hegemony overseas, sending governors and standing armies, making laws, planting colonies, and distributing or selling land in their control.

Politics and Discontent in Rome and Italy

The new empire brought great riches to Rome, but it also brought suffering and dissent. The wealthy, the lower classes, and Rome's allies in Italy all had grievances, and these disputes erupted into the violence that would dominate the last century of the Republic.

Corruption and competition

The rewards of empire were enormous. As well as taxes imposed on the provinces in the west, there were war indemnities, hundreds of thousands of slaves, and a great deal of booty. The booty from Carthage in 146 BC was more than enough to finance a spectacular aqueduct, the Aqua Marcia, the Republic's most expensive building project. The Roman people also benefited from the construction of new roads and the abolition of property tax in 167 BC.

Much of the new wealth, however, ended up in the hands of the elite. As well as senators, this included the *equites*, or knights, members of the upper class who did not pursue political careers – their name comes from their original function as cavalry in the Roman army. Legitimate means of enrichment were abundant, but illegitimate means became ever more attractive, as wealth became the only way to demonstrate honour and prestige. Bribery and corruption were rampant, especially among provincial governors and their staff.

Members of the elite competed to display their wealth and win the political favour of the people. They erected public buildings, put on great specta-cles, and lived extravagantly. The more conservative senators became concerned by this individualism and attempted to stifle these excesses by passing laws against luxurious private entertainment and dress. They also regulated access to public office, instituting minimum ages, compulsory intervals between offices, and a ban on holding the consul-ship more than once.

Rome's businessmen, drawn from the *equites*, did well from building contracts at Rome and the opera-tion of industry and taxation in the provinces. But tensions developed with the Senate over the terms of these contracts, and the *equites* also resented their exclusion from the courts, where only senators could be jurors.

The land crisis

Discontent among the elite was nothing compared to growing rancour among the lower classes, especially the rural peasantry who made up the army. The unceasing warfare that had won Rome its empire had forced Roman soldiers to spend years abroad on campaign. Their farms often collapsed in their absence, forcing them to abandon or sell their land. During the 2nd century BC, the newly enriched

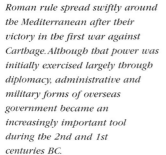

Roman rule spread swiftly around the Mediterranean after their victory in the first war against Carthage. Although that power was initially exercised largely through diplomacy, administrative and military forms of overseas government became an increasingly important tool during the 2nd and 1st centuries BC.

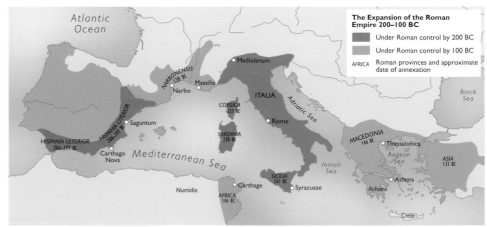

The Expansion of the Roman Empire 200–100 BC

Under Roman control by 200 BC

Under Roman control by 100 BC

AFRICA Roman provinces and approximate date of annexation

A banquet from a wall painting found at Pompeii, on the bay of Naples. Life for the wealthy in Roman Italy was a far cry from the dirt, disease, and overcrowding suffered by most of the urban poor. As the rich took over agricultural land and built country villas, peasants were forced off their land and often into the cities.

elite bought up far more public land than the law permitted. The peasants who had farmed this land had nowhere to go.

It was not only Romans who were suffering: the Italians also fought for Rome and lost their land, and they were now increasingly treated as subjects rather than allies by the Romans, liable to plunder, persecution, and interference in local affairs.

The downtrodden looked to the plebeian tribunes for help, and this era saw an unprecedented increase in the power and visibility of these tribunes. As social concerns came to the fore at Rome, politicians became known as *populares* ("for the people") or *optimates* ("for the best").

Tiberius Gracchus

Tiberius Gracchus, grandson of Scipio Africanus, was elected tribune in 133 BC. He attempted to alleviate rural poverty with a bill that would compel large landowners to give up any public land they held in excess of the legal limit. This land would then be redistributed to the poor. In his speeches, Tiberius claimed to be the champion of those "who fought and died to win luxury for others".

Many senators were opposed to the plan, and persuaded one of the other nine tribunes to veto it. In return, Tiberius removed the tribune from office. He successfully resubmitted his proposal to the people and set up a commission to begin dividing up the public land. In the same year, King Attalus of Pergamum bequeathed Rome his kingdom, which became the province of Asia, and his property. Tiberius proposed to divert the new resources to the people, to provide equipment grants for his settlers. Enraged, his opponents took matters into their own hands when he stood for re-election the next year. While the people were voting, the senators beat Tiberius and more than 300 supporters to death, before throwing his body into the Tiber.

Gaius Gracchus

Ten years later in 123 BC, Tiberius's younger brother Gaius was elected tribune, and he renewed the battle for reform. He passed laws for further land distribution, the foundation of new colonies, subsidized grain, restrictions on military service, the recruitment of the *equites* to the juries, and the protection of provincials from the corruption of Roman magistrates. He also proposed the extension of Roman citizenship to the Latins and voting rights to the Italians, but this did not pass – the Romans were keen to protect their privileges. The Senate opposed Gaius as implacably as they had his brother, and once again politics led to violence. In 122 BC, Gaius killed himself just outside Rome, pursued by a senatorial mob.

Marius' army

The last great popular politician of the 2nd century BC chose practical innovation over confrontation. Gaius Marius was a distinguished soldier, a Roman citizen from an Italian town, and a "new man" – he had no senatorial ancestors. He won his first consulship in 107 BC by denouncing the corruption and luxury of the elite ranks of society, and he amassed forces to defeat King Jugurtha of Numidia by enlisting volunteers as well as the usual conscripts. He settled his soldiers in veteran colonies. In this way, he won the favour of the people and created an army that was loyal to him before the state. The Romans elected him consul again in 104 BC when a German attack seemed imminent. Over the next five years of successful warfare against the Germans he was annually re-elected, a break with Republican tradition that would prove ominous.

The Age of the Generals

The complaints of the Italians and of Roman peasants went unheeded by the Senate, which now found itself under attack. The provinces threatened rebellion. Slave revolts had shaken Sicily, and unemployment and food shortages were driving the urban poor to violence. Powerful individuals with client armies dominated the last decades of the Republic, dismantling its institutions and fighting over its remains.

War with the Italian allies

The Italians became increasingly frustrated by their meagre success in obtaining land grants and voting rights from Rome in return for their enforced alliance, and felt increasingly inconvenienced by the new colonies and settlers that Roman land reform had scattered throughout Italy. In 91 BC, they agreed among themselves to do away with Roman exploitation altogether, and to replace the current regime with a federal state, Italia, with a capital at Corfinium on the other side of the Appenine mountains from Rome. Hostages were exchanged between the Italian communities as pledges of good faith, but the plot was discovered when a Roman agent saw a hostage

Mithridates' image played on that of the famous Hellenistic kings who came before him. Here his lionskin headdress, his hairstyle, and the slight tilt of his head recall portraits of Alexander the Great.

being taken from the town of Asculum, near the eastern coast of Italy. The Roman official responsible for the area hurried to the town, but his threats to the townspeople were in vain: he was put to death along with all the Romans inhabitants of the town, touching off a general revolt which spread throughout central and southern Italy. This war was the first for centuries to pit Roman and Italian troops against each other, and it was a vicious struggle. Velleius Paterculus, writing in the time of the emperor Tiberius, tells us that this war carried off more than 300,000 of the youth of Italy.

It took Rome two years to conciliate most of the combatants with promises of citizenship, and another seven to finally defeat the Samnites, who marched on Rome itself in 82 BC. Sulla defeated them in battle at the Colline Gate, and imprisoned several thousand of them in Rome's election hall for several days before sending his soldiers in to slaughter them all. He followed this up by killing or banishing all the Samnite leaders. With the fiercest rebels neutralized, most Italians were given the right to Roman citizenship, and all Italy came under the full sway of Rome.

Powerful generals and client armies

The 80s also brought trouble from outside Italy, and brought civil war to the city of Rome. Mithridates, the charismatic king of Pontus on the Black Sea, invaded Roman territory in Asia in 88–84 BC. He was welcomed as a liberator by many of the provincial subjects, who were being subjected to extortion by Roman officials as well as the usual taxation and political interference by the Roman state. In Rome, the people wanted to award the command against Mithridates to Marius; the majority of the Senate preferred Marius' old deputy in Numidia, Sulla. Both generals resorted to military force to stake their claim. Sulla marched on Rome with his army, drove Marius out of the city, and imposed martial law. His hold on the city was precarious, however, and after he and his troops left to face Mithridates in Greece, Marius recaptured Rome and was elected to a seventh consulship, but died before he could set out in pursuit of his rival.

In 85 BC Sulla made a lucrative peace treaty with Mithridates in order to return to Rome. Once again, he marched on the city, and by 81 BC he was firmly in control. He revived the ancient office of the dictatorship, by which the Senate awarded supreme power to one individual at times of national crisis, traditionally in order to complete a specific task and for a very short time: six months at most. As sole ruler, Sulla reorganized the magistracies, deprived the people's tribunes of their traditional powers and prestige, and killed more than 90 of his enemies in the Senate after publishing their names on proscription lists. The loyalty of his soldiers on the other hand was not forgotten, and he settled them in veteran colonies all over Italy. These colonies had the added benefit of acting as informal garrisons to counter potential centres of resistance such as Pompeii and Praeneste, where Sullan colonization meant that Roman families and the Latin language swiftly replaced the original inhabitants and the Oscan tongue in the civic records. With his reforms and revenge accomplished, Sulla retired from public life in 79 BC and died the following year.

The tactics of Marius and Sulla were a glimpse of things to come. Soldiers who had once been reluctant to abandon their farms and families for years to fight for Rome were now eager to fight for individual generals who bought their loyalty with shares of land grants and booty. Over the following decades, these generals came to enjoy unprecedented power and freedom of action through "special commands" awarded by the people for years at a time.

Trouble in the West

Even after Sulla's retirement, there was to be no rest for Roman armies: another source of trouble had already appeared on the western horizon. Sertorius was a Roman general in Spain who had been deprived of his command there and placed on a proscription list as a result of the in-fighting between the supporters of Marius and Sulla in Rome at the end of the 80s. After a brief period as a mercenary in Mauretania, he returned to Spain in 80 to organize the indigenous peoples and the expatriate Roman and Italian population in support of a revolt against Rome's current leadership. A brilliant general and a crafty tactician, Sertorius also used religious superstition to secure his authority, in particular by making a pet of a white deer who was thought to have miraculous qualities. He made useful alliances with Cilician pirates and even with Mithridates, the king of Pontus, and for several years had effective control of Spain despite the best efforts of a series of Roman commanders, including Pompey the Great. In the end, however, Roman resources proved stronger than Sertorius's skill, and after a succession of defeats he was assassinated by his own deputy in 73 BC.

In the same year, a Thracian gladiator called Spartacus started a revolt in southern Italy which quickly spread from the gladiatorial schools to slaves and many of the free poor, until Spartacus successfully led around 100,000 troops against Roman generals, including both the consuls of 72. It took the Romans two years to contain this massive insurrection, but eventually Crassus defeated Spartacus in southern Italy and crucified all his supporters. For a brief time there was peace, but resistance continued to simmer under the surface.

This statue of Pompey from the Spada collection in Rome may well be the famous one that stood in the Curia of Pompey, where the senate met on the day of Caesar's assassination. The dictator fell at the feet of a statue of his erstwhile rival.

Julius Caesar was another wealthy aristocrat, six years younger than Pompey, and nephew of Marius by marriage. He first won fame in the 70s as a soldier and orator, and then won the favour of the people by funding generous entertainments and public works, and by extensive electoral bribery. He became *pontifex maximus* (the most senior rank in the Roman priesthood) in 63 at the extremely young age of 37, and obtained the consulship in 59 BC with the support of Pompey. In 58 BC he was given a proconsular command in Gaul, and began a spectacular, decade-long conquest of the region that would bring him both glory and booty on a grand scale. All in all, perhaps a million Gauls died and another million were enslaved as a result of Cauesar's Gallic campaigns.

In 55 BC Caesar's campaign took him as far as the southern shores of Britain; after an inconclusive series of battles with the indigenous population, he imposed tribute on the British commander Cassivelaunus, and departed. The geographer Strabo, writing under Augustus, explained that the Romans scorned to hold Britain at this time because it would have been unprofitable to maintain troops there; this may be an optimistic reading of Caesar's ability to subdue the island.

Debt, hunger, and violence

Meanwhile, back at home, many Romans had lost their land as a result of the recent warfare in Italy, and debt had become endemic. Violence, riots, and political assassinations were part of everyday life. Two aristocrats emerged as lightning rods for discontent. Sergius Catilina led agitation for land redistribution and debt cancellation in 63 BC, and was hounded out of the city amid accusations of arson and conspiracy by the conservative consul Cicero. Catilina raised an army but was killed in battle, whereupon Cicero persuaded the senators to execute those suspected of co-conspiracy.

The poor found another champion – and Cicero another enemy – in Clodius Pulcher, a libertine, with connections to both Pompey and Caesar. Clodius had unsuccessfully (some said deliberately so) prosecuted Catilina in 65 BC, and in 61 got himself into trouble for a transvestite appearance at the strictly women-only Bona Dea festival in the company of Caesar's wife Pompeia. Clodius was acquitted, but Pompeia was divorced by her husband. Nonetheless, Caesar and Pompey combined their efforts to have Clodius adopted into a plebeian family in 59, so that he would be eligible for election to the plebeian tribunate of 58 BC. Once elected, Clodius' legislation included the provision of free corn for the people, and the restoration of the guilds and clubs. These formed the basis of civic and social life for the lower

Pompey and Caesar

The two men who would overshadow the last three decades of the Republic both used popular rhetoric to shore up their personal power, rather than the traditional appeals to senatorial favour and tradition. Pompey the Great originally came to prominence as an ally of Sulla in the 80s, but restored the powers of the tribunes during his first consulship in 70 BC – a consulship that he had obtained, contrary to the usual regulations, without holding previous office, and at the young age of 36. He went on to eradicate the pirates in the Mediterranean who threatened the city's grain supply, having been appointed to this special command for three years by the people, against the wishes of the Senate. Pompey then spent the late 60s defeating a fresh invasion of the eastern provinces by Mithridates, and afterwards devoted several years to annexing territory for Rome in the East, where he also founded cities: activities that led in some quarters to suspicions that he desired kingship himself.

classes, freedmen and slaves, but had been banned by Cicero as a dangerous conduit for political agitation. Clodius' revolutionary credentials were reinforced when he had the Temple of the Nymphs, which housed the census records, burnt down: after this, any individual's claim to citizenship would have been difficult to dispute.

When Clodius was killed in a brawl with a rival in 52 BC, his supporters burnt down the senate house as his funeral pyre. The grand gesture was futile, however: it was to be a much more conservative revolution that ended the Republic.

The final confrontation

In the riots that followed Clodius's death, and in yet another departure from Republican tradition, Pompey was appointed sole consul to restore public order. His relationship with Caesar declined in the following years. Hitherto the pair had maintained an uneasy alliance based on common interests and experience: both had bypassed the Senate in order to take legislation to the people, and to make foreign policy decisions, and both had earned vast wealth from their conquests. But now Caesar wanted a second consulship to mark his triumphant return from Gaul, and Pompey, jealous of Caesar's pre-eminence in Roman politics, co-operated with the Senate to block it. War was inevitable, with both men claiming that they were defending the Republic against the tyranny of the other. In 49 BC, Caesar and his army crossed the Rubicon river, which marked the boundary of his province, to march on Rome.

The civil war that followed was fought all over the Mediterranean. Pompey led his army to a comprehensive defeat in Greece in 48, and was then murdered in Egypt. His supporters held out, but were eventually defeated in Africa and Spain, and by 46 BC Caesar was consul and dictator at Rome. He reformed the Senate and the magistracies, founded colonies for his veterans and for the urban poor, and was even given divine honours. In 44 BC, still consul, he declared himself dictator for life. This was a step too far, and Caesar was assassinated by a conspiracy of senators on the Ides of March.

Julius Caesar emerged as the victor from the military and ideological battles of the late Republic. A patrician who capitalized both on his family's supposed descent from Aeneas and the goddess Venus, and their more recent connection by marriage to the "new man" Gaius Marius, he also gained popularity with the army during his lengthy and lucrative campaigns.

Republican Culture

In contrast to the elegant theatres and athletics of Greece, Roman entertainment was raw and often bloodthirsty: gladiator shows in the Forum, chariot races at the Circus Maximus, and pantomime in temporary theatres. With the conquest of Greece, more sophisticated and literary entertainments emerged, but they never displaced the thrill of the race and the fight for ordinary Romans.

This mosaic panel from Pompeii shows a group of actors with their chorus master rehearsing for a satyr play, complete with masks, costumes, and musical instruments. Satyr plays were originally performed in Greece as light-hearted finales to the trilogies of tragedies that playwrights composed for dramatic competitions.

The small theatre, or "odeon" at Pompeii held less than 1,000 people and was used for recitations and mimes. Plays were produced at the larger theatre next-door, which held 5,000 spectators.

Festivals and games

Festive holidays were central to Roman culture from its earliest days: the rape of the Sabine women supposedly occurred during a festival organized by the city's mythical founder, Romulus. These religious celebrations offered a break from working life, and often featured esoteric rituals. On the Lupercalia of 15 February, for instance, priests sacrificed goats and a dog at the cave where Romulus and Remus were supposedly suckled by a she-wolf, smeared their blood on the faces of two laughing young men, and then ran around the Palatine, naked except for goat-skins, whipping bystanders with thongs. The purpose of this activity was unclear, even to ancient commentators.

The most famous Roman festival, the Saturnalia, was celebrated for several days at the end of December. During this time the normal order of things was temporarily reversed, especially between slaves and their masters. A "king" was appointed as master of public ceremonies, presents were exchanged and private feasts were held.

Games (*ludi*) were held in honour of many of the religious festivals, and were funded in part by the state, in part by individual magistrates. The games featured chariot races as far back as the regal period, in which up to 12 chariots competed over seven laps. The teams were known by their colours: first white and red, later joined by blue and green. The best-known racing arena was the Circus Maximus, which could hold 150,000 spectators.

Mime artists and dancers were later added to the celebrations; later still, there were plays, although at first they were not written down or circulated separately. Literary drama, along with history and epic, developed through contacts with Greeks in the period of Roman expansion.

The Greek conquest of Roman culture

"Captive Greece took her savage conqueror captive, and brought the arts into rustic Latium." So the poet Horace described the extraordinary appeal of all things Hellenic to the Romans of the later Republic.

While Greek culture was never unknown to the Romans, it became increasingly fashionable as they conquered the Mediterranean. Roman military commanders learned Greek and learned to appreciate Greek art and life, often bringing Greek works of art – painting, sculpture, and bronzes – back to Rome as part of their booty.

The first poets and playwrights to record their work in Latin wrote in the Greek epic genre about Roman history and heroes, and translated Greek plays for the Roman stage. Plautus and Terence were the first Latin writers whose work survives in anything more than fragments. They adapted Greek comedies for Roman religious festivals and funeral games in the early part of the 2nd century BC; these were usually performed in temporary theatres or temples. Both writers relied heavily on misunderstandings, mix-ups, and farce for their comic effect. Life is turned upside down in their domestic dramas: prostitutes are virtuous, and cunning slaves routinely save their masters from trouble. Although some of

The Vestal Virgins

As young girls, Vestal Virgins took a 30-year vow of chastity. These priestesses were charged with the care of the sacred fire in the temple of Vesta in the Forum, which guaranteed the preservation of the city. They led unusually public and independent lives for women, under no man's control, with special seats at banquets and the games, and the power to spare condemned criminals. They were regarded as sacrosanct: if someone so much as bumped into a Vestal's litter, he would be put to death. And if a priestess was found to have broken her vow of chastity, she was buried alive.

the details are "Romanized", it is likely that the Greek setting and the topsy-turvy plots gave the plays an aura of escapism. Potentially subversive elements in the population – especially slaves and women – could run riot, but only in Greece, and only on the stage.

While the people watched these dramas, the Roman elite competed to build temples and public buildings in the Greek style, and to adorn their country villas with Greek works of art, commissioning copies if necessary. The culmination of this conspicuous and competitive Hellenism came in 55 BC, when Pompey built Rome's first permanent stone theatre in the Campus Martius.

Greeks in Rome

Greeks themselves also began to arrive in Rome in large numbers, as craftsmen, doctors, and artists, but also as refugees, slaves, and prisoners of war. The Greek historian Polybius was taken to Rome as a hostage in 167 BC, and it was there that he wrote his 40-volume history in Greek of the Roman rise to power in the Mediterranean.

On a famous occasion in 155 BC, philosophers representing the Stoic, Sceptic, and Peripatetic schools in Athens came to Rome as a delegation. Carneades the Sceptic drew large crowds to his public speeches, where he argued persuasively in favour of justice one day and, on the next, equally convincingly against it. Marcus Porcius Cato, the grand old man of Roman politics, was disgusted. He considered Greek philosophers dangerous windbags and had the delegation sent away as quickly as possible.

The new cosmopolitanism was certainly not welcomed by everybody. Historians and orators regularly blamed the troubles of the late Republic on the effects of the conquest of the East, either pointing to the corruption of Roman troops abroad by oriental luxury or, more practically, to the effects of sudden unprecedented wealth on the Roman upper classes. But Hellenism did not entirely suppress the old culture of Rome. As well as Greek adaptations, Roman drama had a strong homegrown tradition of contemporary political commentary and satire, and Latin authors concerned themselves with practical matters such as agriculture and law, as well as the new arts of history and philosophy. Cato himself wrote a treatise on farming, in addition to one of the first historical works in Latin, on the origins of Italian communities.

Latin poets often combined Greek genres and techniques with Roman themes and experience. The poets of the last decades of the Republic used Greek models and techniques to create experimental poetry about the daily lives and love affairs of a dissolute and disillusioned Roman youth. The results were both extremely erudite, and iconoclastic. While this poetry did not avoid passing comment on the harsh realities of war, or the corruption of contemporary politics, it does give us a glimpse of a world in which these matters compete for attention with the more personal preoccupations of sex, friendship, and learning. The best-known of these poets is Catullus, remembered for critical political commentary and miniature epics as well as obscene poems set in the brothels and backstreets of Rome. Many of his poems are about his unhappy love affair with a mysterious woman called Lesbia, rumoured to be a pseudonym for Clodia, the notorius sister of the tribune Publius Clodius.

The Gladiators

Catullus and his fellow poets did not provide entertainment for the masses. Far more popular were the gruesome gladiator shows that had been held in the Forum since the middle of the 3rd century BC. These contests pitted professional fighters, prisoners of war, and condemned criminals against each other in a fight which sometimes ended in death, although the life of a defeated gladiator could be spared by the man who had hosted the games.

Gladiators in Republic and Empire

Notwithstanding their indelible association with Rome, gladiators first appeared in southern Italy on 4th-century vases, and were also early associated with the Etruscans. The first evidence of gladiator fights in the city of Rome comes from 264 BC (not long after the conquest of southern Italy) when an ex-consul, Iunius Pera, held games featuring three pairs of gladiators in the Cattle Market, in honour of his father's funeral. By 174 BC things had become much more elaborate: Titus Flaminius honoured his father with a public distribution of meat, theatrical performances, and three days of fighting between 74 gladiators. In Republican Rome gladiatorial games were always held in association with aristocratic funerals, a private gift from the family of the deceased to the people of the city, as opposed to the public games and festivals held by the magistrates.

By the late Republic, the shows were held in the Forum, with temporary wooden seating erected for paying spectators. A network of corridors to facilitate the games was created below the forum, which can still be traced today. This provided the popular tribune Gaius Gracchus with an opportunity for a symbolic gesture in 123 BC: the night before a big contest, he sent his workmen into the forum with orders to dismantle the viewing stands, so that the poor might watch the show for free.

The popularity and scale of the games continued to grow: in 65 BC, Julius Caesar held funeral games for his father with 320 pairs of gladiators, as well as fights between condemned criminals and wild beasts. Gladiator fights also spread beyond Italy, becoming popular all over the empire.

Although Roman colonies constructed specialized amphitheatres for gladiatorial games and beast hunts from the early 1st century BC, conservatism and the traditional suspicion of public entertainment venues prevailed in Rome itself. It wasn't until 29 BC that the first permanent stone amphitheatre appeared in the city, and not for another century that the Colosseum was built, giving the city of Rome the largest and most spectacular entertainment venue in the entire Mediterranean. Gladiatorial games were no longer family- and funerary events, but public celebrations, often paid for by magistrates. From the late 1st century AD, emperors claimed the sole right to give

The success of olive farming on the coast of North Africa brought great prosperity to market towns such as El Jem in Tunisia; the spectacular amphitheatre there is the largest in Africa, holding 45,000 spectators.

games, and did so on an immense scale: the emperor Trajan celebrated his triumph over the Dacians with spectacles involving 11,000 animals and 10,000 gladiators over 123 days. Gladiators remained popular throughout the imperial period: we last hear of gladiator fights in the Colosseum in AD 434/5.

A day at the games

Under the emperors a pattern emerged for the entertainment: beast hunts in the morning and gladiators in the afternoon, with public executions in the interval between the two.

A banquet would be held the night before for the public and all the participants, including the condemned prisoners. The next morning, the gladiators swore an oath to be burned with fire, chained, beaten with rods, and killed with steel, and were struck with a rod to demonstrate their submission to the rules of the contest before the day's show began with a parade and the beast hunts.

These contests featured animals from all over the Empire, including lions, panthers, crocodiles, and elephants, fighting other animals or unfortunate criminals. Roman citizens could see the fruits of their imperial expansion in these shows, both in the financial resources required to put them on in the first place, and in the exotic prisoners and animals they displayed.

After the beast hunts, the executions of criminals occupied the spectators through the lunchbreak. The prisoners were dispatched in gruesome and often imaginative ways, by machinery or torture, or in re-enactments of famous scenes from mythology and history.

In the afternoon, the gladiatorial contests began, surrounded by elaborate and long-established rituals. Each pair underwent an official weapons inspection, and then a trumpet marked the start of the fight. Typically between 10 and 15 pairs would fight for 10 to 15 minutes each, amid elaborate sets and scenery, overseen by two referees.

There were four traditional types of gladiator, each with different weapons and armour. The Samnite was heavily armed, with a helmet, an oblong shield and a sword. The Murmillo had similar equipment, but could be distinguished by the fish crest on his helmet. The Thracian was more lightly armed, with a round shield and scimitar, while the Retiarius fought with a net and a trident. There were variations on these themes, and horseback and chariot fighters too. These men were professionals, often with years of training and experience, who might be owned by a manager, or by the emperor, or work freelance, hiring out their services to individual festival-givers.

Unless a condemned criminal was involved, fights were not to the death, but until one combatant was

defeated. A gladiator declared defeat by raising his finger or throwing down his shield, and at that point it was up to the man providing the games whether or not to spare the man's life, though the crowd might make its views on the matter clear. Given how expensive it was to find, recruit, train, keep and mend gladiators, the death penalty for defeat must have been rare. The victor was given a palm leaf and often a crown, and, if he were a slave, he might well be awarded his freedom.

Noble fighters

Gladiators were famed for their strength and courage, and the career could seem attractive – to the extent that, in the early Empire, Augustus and Tiberius had to legislate to prevent senators and knights entering the profession. These regulations were not entirely effective in later times: the deranged emperor Commodus (AD 180–192) was said to have taken part in both gladiatorial games and beast hunts in the arena.

There were four different types of gladiators: the Murmillo, with a fish's crest on his helmet, the Samnite, with an oblong shield and a short sword, the Retinarius, who carried a net and a trident, and the Thracian, who had a round shield and curved sword.

The Augustan poet Virgil sits between Clio, the Muse of History, (left) and Melpomene, the Muse of Tragedy (right). Virgil's Aeneid, *an epic poem on Roman origins and identity, was a double-edged commentary on the new world order.*

THE ROMAN EMPIRE: 44 BC–476 AD

By the time of Augustus (27 BC–AD 14), Rome was a huge, chaotic city of perhaps a million people, citizen and slave. Water was scarce, famine a constant threat, sanitation poor, and disease rife. Augustus brought some measure of order to the city, just as he enlarged and organized the Roman Empire, and his successors sought to emulate his example. Life at Rome would never be calm, but it could be controlled.

The institutions of the Republic had grown increasingly outmoded, and with the advent of monarchical power came a shift at every level of society from the collective to the individual. The emperor himself ruled with the authority that had once belonged to a college of magistrates, while the voting power of the people first diminished, then disappeared. Freedom of association was tightly regulated. Power was concentrated in the household of the ruler, who was the source of legislation, adjudicated disputes, and granted privileges to individuals and cities. Rome's citizens old and new had wider horizons, but quieter voices.

Once again, these changes were reflected in the monuments and public spaces of the city itself. Aristocratic competition in building gave way to imperial munificence. The Republican Forum, once the crossroads of the politics and people of Rome, was quickly rendered obsolete. The temples, shrines, and legends of the Forum became a museum of Rome's past, as well as a monument to the imperial family, with new temples and arches erected to celebrate their achievements.

The political functions of the old Republican Forum moved to a series of monumental fora built by the emperors, where the state religious and military ceremonies were now held, and to the imperial palaces. Julius Caesar had begun to build a new Forum abutting the Republican Forum to the east. It was finished by Augustus, who built his own alongside, surrounding a grand temple with statues.

The Campus Martius (Field of Mars) was the plain in the crook of the Tiber outside the city walls, where armies used to gather, and where Pompey had built Rome's first theatre amid temples dedicated by triumphant Republican generals. Now the emperors adorned this quarter with theatres, baths, gardens, and temples. One political institution – a new voting hall – was built there by Agrippa in 15 BC. But the popular vote meant little even by then, and the hall later became an arena for gladiators.

Augustus had kept a relatively modest house on the Palatine hill, above the old Forum. His successors, by contrast, erected vast imperial palaces there, and Domitian's palace still graces the hill today. The various areas of the city had once been united and drawn together by the Republican Forum, open on all sides, where both the nobility and the poor came together in a political context. Now the Republican Forum was a space that separated the palaces, the imperial *fora*, and the popular delights of the Campus Martius. By dispersing the population, the emperors controlled the city and suppressed potential conflict.

Later emperors abandoned Rome, sometimes spending their entire reigns in the provinces. Citizenship was extended to the entire Empire in 212 AD, but it was no longer a guarantee of participation in political life, and was instead a symbol of a relationship with the emperor. Like the city, the Roman Empire never achieved true stability, and what peace and security there was came at the price of tyranny. Religious and political suppression helped to keep the system alive, but could not prevent its decline nor the increasing discontent of the lower classes and subject peoples. The result was that, by the 5th century, the entire Western Empire was easy prey to the incursions of the Goths and Vandals.

Augustus Caesar

If Julius Caesar's assassins had been hoping to restore senatorial authority, they were too optimistic. The surviving consul, Mark Antony, quickly marshalled the support of the people and the army. The Senate fell back on the young Octavian as their champion, and 13 more years of civil war racked the Mediterranean, as Caesar's adopted son gradually eliminated all his rivals to power.

When Caesar was assassinated, his great nephew and adopted son, Octavian, was just 18 years old. With Cicero's support, the young man was appointed to the Senate and given extraordinary powers to protect the state. Once he had gained control of the Roman army, he intimidated the Senate into allowing his election as consul and almost immediately cut a deal with Mark Antony. Along with Lepidus, a governor of Gaul, the two generals established an uneasy "triumvirate". The people awarded the three men special constitutional powers to set the state in order. They appointed magistrates, confiscated land for their veterans, and carried out proscriptions, offering money in exchange for the heads of their enemies.

Octavian gained a reputation as the most hard-hearted and bloodthirsty of the three, although it was Antony who finally defeated Caesar's assassins in Macedonia in 42 BC.

Antony and Cleopatra

Octavian and Mark Antony divided the Mediterranean between them, with Octavian taking the western provinces and Antony the east, where he met Cleopatra. The queen of Egypt already had a child by Julius Caesar, and twins by Antony now followed. His subsequent marriage to Octavian's sister Octavia may have consolidated the triumviral alliance, but it does not seem to have diminished his affection for

Cleopatra VII was the last of the Ptolemaic rulers of Egypt, and the first to learn Egyptian. Inheriting the throne at the age of 18, she became very popular with her subjects, and successfully opposed Roman annexation for 20 years. She was celebrated more for her intellect and conversation than her beauty.

the Egyptian queen. By 36 BC, Antony's relationship with Cleopatra and an unsuccessful campaign against the Parthians had tarnished his reputation in Rome. At the same time, Octavian consolidated his position in the city when his general Agrippa defeated Pompey's outlaw son Sextus, who had been blockading Roman grain ships in the Mediterranean.

Octavian forced Lepidus into a permanent retirement, and his relationship with Antony broke down. Propaganda campaigns became open war in 32 BC, when Octavian had Antony's powers as triumvir revoked in Rome and declared war on Cleopatra. Antony refused to desert his queen, but the royal couple both deserted the decisive battle of Actium in 31 BC and fled to Alexandria, where they committed suicide.

The restoration of the Republic

Octavian now ruled alone. In 27 BC, he handed power back to the Senate and the people, retaining the consulship for himself. In return, the Senate voted him the title "Augustus", a word which had religious connotations, and he was awarded supreme command over the provinces of Spain, Gaul, Syria, and Egypt, which contained almost all the Roman legions. In 23 BC, he went further, giving up the consulship and refusing the title of dictator when the people of Rome pressed it upon him. But these changes were superficial: Augustus remained in control of the state not only by virtue of a grant of tribunician power, and thus the right to propose or veto any legislation, but also because of his special command in the provinces. He called himself the *princeps* – the first man.

The Senate still met, although Augustus revised the membership. He cut their workload by restricting the number of meetings, and decreeing that only those selected by lot to ensure a quorum need attend. Elections also took place with the *princeps* making his preferences known, at first by canvassing in the Republican tradition, but later by simply posting a list. No rivals were permitted, but many nobles were taken into his circle. His brilliant general Agrippa was his most trusted adviser and became almost a partner in government, left in charge of affairs at Rome while Augustus spent long periods in his provinces.

Pax Augusta

It is unlikely that anyone was fooled by the Republican rhetoric, but the peace and plenty of the Augustan era ensured his popularity with the Roman people. Civil war ended, and Italy began to recover. Augustus now compensated for his bloody youth with ostentatious clemency towards his enemies. He restored aqueducts and bridges, gave land to his vet-

This large onyx gem dates from the first decade AD, and unites the Augustan themes of dynasty, piety, and empire. Augustus as Jupiter is being crowned by Oikoumene, the "known world". Alongside him are Livia as the goddess Roma and (far left) the future emperor Tiberius. Below, Roman soldiers are erecting a trophy over barbarian prisoners.

erans, and dispensed cash handouts to the poor. The Augustan peace must have seemed a welcome respite from Republican freedom.

Wars were fought far from Rome. Augustus professionalized the army, and he pacified and enlarged the empire he had inherited. He established dozens of colonies abroad and reformed the taxation and census systems so that even more provincial wealth was channelled to the capital. The expansion met resistance, and the last decade of Augustus' life saw serious revolts in the provinces.

The problem of succession

Augustus married Livia Drusilla in 39 BC, a second marriage for both. It was a devoted partnership, although childless. Augustus brought a daughter, Julia, from his previous marriage, and Livia a son, Tiberius, who became a successful general and politician. Julia was married to Agrippa, while Tiberius was married to Agrippa's daughter Vipsania. On Agrippa's death, however, Julia and Tiberius were forced to marry. The pair detested each other, and Julia's extramarital adventures became embarrassing to her father, who had her exiled in 2 BC. Tiberius had retired from public life to the island of Rhodes in 6 BC, in part to escape his wife, but also because of his stepfather's promotion of Julia's sons by Agrippa, Gaius, and Lucius. Augustus adopted the boys and gave them public commands, but both died young. Augustus had to recall Tiberius and, to Livia's delight, adopted him.

Augustan Culture

The people of Rome were fast losing their political authority – and with it their practical role as Roman citizens. Augustan propaganda sought to reinforce the notion of a communal citizen identity and introduced practical means to do so. Romans followed the same clock and calendar, and worshipped at the same altars, under the common authority of one man – Augustus.

This 1st century AD fresco from Pompeii shows a scene from Book 12 of the Aeneid *where the doctor Iapyx is tending to Aeneas, who has been wounded in battle. Aeneas's mother Venus looks on anxiously in the background, and Aeneas's son Ascanius weeps on the right.*

Augustus filled Rome with new temples, monuments, theatres, and baths, shifting the focus of urban activity away from the Republican political centre into the Campus Martius, previously the army's assembly ground. Augustus boasted that he had found Rome a city of brick and left it a city of marble.

The image of Augustus

Augustus distanced himself from the horrors of civil war and looked instead to Rome's past. He revived old customs and invented new ones. With new laws on marriage, adultery, extravagance, and bribery, he advocated a return to traditional morality. He even barred those not wearing the traditional toga from entering the Forum. In 17 BC, the Secular Games were held, a festival that traditionally marked the passing of an era at Rome. This time it officially designated a new golden age, where peace and the traditions and values of the past would once again predominate.

Augustus transformed the city of Rome with architectural projects that celebrated the themes of his reign: peace, fertility, order, and piety. In 28 BC, Augustus built a massive family mausoleum in the northern part of the Campus Martius. He later added a giant sundial, which also operated as a calendar, to celebrate victory over Egypt. The sundial's pointer was an Egyptian obelisk, underlining the importance of the Empire as an integral part of the Roman order.

The final part of the complex was an altar to Augustan Peace, which the Senate voted to him in 13 BC to commemorate victories over the Gauls and the Germans.

The altar featured the founders of Rome – Aeneas and Romulus – as well as the goddesses Roma and Mother Earth. The imperial family, magistrates, and the people were depicted participating in a sacrificial procession, each group accorded its proper, supporting role within the new order. It is telling that this triumphal monument officially commemorated peace rather than war, and it depicted Augustus himself not as a general, but as a sacrificing priest. The continuity, stability, and authority of the new regime was symbolized by the stories depicted on the altar.

The period of Augustan Peace was followed by a new stage of expansionism. In 2 BC, Augustus finished building his own Forum. This monument was dominated by a grand temple to Mars the Avenger, and a statue of Augustus was placed between serried ranks of individual Roman heroes. This new and bellicose authoritarianism stood in stark contrast to – and was made possible by – the earlier emphasis on peace and order.

Augustus, son of the Divine Julius

Augustus became *pontifex maximus* (chief priest) in 12 BC, and he accumulated many supplementary priesthoods besides. Religion was a cornerstone of the Augustan programme, with ostentatious veneration of both Olympian and traditional local gods existing alongside a nascent ruler cult. Julius Caesar had been deified on his death, and his adopted successor never missed an opportunity to remind the Romans that he was the son of a god.

Augustus blurred the boundaries between the human and the divine. Official state prayers were addressed to his *genius* (spirit), and temples were dedicated to him in the provinces. Ruler cult was not new in the eastern Mediterranean, but temples to Augustus are also found in the West. In Italy,

Mausoleum of Augustus

Horologium of Augustus · Ara Pacis

Aqua Virgo (Agrippa)

Aqua Marcia

Aqua Julia (Agrippa)

Pantheon of Agrippa

Portico of Pompey · Baths of Agrippa

Saepta Julia (voting enclosure)

Theatre of Pompey · Portico of Octavia

Tabularium · Forum of Julius Caesar · Forum of Augustus · Portico of Livia

Theatre and Crypt of Balbus

Amphitheatre of Statilius Taurus

Republican Forum

Servian city wall (C. 4th BC)

Theatre of Marcellus · Temple of Jupiter Capitolinus

Aqua Alsietina

Temple of Apollo on the Palatine

Circus Maximus

Aqua Appia (C. 4th BC)

Tiber

Porticus Aemilia (warehouse)

Augustan Rome
- Pre-Augustan
- Augustan
- Augustan administrative region

Family values

Augustan legislation to encourage legitimate marriage and reproduction among upper-class Romans demonstrates the way in which private life became a public concern in this period. Marriage and divorce were formalized and adultery was criminalized. If a man refused to divorce his adulterous wife and prosecute her, he could be prosecuted for living off immoral earnings. Penalties were introduced for those who did not marry, and rewards given for having children. The new laws were not very popular or successful. The knights demonstrated against them, and senators' wives discovered a useful loophole: they avoided penalties for adultery if they registered with city officials as prostitutes.

he was more reticent, although he did build and restore many temples, including one to Apollo that interconnected with his house on the Palatine. He moved the ancient cult of Vesta into the house itself. It must have come as no surprise to the citizens of Rome that, on his death, Augustus, too, was proclaimed a god.

Political literature

The golden age of Augustus was hailed by contemporary poets, many of whom were supported and funded by Maecenas, who was a close friend of the *princeps*. Horace may have been the closest equivalent to a court poet; Augustus commissioned him to write the choral ode to be sung by children at the Secular Games, the *Carmen Saeculare*. In other poems, Horace thanks Augustus for delivering Rome from the horrors of civil war and the threat of rule by a decadent oriental queen. According to Horace, Augustus "guards the Italian state with arms, and graces it with morals".

The epic poet Virgil often echoes these sentiments. In his *Aeneid* (19 BC), an oracle predicts that Augustus will carry Rome's rule forward to Africa and India. Jupiter announces that he has set the Romans no boundaries in space or time, but given them an empire without end. Despite the friendship between Virgil and Augustus, however, his tale of the wanderings of Aeneas on his way from Troy to Italy is not simple propaganda. The poet explores the tensions in the new era, celebrating it and questioning it at the same time.

Aeneas is Rome's wise and dutiful hero, described as the first of a line of great leaders which culminates with the rule of Augustus himself. When Aeneas escapes from Troy to Carthage, he and his men are rescued by the Carthaginian queen, Dido, and the pair fall in love. Yet Aeneas soon abandons his lover to follow his divine calling to found a great city in Italy. Dido commits suicide, and Aeneas' ships sail out in sight of her blazing funeral pyre. The reader is left to contemplate whether love and civic duty can be compatible; whether piety requires a lack of pity.

Dido is not the only victim of Aeneas' (and thus Rome's) success; the Italian kings must also make way for the new leader, and in the last lines of the poem pious Aeneas completes his mission by slaughtering the courageous Rutulian king Turnus in a moment of passionate cruelty and rage. Order is fragile, Virgil seems to be warning us, and peace has its costs.

The Early Empire

On his deathbed, Augustus counselled Rome to keep the Empire within its present limits. His successors followed this advice for almost a century. There was plenty to occupy them at Rome, where their unconstitutional position was never formalized. With no clear right to rule, they relied instead on a combination of populism, force, and fear.

Tiberius and the Succession

By the time Augustus died in 14 AD, his stepson Tiberius had already been awarded tribunician power and authority greater than any other magistrate except Augustus himself. The succession was not in doubt, although Tiberius himself claimed to be reluctant, and forced the senators to beg him to take up power. Nonetheless, he began his reign as a conscientious and hardworking ruler, concerning himself with the problems of the Italians and the provincials. Unlike Augustus, he refused to have temples dedicated to him – or to his mother – and was not deified, even after his death. An old-fashioned man, fond of learning and suspicious by nature, he did not ingratiate himself with the Senate or the Roman people in the manner of his predecessor, though it could be argued that the senators at least were given more power under Tiberius: elections for public

office were now transferred to them from the people, and the emperor seems to have been largely uninvolved in the process.

The question of the succession quickly re-emerged as a crucial and divisive issue for family and state. Tiberius had two heirs: his son Drusus and his nephew Germanicus, whom he had adopted. Germanicus was a talented and extremely popular general who led the successful Roman campaign against German tribes. He was next posted to Asia, but died there in 19 AD, claiming that he had been poisoned on the emperor's orders. Whatever the truth of this, the intense public mourning for him all over the empire must have given Tiberius and Drusus pause for thought.

Drusus himself died in 23 AD, a loss which seems to have destroyed Tiberius' spirit. In the later part of his reign, the emperor became increasingly suspi-

During the reign of Trajan, the Roman Empire surrounded the whole of the Mediterranean, and encompassed most of continental Northern Europe and Britain. A complex bureaucracy and a large army maintained stability in these regions for a significant period of time, although Trajan's attempt to incorporate areas even further east failed almost immediately.

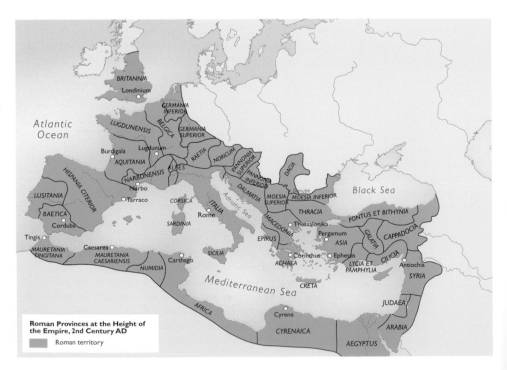

Roman Provinces at the Height of the Empire, 2nd Century AD

Roman territory

cious and vindictive. He was particularly fond of treason trials, and lucrative accusations of slander against the emperor or his family became a commonplace way of bringing about the execution or suicide of prominent politicians. Three years after the death of his son, Tiberius retired to Capri with his household, giving up on most state business. His closest confidant was the sinister head of the imperial guard, Sejanus, who now became the emperor's only link with Rome. Sejanus exercised almost imperial power there, until he too fell from grace and was killed in 31.

Thereafter, Tiberius devoted himself to a life of leisure, and, later writers alleged, extraordinary vice. He was joined on Capri by Germanicus' son Gaius "Caligula" (Little Boots), a youth already notorious for an unusually close relationship with his own sister, and who took to the pleasures available on the island with enthusiasm.

When Tiberius died in 37, Gaius was named joint heir in his will with Tiberius's grandson Gemellus, but engineered the invalidation of the document by the senate, and his own sole inheritance of the principate. Gemellus was executed within the year.

After the sullen terror of Tiberius's last years, Caligula started his reign with much public goodwill, especially after he returned the elections for public office from the Senate to the people. But he quickly became intoxicated by his own power. He was the first emperor to declare himself divine in his own lifetime, and he installed a life-sized golden statue in a shrine to himself, which every day was dressed in clothes to match his own. Worse, he treated the Senate with outright contempt, and it may be this that led to rumours that he was planning to award a consulship to Incitatus, his favourite horse. His short reign was ended by assassination in 41, at the hands of the imperial guard.

Claudius and Nero

In the immediate aftermath of Caligula's death the senators attempted to seize the opportunity to restore the Republic and reclaim power for themselves, but the imperial guard forced them to accept Germanicus's scholarly and hitherto politically insignificant brother Claudius as emperor. His physical disabilities and diffidence caused many to perceive him as weak, but Claudius seems to have been a competent emperor, if always more popular with the army than the politicians. He took care of Rome's grain supply, building a harbour on the coast at Ostia to ensure the prompt and safe delivery of grain to the city, and it was under Claudius' rule (although not his command) that the first significant territorial gains since the Augustan period took place, with the conquest of southern Britain in 43.

Bread and circuses
Roman politicians traditionally won popular support with distributions of grain or cash, and extravagant public games. In the Julio-Claudian period, the emperors came to monopolize these activities. Vespasian and his sons asserted their popular credentials after the megalomania of Nero's reign by building the Colosseum where the Golden House had stood. Trajan established a new formula for public welfare in Italy – the alimentary scheme – whereby capital improvement mortgages were issued to farmers from the imperial treasury at a fixed 5% interest rate. The proceeds were distributed to poor children in the locality – 16 sesterces for boys and 12 for girls.

As well as expanding Rome's dominions, he was keen to expand the Roman citizenship, and controversially allowed Gauls to be admitted to the Roman senate. His reliance on his freedmen and wives as advisors also caused concern, perhaps with some justification: when he died in 54, he was said to have been poisoned by his fourth wife, his niece Agrippina, in order to ensure the succession of her son Nero.

The new emperor was young, popular, and immensely brutal. As had often been the case with his predecessors, his reign started well, with an undertaking to return to Augustan values, and to govern in partnership with the senate. He enjoyed enduring popularity with the Roman people, but his domestic life was less happy. In 55 he murdered his stepbrother Britannicus, and in 59 his own mother. In 62, he divorced then murdered his wife Octavia and married his mistress Poppaea, whom he kicked to death in 65. This was the same year that he forced his tutor, the philosopher and playwright Seneca, to commit suicide. Nero's public life became increasingly dissolute, and confiscations fuelled his expensive tastes. When a great fire destroyed much of Rome in 64, he took advantage of the devastation by building an enormous palace in the centre of the city, the Golden House. Things came to a head with the rebellion of Judea in 66, and a revolt by the governors of Gaul and Spain in 68. Nero panicked and

THE EARLY EMPIRE 97

killed himself. The Julio-Claudian dynasty had wiped itself out.

The Flavian dynasty

Sixty-nine AD was The Year of Four Emperors: events demonstrated that outsiders could become rulers at Rome. Four provincial governors in succession seized power, the last being Vespasian, an obscure general from a non-senatorial family who had been appointed by Nero to put down the Jewish revolt in 66 AD. After taking power by threatening to cut off the Egyptian grain supply to Rome, Vespasian proved himself a disciplinarian, and he quickly solidified his position and that of his two sons.

The elder, Titus, took over his father's campaign in Judea, captured Jerusalem and was responsible for the burning of the Temple in AD 70. This victory helped to guarantee his succession to his father's seat in 79, but his reportedly benevolent and popular rule ended with his death in 81 at the age of just 40; there were rumours that his younger brother Domitian had poisoned him.

Domitian, much less of a general than his brother, was also much less of a leader. He insisted on being addressed as "Lord and God", and saw conspiracies everywhere. Constant denunciations and treason trials did indeed lead to several attempts at revolt, and he was finally stabbed to death in a plot that involved his wife.

Emperors by adoption

Dynasty fell out of fashion with Domitian. His successor, Nerva (r. 96–8), was nominated by the Senate, and founded a tradition of adopting an heir from among the promising senators. This proved to be a stable and less bloody way of organizing the succession. After a short and uneventful reign, Nerva's choice of successor was the Spanish-born Trajan, a renowned general and the governor of Upper Germany. Not only could an outsider now become emperor, but even a soldier from the colonies.

Trajan's accession caused so little controversy that he did not even feel the need to come to Rome for more than a year. For contemporary authors, whose point of comparison was Domitian, Trajan was a diplomatic and just ruler. But he was also ambitious, and turned again to imperial expansion. In 106, he annexed Dacia (roughly modern Romania) with its gold mines, and in the same year he established the province of Arabia. His greatest success occurred in 115 when he conquered and provincialized Assyria and Mesopotamia; it is appropriate that the largest extent of the Roman Empire should have been won by its first provincial emperor. Yet, even before Trajan's death in 117, revolts were under way among the Jews and Mesopotamians, and the Empire began to shrink again.

His reign left its mark on the city, however, with an immense building program, including a new forum, libraries, baths, and the famous column which still dominates the city's skyline, and narrates the events of the Dacian campaign in a 200m- (656 ft-) long frieze wrapped around the exterior.

Trajan had adopted as his successor another Spaniard, Hadrian, a philhellene who had served as his adoptive father's speech writer. Faced with the precarious results of the recent wars of conquest, he abandoned the new provinces, and made his reign one of consolidation rather than expansion, and one of culture rather than conflict. Revolts in Britain, Mauretania, and Judea were suppressed, and Hadrian made several tours of the Roman empire, inspecting frontiers and reorganizing the administration of Rome's subject territories. For Britain this meant the building of the wall that is known by his name. His extensive travels also gave Hadrian the chance to indulge his devotion to Greek culture, and to the city of Athens in particular. His Greek habits extended to his passion for Antinous, a young man from Bithynia, whose death by drowning during a tour of Egypt devastated the emperor. He declared his lover a god, inaugurated his worship across the empire, and named a new city on the Nile Antinoopolis.

State and Empire

Over the decades, the ideal of restoring the Republic faded from the hopes of the people and from the rhetoric of the politicians. Nonetheless, while the position of the emperor at the head of the civic and imperial hierarchy came to seem normal, it was never completely regularized. The Senate continued to meet, and to appoint some of the magistrates, and the emperor would often seek senatorial advice or support. But, in practice, he relied at least as much on his household staff and personal friends in devising and implementing policy.

Rome's finances were the subject of confusion as well: although officially state finances were separate from those of the imperial household, the emperor often ostentatiously subsidized the public treasury, and drew on it without hesitation for his own political projects.

Over time, the emperors also consolidated their authority in the provinces, where, since the time of Augustus, they had officially had greater power than any other magistrate, including the provincial governors appointed by the senate. Military functions throughout the empire were gradually removed from these senatorial governors and given to imperial appointees. The emperors also benefited from the rudimentary nature of Roman imperial administra-

tion, in which a small number of administrators were sent from Rome with a skeleton staff to take responsibility for tax collection, military operations and justice over vast areas. The small numbers of people involved meant that emperors could take a personal interest in the conduct and achievements of Roman officials abroad.

The Roman empire did not need a complex bureaucratic structure, as its purpose was above all to collect taxes from the pacified provinces for use in metropolitan Italy and for maintaining the armies on the frontiers. There was no standard system for extracting these taxes, and practice tended to be based on pre-Roman regimes in the area concerned. Roman officials rarely had the time or inclination to become involved in day-to-day politics in their provinces, and a great degree of independence in local affairs was both granted to and expected from subject cities. Nonetheless, requirements to clear all new civic taxes and public buildings with the emperor served as a useful reminder to these cities of where power really lay.

Imperial Life and Literature

Tacitus described the accession of Trajan as "the dawn of this most happy age". After the reign of Domitian, the return of free speech with the new emperor came as a great relief to writers and politicians. By now, no one dreamt of a restored Republic; an emperor was a necessary evil to ensure peace, and good emperors were a rare delight.

Historians of Empire

The best history is often written by those with an awkward relationship to power: among historians of Rome, Polybius was a Greek hostage in Italy, Sallust was a disgraced senator, and Seneca combined teaching, philosophy, and playwriting with a career in politics until his ex-pupil Nero forced him to commit suicide for his alleged involvement in a plot on the emperor's life.

Tacitus was a politician during the reign of Domitian, an emperor whom he thought worse even than Nero, for "even Nero looked away, and did not gaze upon the atrocities he ordered". Tacitus appointed himself the historian of the households that ruled the Roman Empire, preserving them in vivid colour and biting prose. Beginning with the accession of Tiberius, he describes the descent of the Roman political system from, as he saw it, Republican freedom to imperial tyranny. His bitterest comments are reserved for politicians who collaborated with the regime, and thus in their own enslavement. The books dealing with Domitian are now lost, but Tacitus' own involvement in the politics of the day seems to haunt his writing.

Upper-class life

If Tacitus recorded the lives of the imperial family, the writings of his friend Pliny, consul in 100 and governor of Bithynia from 110–12, paint a broader canvas of upper-class Roman life. Pliny wrote nine books of letters in the first decade of the 2nd century, intended for publication. As well as including the conventional praise of his emperor, Trajan, Pliny's major themes are land and the extraordinary wealth of the Roman elite. At a time when the average daily wage of a labourer was around 3 sesterces, and a soldier earned 1200 sesterces a year, Pliny had no difficulty raising 3 million sesterces to buy another estate, although he complains at the same time of financial problems. The minimum property requirement for a senator in the imperial period was one million sesterces.

Most income was derived from the ownership of land. Pliny himself possessed several estates and rented land to tenant farmers. The early Empire was a time of rural prosperity and increasing population in Italy, although tenants had little security, and relied on the goodwill of the landowners. Intensive cultivation made marginal land agriculturally viable, and there is evidence of a great variety of farmhouses, villas, and ranches throughout the peninsula. That vines and olives, which required space, investment, and a good supply of seasonal labour, were a popular choice for farmers demonstrates the stability of rural life.

Lower-class life

Few lived like Pliny, especially in Rome itself. The urban population was large, loud and often hungry. Many were immigrants to Rome or members of recently arrived families, and freed slaves made up much of the rest of the populus. There were job opportunities in the capital for labourers, and artisans and small businesses could flourish, with women as well as men finding ways to make money from various crafts and selling their goods at markets. Yet many city dwellers were crowded into rickety apartment blocks, expensive to rent, easy to burn, and quick to collapse. Homelessness was common, and

This model of Pliny's villa at Laurentum, on the coast south of Rome, has been reconstructed from the descriptions in his letters. Archaeologists have yet to locate the site of the villa itself.

the state welfare of grain and cash distributions often failed to reach those who needed it the most. Outside the monumental centre of the city, open sewers ran through the streets, and the public water supply was insufficient to meet the needs of the population. Disease was endemic. Unfortunately, the only first-hand accounts of conditions come from the privileged pens of elite writers such as Martial, who wrote exuberant, comical and often scurrilous poems about Roman life and characters, while courting rich and powerful patrons, especially the emperor Domitian. Martial's vignettes tend to look on the bright side of Roman life, while his contemporary Juvenal's satires are darker, but also ironic: he complains with a typical sneer of the "thousand dangers of the savage city": the fires, building collapses, and "poets reciting in August".

Slaves and freedmen

The great imperial wars of the last centuries of the Republic had flooded Rome with slaves, mostly from the Greek East. By the early Empire, much of Roman industry and agriculture relied on slave labour, and domestic slaves were also in plentiful supply.

The casual acceptance of slavery in the Roman world is a constant reminder of the Romans' conceptual distance from us. But Roman slavery was of a distinctive sort even in the ancient world, and in particular the popularity of the institution of "manumis-

sion" (liberation) may explain why the system lasted so long, and why using it made chilling logical sense as an economic choice for Roman citizens – and even for some slaves.

The practice of liberating individual domestic slaves after a certain amount of time or service, at which point they received many of the rights of Roman citizenship, resulted in extraordinarily high proportions of freedmen and women in the towns of central Italy. According to funerary inscriptions from Republican Rome, the freed outnumbered the free by three to one; by the time of the Empire, the figure for Puteoli on the bay of Naples is 10 to one. These figures can't be treated as an accurate census – for one thing, freed slaves may have been keener to record their status in their epitaphs than those who had been citizens from birth – but they give a graphic indication of the scale of the phenomenon in some Italian cities.

The location of freedmen and women is also an interesting phenomenon: outside Rome itself they are concentrated in centres of commerce, production and trade. Their involvement in these sectors of the economy is also recorded, from carpentry to building to the naval trade and money-lending. Their commercial success, on both a small and a large scale, was no doubt aided by the way that slavery provided access to training, funding and contacts. In return, the expectation of liberation, at least for educated

This depiction of a donkey mill, including the donkey and, presumably, his owner, is a typical tomb decoration in the cemetery near Rome's port of Ostia, and typical of the confident and commercially oriented self-representation of freedmen in the early empire.

This portrait of a young couple was found in a house at Pompeii belonging to Terentius Neo, a baker. The woman's hairstyle dates the painting to the period of Nero. The couple seem well-to-do, and the painting emphasizes the intellectual pursuits of both husband and wife: he holds a scroll, and she seems about to write on a tablet with her stylus.

domestic slaves, might well have encouraged slaves to work conscientiously for their masters while in their ownership.

The growing commercial importance of freedmen and women also parallels a sharp rise in Roman economic activity and even growth from the 1st century BC, and it is very likely that the extraordinary social mobility and economic dynamism of the towns of central Italy in the 1st century AD owed much to the institution of manumission, and through that to the institution of slavery.

The Bay of Naples

Pliny was also the chronicler of seaside life in the Bay of Naples, where the wealthy maintained holiday villas, in addition to their country homes outside Rome and their agricultural estates. But the area was not just a haven for holiday-makers: the natural harbours had made it a centre of colonization and trade since the 8th century BC, and the volcanic soil and mild climate made it excellent for agriculture. The towns around the bay were wealthy resorts, servicing visitors and the local elite in bars, baths, and brothels in the shadow of Vesuvius, a volcano thought to be long extinct.

Pompeii

Of these towns, we know most about Pompeii. Founded in the 7th century BC at the outlet of the Sarno river, for several hundred years Pompeii remained a small harbour town of little economic importance, inhabited largely by Oscan-speaking Italians. From around 200 BC it began to grow, with new quarters laid out every few decades, and increasing wealth, trade and industry. By the time the town joined the rebellion against Rome in 91 BC, it was a sizeable and prosperous port. Sulla took the city by storm two years later, and installed a Roman veteran colony as a punishment. Two thousand Roman ex-soldiers arrived, and the city's administration was immediately transformed: the official language was now Latin, the coinage, measurements and magistracies, Roman. An amphitheatre seating 20,000 spectators was built on the edge of the town, and was the scene of a famous riot between the townspeople and visiting fans from nearby Nuceria in 59 AD. The beginning of the end came in 62 when a major earthquake almost flattened the city, and damaged many other towns in the area – no one realized that this calamity signalled that even worse was to come.

A living city

The surviving city blocks of Pompeii gives us a striking illustration of the mixed residential, commercial and industrial use of districts, and sometimes even buildings, a common custom in the ancient world which seems odd to modern sensibilities. Brothels, workshops, and foul-smelling factories sit next to fancy houses – and sometimes inside them. There is evidence of lime-production, metal workshops, urine-fuelled launderettes, dyers, fish tanks, and the production of fish sauce (*garum*) – a process which involved leaving large quantities of the creatures' entrails to ferment in the sun. It must be admitted that some householders seem to have been more enthusiastic than others about embracing these economic opportunities!

Other specialities were gentler on the senses: in particular, gardens inside and outside the city produced flowers and perfume. Not all local production was entirely successful: Pompeian wine was famous for inducing hangovers, and even the locals seem to have switched to imported wine when they could. Another danger of urban life is indicated by the large stepping-stones that enabled pedestrians to cross streets above the mud and sewage on the road itself.

We can also see the social and economic rise of freedmen at Pompeii, most strikingly from an inscription commemorating one Numerius Popidius Celsinus, who had paid for the rebuilding of the Temple of Isis, in return for which he was appointed to the local council – at the age of six! The explanation is straightforward: his father was a wealthy freedman, and thus ineligible to serve on the council himself, but he could achieve the same social and political status through his little son, and a large public benefaction. A similar gift gave the wool-workers a guildhall in the forum – though the benefactor in this case was not a freed slave but a woman called Eumachia, also of course barred from direct political participation, but allowed to buy a place in civic life.

Herculaneum

Further north on the Bay of Naples, Herculaneum presents an example of a different kind of town: smaller, sleepier, less industrial, but more elegant. One of the most spectacular houses in the town, the Villa of the Papyri, has yielded a vast number of papyrus manuscripts; it is unfortunate that the owner's love of Epicurean philosophy apparently precluded the collection of texts of literary or historical interest.

The eruption of Vesuvius

We have an eye-witness account of the eruption of Vesuvius on 24 August 79 from the pen of Pliny, whose uncle was commander of the imperial fleet at

Misenum on the northern tip of the Bay of Naples. This great local character, known now as Pliny the Elder, devoted much of his life to writing a vast encyclopedia of knowledge, including science, ethnography, and geography: such subjects were highly fashionable in the 1st century AD, codifying the new knowledge from the imperial domains.

The younger Pliny later described in a letter how his mother drew his uncle's attention to an unusual cloud that was forming over the bay. The elder Pliny could not resist going to investigate this extraordinary natural phenomenon. On closer inspection, it became clear that ash and stones were raining down from the mountain. The admiral sprang into action, leading boats to the rescue of the fleeing population. They were forced to put in at Stabiae as the eruption worsened. Flames were shooting out of the volcano and the ground was shaking. By the morning, the massive eruption had destroyed the towns of Herculaneum and Pompeii. Pliny the Elder was himself overcome by the smoke and died alongside thousands of local residents, most of whom were drowned in lava or mud.

The afterlife

Vesuvius both destroyed and preserved the towns and villages it buried, creating an astonishing record for posterity of the daily life of these bustling cities, stopped dead in an instant. Modern visitors to the Bay of Naples can walk around Pompeii's fancy houses, shops, and restaurants, marvel at the town's open spaces and gardens, and sit in the theatre and amphitheatre alongside crowds of tourists: nowhere else can we get closer to the world of the ancients than in these two towns. At Herculaneum, household effects can be inventoried, business records and graffiti still read, and an incomparable picture of small-town Italian life emerges, including competing endorsements for elections, advertisements for bars and price-lists for prostitutes.

The last moments of some of Vesuvius's victims have been preserved in tragic detail. Lava buried this young Pompeian woman alive as she fled the volcano, and then hardened around her. When the city was excavated many centuries later, although her body was long gone, the space it had created in the lava remained to be filled by the archaeologists. This cast and others like it are displayed at Pompeii, and serve as a counterpoint to the deserted buildings.

Architecture and Urbanism

The cities of the Roman provinces prospered in the 2nd century AD. Growth, wealth, and magnificent public architecture reflected the new importance of provincial politicians and soldiers in the Roman Empire, as well as the increasing "globalization" of politics, trade, and culture in the Mediterranean world.

The new architecture

Roman architecture was heavily influenced by Greek building styles, but new developments and inventions gave it a different character. In particular, the use of arches, concrete, and sophisticated vaulting techniques meant that Roman architects, unlike their Greek counterparts, were at least as concerned about internal space as external structure.

Towards the end of the Republic, the building trade adopted standardized industrial production techniques, and under the early emperors Romans learnt how to combine reliable concrete with weight-relieving brick arches in order to build domes. These became the hallmark of ostentatious Roman imperial architecture. Hadrian's Pantheon, built in the 2nd century and still standing in the middle of the Campus Martius, is a perfect example of the possibilities of these new techniques. From the outside it is a conventional square-fronted temple, but that is only the porch. The classical columns lead to an echoing rotunda lit through an opening at the top of a vast dome. The art of the dome was lost for a millennium before the Renaissance, and the diameter of the Pantheon's dome was unequalled until the construction of the CNIT building at La Defense in Paris in the 1950s.

Alongside new techniques, distinctive versions of Greek building forms developed in the Roman period. Theatres were enclosed and were given sub-structures, wide stages, and façades; bath-houses acquired central heating and elaborate architectural elements; and Greek *agoras* (market places) were surrounded by colonnades to make Roman fora. Etruscan and Italic forms also formed important ingredients in Roman architecture. Roman temples, like Etruscan ones, had a high podium and steps

"Roman"-style theatres spread across the provinces during the Empire. This spectacular example from the city of Sabratha in Tripolitania (modern Libya) is 92 metres (322 ft) wide, and 108 columns adorn the wall which served as a backdrop for the performances. The front rows were reserved for local magistrates and other dignatories.

only at the front; and wealthier Romans retained the traditional Italian house, built round an open-air atrium.

Although these building forms are associated with Rome, they did not develop in the city itself. The earliest "Roman" theatres, baths, amphitheatres, and even domes are found around the Bay of Naples, although more monumental versions were soon built in the capital. New architectural and urban forms developed almost simultaneously in Italy, Gaul, and Africa, with Rome sometimes lagging a little behind. The only building form which is first encountered in Rome is the basilica, a large covered hall, often used for state or legal affairs. It is recognizably related to the Greek *stoa*, a covered colonnade, but different in function. The first basilica was built in Rome in the 2nd century BC, and with the forum and temples it became the trademark of a "Roman" town.

Urbanism in the Roman world

From the 1st century AD, the cities of the Roman world came to have more and more in common. As well as similar public buildings, there is evidence for shared tastes in pottery, food, dress, and many other aspects of culture. These changes can be seen as part of broader economic and social developments, including industrial production, more extensive trade, and better communications. Provincial elites were also connected with each other through the new political and military opportunities available in the Roman imperial system.

Great differences persisted between the regions, and strong continuities remained within pre-existing cultures. Greek *Agoras* and *gymnasia* remained common in the East; Gallic or Celtic architectural features were prevalent in the West. African buildings and town plans were often of recognizably Carthaginian inspiration. Similarly, local gods retained a great many of their "native" characteristics even if they adopted Roman names, and local languages often outlived Latin. Towns were more likely to develop the new "Mediterranean" culture the larger they were, the closer to the sea, and the more politically and commercially important. Cultural life in rural areas, by contrast, did not change much at all.

Urbanization in itself was often seen by the ancients as a sign of Roman influence and control. Cities were a mark of civilization, and ancient authors can give the impression that Roman colonialism introduced the urban form to backward nomadic natives in Britain, Gaul, and Africa. In fact, cities usually pre-existed the coming of the Romans. This was true not only in the Greek East, and on the coast of the Mediterranean, but also in the West and the interior. The urban forms may have looked different in these places, but the functions remained the same.

Hadrian's Wall

This continuous barrier across the north of England is unique, the only permanent defensive frontier in the Roman Empire. It was built between 126 and 126 AD and abandoned around the end of the 4th century. The wall is 3 metres (10 ft) thick and 4 metres (15 ft) tall, with a wide ditch a few metres to the north. There are fortified gateways every Roman mile, and 12 major forts straddle the wall. Much of it survives today, and the forts have yielded a great deal of evidence of the lives of ordinary soldiers posted overseas. This includes reports, accounts, and, most fascinating of all, many private letters. Elsewhere, frontiers were flexible, and forts were mainly used to channel and control communications. Hadrian's Wall divided Roman from barbarian land, and it was probably of more symbolic than military importance: it could not have withstood an army.

Colonization and cultural change

Roman expansion created many opportunities for elite cultural convergences, but those convergences did not necessarily follow the Roman frontier. Settlements in Gaul and Britain shared architectural and cultural features with contemporary Italian towns long before they became Roman territory. Conversely, when Roman colonists were added to existing populations in the provinces, the physical effect on the town was often negligible, with new buildings imitating the local style rather than the imperial one.

Cities outside the Roman Empire could have much more "Roman" architecture than many within it: Lepcis Magna on the African coast had a forum, Italian temples, and an Italian-style theatre with a dedication to the Roman emperor in the Augustan period, even though it did not officially become a Roman town until at least the time of Vespasian (*c.*69–79). Septimius Severus, the first emperor from Africa (193–211), was a native of Lepcis Magna, and it was he who rebuilt the city. He gave it a Hellenistic colonnaded street with Roman arches, and a new Roman forum and basilica with decorative touches in an Asian style. These Eastern influences on architecture in an African city built by a Roman emperor perfectly exemplify the complexity of imperial culture.

Religions and Rome

When Polybius encountered Roman state religion in the mid-2nd century BC, he was cynical: "I believe that it is fear of the gods that holds the Roman state together." Religion was so theatrical in Rome, and so embedded in public and private life that he suggested these "invisible terrors and pageantry" were a tool used by the elite to control the mob.

The lives and loves of the traditional Roman pantheon of gods were a favourite subject in Roman art. In this fresco from a house at Pompeii, Venus, the goddess of love, is marrying Mars, the god of war.

Religion and the state

Religion was a structural part of Roman life and politics, and Polybius's words show how bewildering this was to an educated Hellenistic Greek. Even he, however, admitted that Roman magistrates never broke religious oaths. From a Roman perspective, Cicero put it differently: because candidates from the same political elite filled both the priesthoods and the magistracies, religion was upheld by the proper administration of the state, and vice versa.

The Romans themselves traced this relationship back to Numa, their legendary second king, who was supposed to have established the traditional priesthoods and the Roman ritual calendar, in which some days were designated as business days, and others as religious festival days, on which no courts could sit or assemblies meet.

Religious observances remained central to the political system. As we have seen, state festivals were all linked to religious celebrations. No votes took place in Rome without favourable auspices, all meetings and elections had to be held in ritually sanctified spaces, and mistakes in the ritual procedure could invalidate the political proceedings.

Priests were consulted by the Senate about all matters of ritual, prodigy, and sacred law that affected the political process, and made up several different priestly colleges. The pontiffs dealt with legal matters, record keeping and the calendar; the augurs' job was to divine the will of the gods by interpreting the flight of birds, thunder and lightening, or the feeding patterns of the sacred chickens; the fetial priests were in charge of the just declaration of war, an archaic procedure which involved flinging a spear across the boundary of enemy territory.

As Cicero noted, all these priests were drawn from leading senatorial families, co-opted into the priestly colleges by existing members, or, in the case of the *pontifex maximus* (chief priest), elected by the people. But the diversity of roles and personnel

This map of bishoprics, church councils, and other Christian communities shows how far the religion had spread by the time the Emperor Constantine converted to Christianity in 310. It was more popular in the East than the West and very much an urban religion; however, Christians could be found in every corner of the Roman world.

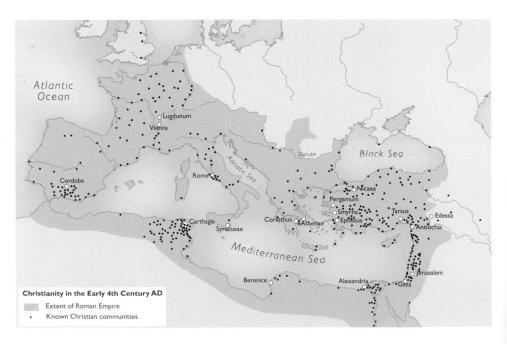

meant that there was no one centre of religious power in the state until the early imperial period, when emperors began to assume the role of *pontifex maximus* as a matter of course, thus retaining both religious and political authority for themselves.

Domestic religion

Not all Roman religious practice revolved around the state cults. The head of any household (the *pater familias*) was responsible for maintaining a shrine to the household gods (the *lares* and *penates*) and overseeing rites of birth, marriage and death. Outside Rome, there were rural shrines and healing sanctuaries, where the sick would dedicate terracotta body parts in the hope of divine assistance. The prevalence of curse tablets – small lead sheets imploring the gods to take revenge on a personal enemy – also demonstrates the way in which respect for supernatural forces was an intrinsic part of Roman life.

The Roman gods

The Roman state gods were partly adopted from the Greek pantheon and partly from local and Italian traditions. Unlike the Greeks, the Romans were not particularly interested in the morals and characters of their gods, and in the earliest times they didn't even make visual representations of them.

The most important Roman gods were the "Capitoline Triad" of Jupiter, Juno, and Minerva (Zeus, Hera, and Athena to the Greeks), whose temple on the Capitol had been dedicated in the first year of the Republic. But the Romans also worshipped less imposing gods connected with nature and agriculture, and personifications such as Hope, Victory and Concord.

As polytheists, the Romans saw all gods as manifestations of the same divine powers, and were open to accepting new gods into the official cult, especially at times of national crisis. In some cases the cult objects of these new gods were physically uprooted from their homelands and brought to Rome, in others the process was more one of gradual assimilation. They were even quicker to identify gods they found in the provinces with Roman deities, and religious freedom was a notable feature of the Roman Empire. Even when local gods came to be worshipped under their Roman names, they retained many of their characteristics, just as "Greek" gods were worshipped at Rome in ways that would not have been very familiar to visiting Greeks.

Imperial cult

One of the most controversial religious innovations of the imperial period was the practice – never automatic – of deifying emperors after their deaths, and

The Bishop of Hippo

The greatest of all the Church fathers, Augustine of Hippo (354–430), is best known today for his extraordinary Confessions, a long, autobiographical prayer. Memorable moments include his meditation on his youthful theft of some unripe pears, his adolescent prayer to "Grant me chastity, Lord, but not yet!", his Christian mother Monica's frequent weeping, and a vision in a garden in Milan which prompted his baptism by the local bishop Ambrose. Abandoning his common-law wife, Augustine returned to his native North Africa, becoming Bishop of Hippo in 395 and completing his vast book The City of God against the Pagans in 426.

sometimes even during their lifetimes. Shortly before his death, Julius Caesar was given divine honours, if not quite divinity: a priest for his cult, the right to add a pediment to his house (as if it were a temple), and the right to include his own image in processions of the gods. After his death, more starkly religious symbols were offered to the dead emperor: altars, sacrifices, and a temple. In 42 BC he was formally deified. His nephew and adopted son, Augustus, made much of his filial relationship with the new god, and was in turn deified on his own death. The emperors Tiberius and Caligula were not so honoured, but the tradition was resurrected after the death of Claudius.

This new imperial cult was not quite as innovative as it might appear. The boundary between the human and the divine was never absolute in Roman religion: a striking example of this was the Roman triumphal procession, led by the victorious general dressed as Jupiter – and accompanied by a slave whose job it was to remind him that he was, after all, only a man. The disputed example of Romulus's apotheosis might have given encouragement to a political leader who wished for more. And there were foreign precedents, including the ruler cult of various kinds that had been common in the Eastern Mediterranean for centuries – and which was on occasion extended to Roman generals serving in those areas, including Pompey the Great. The difference in 44 was that Caesar was now worshipped in Rome.

The imperial cult quickly became widespread even at home, where images of the imperial family were added to domestic shrines, and throughout the empire, where provincial subjects were expected to show proper reverence for the cult of the imperial family and the *genius* (spirit) of the emperor, as well as their own gods.

New Religions

Traditional Roman religion, public and domestic, was essentially a practical rather than a spiritual phenomenon. Rituals were performed, sacrifices offered, vows made, but there was no call on participants to make their religious observances a central part of their thoughts and identity, or even to "believe" in the gods they worshipped.

The Roman catacombs were used for burials between the 1st and 5th centuries AD. Most of those buried in these underground networks of corridors were Christians, though there were also some pagans and some Jews. This scene from the S. Callisto catacomb shows seven disciples.

In ancient Rome, there were no charismatic individuals claiming particular spiritual authority, no prophets or holy men. There were no holy books, and no comforting story of life after death. But in the late Republic, and especially under the emperors, a new set of cults started to offer a different kind of religious experience, and one that was quite separate from the state – though usually tolerated by the authorities. Initiation ceremonies and social rituals in small communities were at the heart of these new religions, and may account for a great deal of their popularity.

Another distinctive feature of these cults was the central, in some cases exclusive, role offered to a single god.

Mystery cults

The cult of the god Mithras was supposedly founded by the Persian sage Zoroaster, though no evidence for it has been found in Persia itself. It was extremely popular in the Roman West in the 2nd and 3rd centuries AD, a religion for men only, many of them low-ranking soldiers, slaves or freedmen. A typical Mithraic chapter would have 20 or 30 members, working their way up through seven grades of initation: raven, male bride, soldier, lion, Persian, sun-runner, father.

There were 40 Mithras sanctuaries in Rome alone – secluded, underground rooms, usually in established in private property. Elsewhere they are often found in army camps. At one end of the "cave" there was always a cult image of Mithras sacrificing a bull, surrounded by numerous symbols relating to the zodiac.

Unlike Mithras, the Egyptian goddess Isis became popular even among the elite, and was eventually incorporated into the official state religion by the emperors. Although these cults were secretive, they were not incompatible with the official religion; a devotee of Isis could also sacrifice to Jupiter, and images of more traditional gods have been found in Mithras sanctuaries. Problems only arose when foreign gods demanded exclusive rights to their worshippers.

The cult image of Mithras always contained the same symbolism: note here the god's companions, a dog, a snake, a scorpion, and a raven, the sun (Sol) and the moon (Luna) flying above him, and the way in which the bull's tail has become an ear of wheat. The meaning of the iconography is highly obscure.

Rome and the Jews

Like Rome, Judea offered an example of religion and a state intertwined. Until the final destruction of the temple in 70 AD, Jews all over the Mediterranean sent money back to Jerusalem. Military and political alliances with the Romans meant that the Jews and their kings were given a lot of leeway in interpreting the imperial cult, though they were also subject to a special tax.

A sizable Jewish community grew up in Rome itself, not least as immigrants and slaves after attacks on Jerusalem. Numbers reached several thousand by the Augustan period, largely Greek-speaking, and worshipping in at least 11 synagogues. Their special dietary rules, calendar, and separate burial grounds marked them out in the city.

Judea became a province of the Empire in 6 AD, but it was not completely pacified, and corrupt governors did not help the Roman cause there. Resistance movements started to spring up among the poor, and rural leaders became the focus of popular discontent. It was in this context that Jesus was put to death by the Roman authorities. Whether or not he himself was a political revolutionary, he had amassed a large following both in Galilee and in Jerusalem, and therefore presented a credible threat to the stability of the Roman province.

The spread of Christianity

The followers of Jesus believed that he had been resurrected after his death, and they gradually distanced themselves from other types of Judaism and began to recruit among gentiles (non-Jews). The cult spread throughout the cities of the Mediterranean, though it remained very small, and its adherents tended to be of low social status. Christians in Rome attracted little attention from the authorities at first, with one notorious exception: Nero arbitrarily made them the scapegoats for the Great Fire of 64 and executed a number of them, throwing some to animals, and burning others to death as torches for his gardens.

The Christians demanded allegiance to one god, and their faith forbade the worship of others, which did not sit comfortably with the Romans' religious toleration and polytheism. They often refused to swear by the *genius* of the emperor, and their allegiance to him was therefore deemed suspect. Nonetheless, persecution was very limited until the mid-3rd century, and it was almost always in response to specific local circumstances rather than empire-wide policy. Just a few hundred names are recorded altogether, although the "Passions" of these martyrs, written on the eve of their executions, are compelling. In North Africa, St Perpetua was among a small group of Christians mauled by wild animals in the amphitheatre before being executed in 203. In

her Passion, she describes how her devotion to her new religion carried her through her trials. Martyrs were good for Christianity; they encouraged converts and increased popular support and sympathy. Around the time Perpetua died, the bishop Tertullian declared that blood of the martyrs was the seed of the Church.

Under the 3rd-century emperors Decius and Diocletian, with the values of the Empire under strain, Christians were imprisoned and executed in larger numbers for their refusal to participate in the religious and military apparatus of the state. The emperor Constantine brought relief. After experiencing a vision and receiving certain omens in 310, he began to worship the Christian god, and gave legal privileges to individual Christians and to priests. He built many churches, giving Christianity a prestige and official acceptance it had previously lacked – and thus began the process of making Christianity the official religion of the Empire.

Given the growing popularity of the Christian cult, this imperial conversion may have been political in its motivation. Nonetheless, it had a profound effect: by the mid-4th century, Christianity was a central and influential part of the Roman Empire.

But not all later emperors worshipped the Christian god, and other religions were practised in the Roman world for many decades to come. Celebrations of pagan festivals were still practised in Rome in the 5th century.

The circular Santo Stefano Rotondo on the Caelian hill is one of the most interesting and earliest churches in Rome, dating from the late 5th century. This 7th century mosaic in the apse shows the martyrs Felicanus and Primus, whose relics were kept in the church. In the 16th century the interior walls of the church acquired dramatic scenes of modern martyrdoms.

The Decline and Fall of the Roman Empire

Despite the prosperity of the 2nd century, the Roman Empire began to show some weaknesses. Although rebellions and invasions were contained by the Roman army, it proved impossible to preserve the unity of the Roman world. The award of universal citizenship in 212 did nothing to stop the disintegration, and the Empire soon lost its metropolis.

The Antonine Emperors

After Hadrian's death in 138, three generations of the Antonine family ruled Rome for almost 50 years. Antoninus Pius succeeded Hadrian, and unlike his predecessor spent his entire reign in Italy. Imperial activity was confined to maintenance in this period: Antoninus' armies reconquered part of Scotland (up to a new "Antonine Wall"), and suppressed revolts in Africa and on the Danube.

Following in the established tradition, the emperor adopted as his son Marcus Aurelius (*r.*161–180), who passed much of his time as emperor abroad – not as a tourist, like Hadrian, but in response to attacks by the Germans across the Danube, the first invasion of Italy for more than 200 years. While on campaign Marcus comforted himself with philosophy, writing a book of *Meditations* which became a central text in the Stoic tradition. When he had finally defeated the Germans, he erected a 30.4 metre- (100 ft-) high column with graphic scenes of his victorious campaigns, which still stands in the centre of Rome, a companion piece to Trajan's column commemorating his wars against the Dacians.

In a break with custom, Marcus Aurelius was succeeded by his natural son. This was a mistake, however: Commodus was a weak and corrupt ruler whose main enthusiasm was for gladiatorial fights, both as spectator and participant. His increasingly erratic behaviour led to his assassination in 192, at which point the elite praetorian guard effectively offered the imperial throne for sale. A period of intense civil warfare followed as four men in a single year gained and lost power.

The army's Emperors

The fifth, Septimius Severus (*r.*193-211), was the last of the Roman emperors to aim seriously at further conquest. A native of Lepcis Magna in modern-day Libya, Septimius had had an outstanding military career in the service of Rome, and in 192, as prefect of Upper Pannonia on the Danube, he was proclaimed emperor by his troops. He spent the first four years of his reign disposing of his rivals and their partisans in the Senate, with the strong support of the army. In return, he increased the number of legions, raised military wages, and improved conditions – including lifting the ban on marriage for soldiers. He himself married a Syrian woman, Julia Domna, who gave him two sons, Caracalla and Geta, and whose family provided a new, Syrian, set of Roman emperors to follow them.

Septimius' career was spent mainly on the frontiers, responding to attacks and revolts in the East, Africa and Britain, and conquering two new provinces out of Parthian territory beyond the Euphrates river. War was not his only occupation, though, and he spent a great deal of effort and money on the architectural adornment of both Rome and his hometown of Lepcis, where his immense enclosed forum remains one of the most impressive monuments of the ancient world. He died at York in 211, whiile attempting to conquer Scotland.

His son Caracalla at first shared imperial power with his brother, but murdered Geta in 212, and ordered his name and picture to be effaced from memory. He then travelled East, stopping at Alexandria in 215 to have the male youth slaughtered for reasons which remain unclear, before continuing on to confront the Parthians with some success. He was murdered by one of his bodyguard in 217 before he could conclude his campaign. The most important event of his short reign was his decision in 212 to extend Roman citizenship to the entire free male population of the empire.

Fragmentation of the Empire

Caracalla's 3rd-century successors, of whom there were 20 in less than 70 years, faced not only internal competition, but also invasions from the north and

east. The Germans and Goths threatened the whole of the Danube frontier, parts of which had to be permanently ceded to them. The rise of the Persians in the East destroyed the Parthian empire and posed an increasing threat to the Romans themselves, culminating in the sack of Antioch in Syria in 253.

In response to these rebellions and invasions, the army effectively took control of the imperial machine, appointing and dispatching emperors according to their military prowess. Most were military commanders from different regions, and some never even saw Rome, where the central administration became more bureaucratic and authoritarian at the same time that it lost its real authority.

The lowest point occurred in 260 when the emperor Valerian himself was taken prisoner by the Persians at Edessa, and subsequently died in captivity. The Empire splintered as a result. In the East, the oasis city of Palmyra asserted its independence, and pursued an empire under the charismatic leadership of Queen Zenobia, who briefly captured Egypt and much of Asia Minor. At the same time, the governor of Lower Germany established a "Gallic empire" comprising the Western provinces of Gaul, Germany, Britain and Spain which lasted for more than 10 years.

But things did improve again for Rome: after a decade of chaos, emperors in the 270s and 280s put much of the Empire back together again, and convincingly defeated the Goths and Persians. But the effects of the preceding years were never entirely overcome.

Economic crisis

Foreign enemies were not the empire's only problems in the late 2nd and 3rd centuries. Without fresh conquests, Rome lost its supply of slaves and booty. Without a reliable, cheap source of slave labour, traditional agriculture and industry were in jeopardy, and in the absence of new technology, production decreased. Prices rose sharply under the Antonines and Severans, and the currency became increasingly debased, with "silver" or relatively high-value coins containing increasing amounts of lower-value bronze, and bronze denominations ceasing production altogether. Local communities were forced to produce their own low-value coins for day-to-day spending.

Cities declined, construction stopped, and the rural population had to cope with the devastation of war and the disease that followed in its wake, leading to uprisings in the countryside.

The effects of the crisis were long-term: the rising cost of transport encouraged localization of markets in all but luxury goods, and taxes and rents were increasingly paid in kind rather than cash. The global empire was becoming local once again.

The reforms of Diocletian

Diocletian (*r.*284-305) was the first authoritative emperor for many years. He quickly established a firm basis for his power, and tried to reverse the process of decentralization in some respects. In particular, he increased the size of the army in order to strengthen the Empire's frontier defences. All the new soldiers and administrators had to be paid, so Diocletian reformed and regularized the taxation system. He attempted to fix maximum prices and wages, and to create a unified currency across the provinces; however, these measures were out of keeping with the times, and were largely ignored. At court, changes in nomenclature and ceremony reinforced a new and realistic recognition of the realities of imperial power: the emperor was not a mere

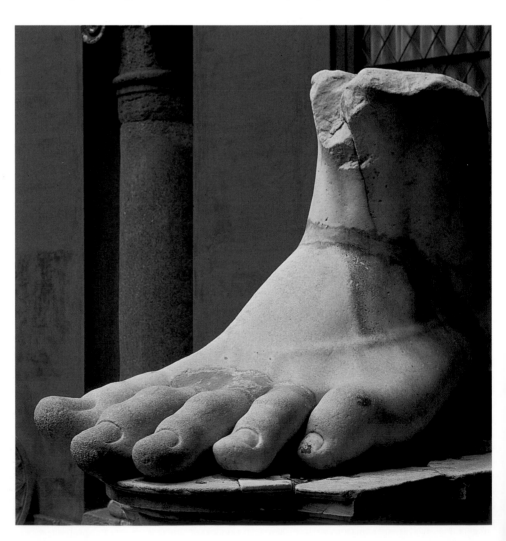

This enormous foot belongs to a colossal seated statue of the emperor Constantine, from his Basilica in the Forum. Made at the beginning of the 4th century, the complete work would have been over 9 metres (30 ft) high.

citizen, governing in concert with the senate, but instead *dominus et deus*, Lord and God, whose subjects prostrated themselves before him. Diocletian's large-scale persecution of Christians may also have been part of his attempt to impose his own central and visible authority on the provinces.

In another sense, Diocletian embraced decentralization: he formalized the fragmentation of the Empire and by doing so checked it temporarily. He divided the provinces into smaller, more manageable units – and thus reduced the power and resources of potential rivals among the provincial governors. He also separated the civil and military roles of Roman officials abroad, with similar results. Finally, he brought an end to the constant internecine warfare among the army commanders by dividing the imperial power between two "Augustuses", who were to rule as equals, one in the East and one in the West, with two Caesars as deputies and presumptive heirs. This institution, known as the tetrarchy, provided the basic pattern for imperial rule during the last centuries of the Western Empire, and by the end of the 4th century the Eastern and Western empires were effectively independent of each other. It was frequently modified, however, and did not prevent civil war breaking out again on Diocletian's retirement.

Diocletian's most lasting innovation was in the realm of agriculture and rural life, where he is credited with the establishment of the colonate, a distinctive tenancy arrangement that directly prefigured medieval serfdom. *Coloni* were tenant farmers who leased land from larger owners or municipalities in return for rent in cash or, as time went on, crops. As part of his taxation reform, Diocletian tied peasants to the places where they were registered. Now that slaves were scarce and expensive, landlords gleefully enforced this rule on their tenant farmers to ensure a permanent source of labour and rent at no ongoing cost to themselves. The rural population had no escape route, and this added to the misery brought by increased taxation and oversight. The world of the peasant farmer grew smaller and more wretched.

Constantine to Theodosius

In 305 Diocletain handed power from himself and his fellow-Augustus Maximian to their junior colleagues in the tetrarchy. When the new western Augustus, Constantius, died in 306, his son Constantine was recognized by some as emperor, but others supported Maximian's son, Maxentius. After several years of civil war, Constantine the Great (*r*.307–37) emerged as victorious in the West. In 324, he defeated the Eastern Augustus and temporarily reunited the Empire under a single ruler. He also campaigned against the Germans and the Goths, and founded the city of Constantinople in 330. It show-

cased his wealth and his new religion of Christianity, and also symbolized the new importance of the eastern half of the Empire. Meanwhile, the Western capital was moved from Rome itself to Milan.

Constantine's successors in the 4th century faced renewed invasions from the Germans, and Persia made large gains in Roman territory in the East. The Goths, under pressure themselves from the Huns, crossed the Danube in 376, and they defeated the Roman army at Hadrianople in 378.

The East-West divide soon reasserted itself, and Theodosius the Great became Augustus of the East in 379. He fought the Goths without success, then made an alliance with them, giving them land in the Black Sea provinces. In 386, he treated with Persia, again ceding disputed land. Theodosius was a fervent Christian and banned pagan religion, further entrenching the relationship between the Christian Church and the Roman state. He left his two sons as the Augustuses of East and West. In the East, the Roman Empire recovered, especially under Justin and Justinian, but by the 6th century, there were new rulers in the West.

The final years of the Western Empire

The various Gothic peoples in the Roman Empire united as Visigoths under Alaric in the early 5th century, and moved west from the Balkans and the Black Sea. The Western Roman government retreated from Milan to Ravenna. The Visigoths sacked Rome in 410, then carved out their own kingdom in Gaul and Spain. Worse was to follow: the Vandals travelled to North Africa in 429 and had conquered it entirely by 442. At the same time, the rural peasantry was staggering under the weight of taxation and the colonate, and sporadic revolts had become continuous guerrilla warfare against local commanders and officials.

The Western Empire did not so much fall as peter out. In what was left of the Roman administration, Visigoths attained high commands and influence. The last Western emperor, Romulus Augustulus, was forced to abdicate by the Visigoth king Odoacer in 476. The Goths reunited Italy, Spain, and southern Gaul, cultivated the Church and the Eastern emperors, and ruled with Roman-style administration. It is unlikely that the provincial population knew or cared that their rulers were no longer Roman.

But the Romans were the first to unite Europe in a common citizenship, and their legacy endures. Their language, their roads, and their laws are some of the foundations of modern Europe, building on older traditions and built on in turn by the cultures that took their place. Every generation has reinvented its Roman inheritance: poets, soldiers, tyrants, revolutionaries, and architects have all found something Roman to claim as their own.

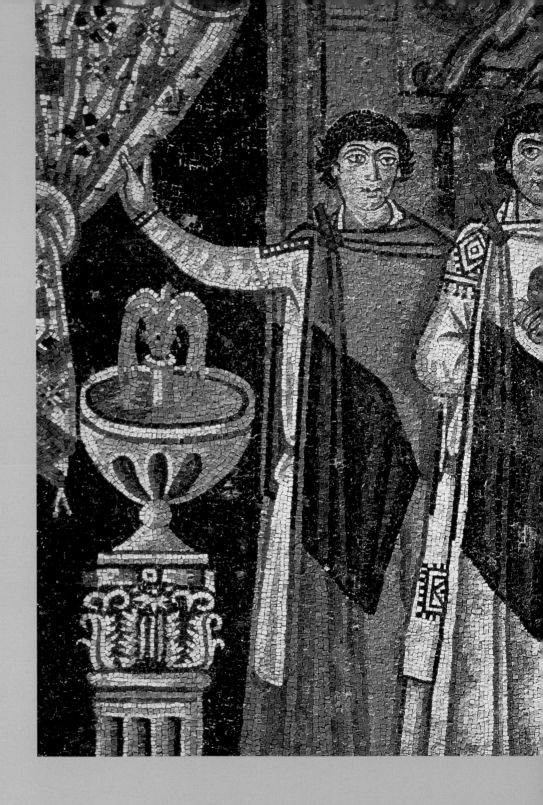

YZANTIUM AND THE RISE OF THE WEST

500–700

POLITICS AND GOVERNMENT

410 Sack of
Rome by Alaric
the Goth

476 Last Western Emperor
Romulus Augustulus driven out by
Goths and abdicates. The Greek-
speaking, Eastern Empire survives
as Byzantium.

527–65 Reign of Justinian I, Emperor of East Rome,
whose conquest policies and massive artistic
patronage created the Byzantine Golden Age.

535 Byzantine general Belisarius invades Southern Italy.
The Byzantines complete the conquest of Italy by 555.

493–526 Theoderic, King
of the Ostrogoths in Italy,
preserves many Roman
institutions and values.

400

475

SOCIETY AND CULTURE

*c.*480–550 St Benedict of Nursia,
monastic founder and writer of the
single most influential monastic
guide – The Rule of St Benedict.

538 Inauguration of the rebuilt, domed
Church of Hagia Sophia in Constantinople
sets new standard for Christian
architecture in the Mediterranean.

*c.*580–620 Slavic occupation of the Balkans and beginnings of Slavic domination between the Carpathian Mountains and the Baltic Sea.

632–655 Islamic Arab conquests of the old Persian Empire, and of the Near East and Egypt from Byzantium destroy the ancient world order which saw Europe dominated by the Mediterranean.

625

700

*c.*580–632 Life and teachings of Muhammad in Arabia generates the Islamic religion

597 Arrival in England of the Roman mission, led by Augustine of Canterbury. Opens new era of spreading the Gospel in Europe.

*c.*630 Sutton Hoo ship burial in East Anglia; amongst its treasures is fabulous jewelry in the Hiberno-Saxon style.

*c.*700 production of the *Codex Amiatinus* in Northumbria, with fabulous illuminations in a realistic, classicizing style.

679–754 St Boniface, the "Apostle of Germany", missionary and Church reformer who spreads the Gospel in Germany and the Low countries until his martyrdom.

Byzantine emperors saw themselves as appointed by God to rule the entire world. This silver dish produced on the 10th anniversary of the reign of Emperor Theodosius I celebrates unbreakable, divinely inspired imperial order. The emperor sits in state holding the orb that symbolizes his authority over the earth.

BYZANTIUM: APOGEE AND DECLINE

In AD 500, Byzantium – the eastern half of the Roman Empire – was emerging triumphantly from a very difficult century. Its Western Roman counterpart had fallen in the 5th century, and its own territories had been repeatedly invaded. Yet in the 6th century, Byzantium entered an era of renewed prosperity, first under Anastasius, then under an uncle and nephew, Justin and Justinian.

In this era, Byzantium stretched its boundaries over Greece and the Balkans, across Asia Minor as far as the Caucasus, and through the Middle East. However, difficulties remained. In the east, Persia, its traditional foe, was also enjoying respite from northern threats. Internally, imperial politics remained unstable. Nonetheless, 6th-century emperors, particularly Justinian, were able to mobilize the powerful resources of this state. Two of the barbarian kingdoms that had replaced the Western Roman Empire – the Vandals and the Ostrogoths – were destroyed, bringing North Africa and Italy under Byzantine control. Dissensions in the kingdom of the Visigoths were also exploited to add parts of southern Spain.

Culturally, this period of Byzantine greatness is famous for the emergence of a new Christian art, manifesting itself in the magnificent domed churches of Istanbul, decorative mosaic on church walls, ivory, metalwork, and textile.

The peak of Byzantine greatness was not to last. After Justinian's death, the nomadic Avars rose in the north and conflict was renewed with Persia. Disaster came from an unexpected quarter – the Arabian peninsula – and when Byzantine–Persian coexistence collapsed into war in the early 7th century, the resulting weakness of the two empires was exploited by the newly united power of Islamic Arabia. By 651, the Persian Empire had been extinguished and Byzantium stripped of its richest territories. By the end of the 7th century, Byzantium had ceased to operate as an imperial power and became an unwilling satellite of the Islamic world. However, Byzantium survived for another 800 years, and its influence on the course of European history was immense.

Between 527 and 565, the Emperor Justinian added enormous tracts of territory, but much more was lost to the Arabs and others. Reduced drastically in size by 651, the Empire was forced to refinance its armies by granting them heriditary landholdings in the themes of Asia Minor.

The Rise and Fall of Byzantium in the 6th–7th Century AD

- Byzantine Empire 527
- Byzantine Empire 565
- Territory always under Byzantine control

The Renewal of Empire

The late 5th and early 6th centuries saw the dawn of a new era in Byzantine history. The external and internal threats of the previous century had been overcome, and the economy was booming. The problem lay in politics: ever since the end of the Theodosian dynasty in 451, one childless emperor had been replaced by another.

Between 491 and 517, power was exercised by the able Anastasius; however, on his death, his adult nephews were passed over in favour of a well-connected guards officer, Justin I. Justin was also childless, but he had his own highly ambitious nephew Justinian, who, over the next decade, so entrenched himself in power that he was able to succeed his uncle in 527.

In Roman thought, "victory" represented the seal of divine approval upon any reign. Needing to

The Emperor Justinian victorious. Christ, portrayed at the top of this ivory, makes the mounted Justinian (surrounded by female embodiments of victory) dominant over the entire world, whose different peoples – note the varieties of costume and animals – bring him their tributes, bowing down before him in submission.

secure his position, military adventurism was thus a natural choice for Justinian to make, and he immediately picked a fight with Persia, which was the traditional enemy of Constantinople. After initial successes, Byzantium suffered a major defeat at the hands of the Persians in 532, and Justinian was forced to pay for the humiliating "Endless Peace". Defeat inspired plotting against him, and attempts were made to replace Justinian with the nephews of Anastasius during the Nika riot. After a week of violence in which most of central Constantinople was burned down and 20,000 people (including Anastasius' nephews) were killed, Justinian only just held on to power.

He decided to gamble on still more military adventurism, sending a small expeditionary force under Belisarius to Vandal North Africa, which was in the middle of its own succession dispute. Against all expectations, the Vandals were decisively defeated, and the entire kingdom was conquered between 532 and 534. The rewards for Justinian were huge. He was politically unassailable, and a massive victory parade was held to display the captured enemy and all his gold.

The next acquisition was also painless. Sicily was conquered from the Ostrogoths in 535 with minimal opposition, but this was only a prelude to the main assault. Belisarius, again, landed in southern Italy in the spring of 536, and by 540 seemed to have won a great victory when the Gothic king Wittigis surrendered. But only some of the Goths had been defeated; most had simply gone home in what was more of a truce than a peace.

The Persians, too, were becoming worried by the extent of Justinian's success in the West, and they launched a massive raid towards the Mediterranean in the summer of 540, sacking the city of Antioch. When Belisarius and some of his troops were withdrawn from Italy, the undefeated Goths revolted. This established a pattern for the next decade, with Persian affairs making it impossible to defeat the Goths decisively.

Only in 551, when peace was again negotiated with Persia, could a large army under the leadership of Narses be sent to Italy. By 553, Italy was finally in Byzantine hands. Justinian had also taken advantage of a civil war in the Visigothic kingdom to conquer a thin strip of territory in southern Spain.

Internal affairs

Justinian was equally energetic within his empire. Here his greatest achievement lay in the field of law. By the early 6th century, legal authority reposed in a confused mass of expert opinions given between the 1st and 3rd centuries, and a host of ill-edited imperial rulings. Under the leadership of Tribonian, every-

Mosaic of Justinian from Ravenna
The famous mosaics of St Vitale in Ravenna, Italy, are a contemporary representation of the Emperor Justinian and his court. It has often been claimed that he came to the throne determined to reconquer the lost Roman lands in the West, but his armies attacked the Persians first, and only turned west when this war failed. A chain of victories followed in North Africa, Sicily, Italy, and Spain; however, they came at a price. The historian Procopius eventually condemned Justinian: "He made a desert and called it peace." Historians remain divided as to whether the gains were worth the cost.

thing was pulled together by 535 into one simplified code: *The Corpus Juris Civilis* (Body of Civil Law).

In Church affairs, Justinian tried to end the monophysite dispute, a debate over how to understand the mixture of the human and divine in the person of Christ, revolving around the definition of faith agreed at the Council of Chalcedon in 451. By Justinian's reign, two separate parties with their own bishops, priests, and church organization existed, and there was little he could do to resolve the schism.

His other reforming efforts were geared to the problem of raising money to finance both his huge campaigns and a vast building programme. These certainly aroused hostility among certain taxpayers, but there is no sign that they caused serious damage to the economy.

The balance sheet

In time, Justinian's new North African provinces became useful parts of the Byzantine Empire, their revenues more than paying for the costs of their conquest and upkeep. The same was true of Sicily.

Shortly after Justinian's death in 565, however, large parts of mainland Italy fell to the Lombards, and the Gothic war had been very damaging to the Italian economy. Justinian's reign also saw an outbreak of plague, and much of the Eastern Empire was to fall into Arab hands in the 630s. The suggestion is often raised, therefore, that the plague and conquests had between them overstretched imperial resources. The later losses of territory were born of quite different circumstances, however, and large areas of Italy remained useful parts of the Byzantine Empire for centuries, despite the losses it suffered. The 6th-century plague also seems to have been too minor a phenomenon to have caused serious dislocation. Overall, North Africa, Sicily, and southern Italy, at least, were important strategic gains, and the great Arab successes occurred three generations after Justinian's death and were not of his making.

Art and Architecture

The later 5th and 6th centuries were an era of huge artistic and architectural achievement in the Byzantine Empire. The booming economy provided funds for artistic patronage of all kinds and on every scale, from huge imperial monuments to smaller-scale local activities. This was the period, too, when traditional Graeco-Roman artistic forms merged with newer cultural concerns to generate a properly Christian art.

Architecture

Some of the Emperor Justinian's buildings survive intact, above all the Church of Hagia Sophia in Istanbul; others are known from archaeological investigation, with a long account of them written by Procopius in the *Buildings* of 561. In religious architecture, Justinian's reign was marked by the development of a distinct Christian structural style: the domed church. Large churches had previously been constructed as basilicas, the standard rectangular form used for most large Roman public buildings. In the 6th century, starting with the Church of Saints Sergius and Bacchus in Constantinople in 530, such churches were increasingly replaced with domed structures, either of wood or masonry, and resting on squinches or more advanced pendentives. The apogee of this new form was achieved in the rebuilding of Hagia Sophia (previously a basilica) between 532 and 537. The architects were able to suspend the top of the dome a staggering 56 metres (182 ft) from the floor and create a vast space beneath. Repairs had subsequently to be made because of earthquakes, but the new church was a triumph and set the form for all the major constructions of the 6th century, such as San Vitale in Ravenna and the pilgrimage Church of St John the Baptist in Ephesus.

Secular building was not ignored. Most cities already had a stock of forums, baths, circuses, and council buildings, but these had to be maintained, and, where new settlements were founded, or earthquakes intervened, they were built from scratch. Justinian transformed his birthplace in the Balkans (Justiniana Prima, now Caricingrad) from a village into a classical city. After the Persian sack of 540, likewise, Antioch underwent a magnificent reconstruction, with porticoed main streets and fora. But in the midst of all the splendour, there was a sense of threat. Much of the construction recorded in Procopius' *Buildings* was of fortresses. Every major city had huge fortifications, the countryside was dotted with refuge centres, and chains of castles and watchtowers guarded the frontiers.

The Arts

A handful of beautifully illuminated manuscripts survive from this era of Byzantine greatness, above all the Vienna *Genesis* and fragments of the *Cotton Genesis*. These used to be seen as the tip of a vast iceberg of lost artistic achievement, but are now understood to be items produced for very special purposes. Such manuscripts would have been extremely rare even in their own time. The first flowering of a specifically Christian art involved a much wider range of media than the illuminated book. The ancient art of lifesize (or greater) statuary in three dimensions fell into disfavour and was replaced by the bust. Otherwise, a full range of traditional media continued to be employed. Carved ivory was used to provide covers for imperial letters of appointment,

Hagia Sophia. Justinian's revolutionary domed church design created a central open space of breath-taking size and beauty. Richly decorated, and lit by countless windows and lamps, this became the setting of spectacular liturgies and imperial ceremonies. In the East, it replaced the basilica as the classic form for church buildings.

Golden, luminescent mosaic
decoration had emerged by the
6th century as a central feature of
Byzantine Christian art. In this
example from the south vestibule
of Hagia Sophia, the Virgin and
Child are framed by two emperors.
Constantine offers them the
original Hagia Sophia he built
in the 4th century, Justinian the
still surviving church of the
6th century.

particularly to the highest dignitary of state, the consulship. Many consular diptychs survive, carved in
high relief, in a realistic, classicizing fashion. Ivory
was also employed in many religious contexts,
whether carved as part of reliquaries or in such prestigious items as the so-called ivory throne (perhaps in
reality a book rest) of Bishop Maximian from 6th-
century Ravenna.

Equally wide use was made of silver. Gifts of fine
silver were often made by emperors to their loyal
officials to commemorate great events. The "David
Plates", discovered in Cyprus, are a striking survival.
These were issued by Emperor Heraclius to celebrate
his astonishing comeback victory against the Persians
in the 620s – David's victory over Goliath having perhaps provided the original inspiration – and illustrate
episodes from the Biblical king's life. Most of the
silver to survive from this era, however, was originally church plate: chalices, pattens, ewers, and
candlesticks. Churches were not only endowed with
rich silver, but also extraordinary textiles. Some
examples from Egypt survive in fragments.

The new Christian art also flourished on the walls
of churches themselves. Hagia Sophia was decorated
only with bare mosaic crosses, but, elsewhere,
Byzantine churches were evolving their standard
cycle of mosaic decoration, which sought to make
the inside of the church representative of the entire
Christian cosmos. Christ and the Virgin Mary were
represented only at the highest physical points, at the
apex of the dome. The next level was occupied by
the angels and the panoply of heaven, and, finally,
closer to eye level, human saints. The earliest surviving example of the full cycle comes from the rotunda
of St George from Thessalonica (dating c.450–500).
Variations on the basic scheme were possible: in San
Vitale in Ravenna, after the destruction of the
Ostrogothic kingdom, the famous pictures of the
Emperor Justinian and the Empress Theodora and
their courts were placed between heaven and earth.
As in so many other areas, the era of Byzantine greatness set a standard for Eastern Christian art which
was followed throughout the Middle Ages.

Patronage

To flourish to such an extent, Christian art required
massive patronage. Hence, larger projects were
funded by the state. Justinian and other emperors followed the pattern established by Constantine two
centuries before in channelling building funds and
tax revenues towards grandiose structures such as
Hagia Sophia. Many smaller churches were built
through local efforts. The great and recently excavated Church of St Polyeuktos in Constantinople was
the brainchild of one great aristocrat – Anicia Julia –
in the 520s. Smaller churches were built and decorated by local bishops, priests, and aristocrats, with
mosaics sometimes recording their efforts, as in the
Church of Saint Demetrius in Thessalonica. The same
was true of all church silver, several pieces of which
are engraved with the names of their donors. Much
of the public and private patronage which used to be
expended upon the classical city was now redirected
towards Christian art.

The Arab Conquests

In the mid-7th century, a new force suddenly appeared to change the course of European history. Muhammad's new religion united the previously divided tribes of the Arabian peninsula. The military force unleashed was powerful enough to destroy the Persian Empire entirely, reduce Byzantium to a fraction of its former strength, and definitively separate the northern and southern shores of the Mediterranean.

An Umayyad-period desert palace, combining mosque, baths, and a decorated dining hall, at Qusayr Amra in Jordan. In entertainment complexes such as these, 7th- and 8th-century caliphs courted the Bedouins who were the source of the military power that enabled them to conquer Persia and most of Byzantium.

The Great Mosque of Damascus, completed in 705, was the first great public building of the Islamic world. Decorated in sumptuous mosaic (this detail shows the treasury) and laid out as an open courtyard and building complex, it is a stunning monument to the new dominance of Islam created by the 7th-century conquests.

Within the Arabian peninsula, important structural transformations worked themselves out in the late Roman period. Up to the early 3rd century, this had been a world of very small political units, consisting of mixed populations of agricultural producers and nomadic Bedouin. These steppe and savannah regions, on the fringes of the true desert, then came to form a southern front in the ongoing great-power confrontation between Byzantium and Persia. To secure the southern front, both empires recruited, armed, and paid client Arab forces. By process of competitive escalation, the allied groups became ever larger, until by the 6th century both sides were dealing with just one Arab entity each: the Byzantines with the Ghassanids and the Persians the Lakhmids. The constituent smaller groups continued to exist within these confederative umbrellas; however, both the Lakhmids and Ghassanids were powerful enough to pursue their own agendas, which were sometimes threatening to the imperial powers. In the early 580s, the Emperor Maurice destroyed the

power of the Ghassanids by military action. But the clock could not be turned back. The tribes of Arabia had become used to working in larger alliances.

Great-power conflict

Many shorter term events also contributed to the Islamic revolution. Throughout the 6th century, competition between Persia and Byzantium was endemic, and had been so since the 3rd century. Fighting was limited, however, to raids for prestige and profit, and the occasional siege. In the later 6th century, the conflict ran out of control. In 602, the Byzantine Emperor Maurice was murdered and his son, Theodosius, fled to the Persian Shah, Chosroes. Chosroes had previously been restored to the throne by Maurice and tried at first, it seems, to repay the favour, invading Byzantium on Theodosius' behalf. His aims, however, escalated. Chosroes' unprecedentedly successful conquest of Egypt, Palestine, and Syria by the mid-610s convinced the Persian to attempt the total conquest of Byzantium. In 626, his forces moved as far as Chalcedon on the southern side of the Bosporus, and their Turkic-speaking nomadic Avar allies, now based on the Hungarian Plain, were outside the land walls of Constantinople to the north. The Byzantines, however, still ruled the waves, and their enemies were unable to unite. The Emperor Heraclius, in the meantime, launched a counter-offensive from the north-east, which outflanked and defeated the Persian army. Chosroes was deposed in 628. Heraclius' victory was in essence a draw, brought about by exhaustion on both sides.

Muhammad and Arabia

This draining war gave the Prophet Muhammad an opportunity to add another key ingredient to the revolution brewing inside Arabia. In creating his new religion, Muhammad took elements from Judaism and Christianity, both of which had been present within Arabia from the 4th to the 6th centuries, and refashioned them into an entirely new mix. Muhammad's message, preserved in the Koran, presented him as

the culmination of the Jewish prophetic tradition transmitted via the Old Testament, and the necessary successor to Jesus. Muhammad proclaimed that all the faithful should form one political community and set about uniting the Arab world behind him. Within Arabia, his message and military leadership, eventually based at Mecca in the Hijaz, provided a political superstructure independent of Byzantium or Persia. The new unity led to unprecedented military success, providing healthy profits to those participating in the new enterprise. During Muhammad's lifetime, military activity was directed towards uniting the peninsula and preying on its fringes. After his death in 632, his successors looked outwards to the richer prizes available in Persia and Byzantium.

Here, the postwar weakness of these empires played a critical role. Muhammad's religion and authority had created an Arab entity of unprecedented power. Yet it is unlikely that Arabia would have conquered so much had its imperial neighbours not been so devastated by their great war. Victory over the Byzantines at Yarmuk in 636 allowed the Arabs to capture Syria and Palestine. Egypt was conquered in the 650s. In the meantime, similar gains had been made in the Persian Empire, with the last Shah, Isdigerdes III, defeated and killed in 651, by which time the Arab conquests stretched over all of the territory now covered by Iraq and Iran. The Byzantine emperors survived, but only just. Two major Arab sieges had to be fought off in the 670s and 710s, and the Empire was only a shadow of its former self. By the year 700, its North African provinces had also been lost to Islamic conquest, reducing Byzantium to between a quarter and a third of its former size. By the early 8th century, the Muslim world stretched from India to the Pyrenees, with the bulk of Visigothic Spain falling into its hands in the 710s.

A satellite state

The consequences for Byzantium could not have been more profound. It became a second-rank regional power at the eastern end of the Mediterranean, confined to the southern Balkans and northern and western Asia Minor. In the face of constant Arab raiding, its economy suffered so much that former large cities shrank into refuge fortresses. The population of late 7th- and 8th-century Constantinople likewise collapsed to one-tenth of what it had been in its 6th-century heyday. Byzantium became an unwilling satellite of the Muslim world. When the latter was united, Byzantium could only suffer, and it was only when Muslim unity collapsed in the late 9th and 10th centuries that a limited Byzantine expansion could follow. When the Seljuk Turks reunited the world of Islam in the 11th century, Byzantium quickly shrank back to its now core territories in north-western Asia Minor and the Balkans. For Europe as a whole, the rise of Islam brought the ancient world order to an end. The conquests divided the Mediterranean world in two and freed the rest of Europe to chart its own historical course.

This fabulously ornate initial page introduces the Gospel of St Mark in the 8th-century Book of Kells. It is a perfect example of the Hiberno-Saxon pictorial style of the Dark Ages, which combined interlacing, abstract monsters, and geometric patterns into explosions of multicoloured decoration.

THE BARBARIAN KINGDOMS

By AD 500, the Western Roman Empire was no more than a memory. A broader Roman legacy was still alive, however, in territories around the rim of the Mediterranean, where Roman landowners survived alongside barbarian armies. They preserved Roman governmental systems and Roman cultural values in their Christianized form. In Anglo-Saxon England and north-eastern Gaul, the Roman legacy was rejected. In some areas, Latin education was not maintained, and Christianity was thrown over in favour of pagan religious cult.

Over the next two centuries, the differences between northern and southern kingdoms in the post-Roman west were eroded. Justinian's campaigns destroyed two of the Mediterranean states – the Ostrogothic and Vandal kingdoms – and, in the longer term, a pattern of dual evolution set in. The northern territories came to accept parts of the Roman value system, turning to Christianity and trumpeting the civilizing importance of written law. Further south, Roman value systems survived, but not the structures of centralized Roman rule. A simpler kind of state, with rudimentary low-yield tax structures and small unspecialized bureaucracies, became the norm in both north and south. Political power was switched from the centre to the localities.

The late Roman world was characterized by extensive literacy among the secular aristocracy, due to years of private education. This allowed the elite to participate in the lucrative bureaucratic careers of the Roman world. As these careers disappeared, so did the willingness of elite parents to pay for education, and it quickly became the preserve of the Church. At the same time, new cultural modes were introduced by the immigrant barbarian elites and began to coexist alongside such classicizing cultural elements as were preserved by the Church.

Simultaneously, east-central and eastern Europe was undergoing a massive revolution of an entirely different kind. Up to about 500 AD, Europe as far east as the river Vistula, the outer arc of the Carpathian mountains, and their eastern approaches north of the Black Sea were all dominated by Germanic-speaking groups. From that date, Slavic-speakers spread from their original homes in the wooded steppe zone of the East European plain. In the later 6th and 7th centuries, they came to dominate most of Greece and the Balkans and swept through central Europe. By the time that written sources start to cover these regions in the 9th and 10th centuries, all of Central and Eastern Europe from the Elbe to the Volga was divided between different Slavic tribes. How this revolution was achieved continues to be debated, but it clearly involved the Slavicization of indigenous populations.

The Successor States

⌒ Approximate frontiers of barbarian kingdoms

➙ Lombard invasion 568

By 500 AD, Roman Europe had been carved up between a host of successor states. These states were built around the military might of intrusive "barbarian" groups, but incorporated, to differing degrees, Roman land-owning elites who had survived the Empire's fall. Over the following two centuries, the boundaries were redrawn as the various kingdoms quarrelled among themselves and struggled against Byzantium and the rising power of Islam.

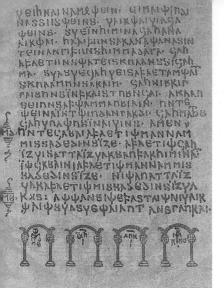

Kingdoms of the Mediterranean Rim

After the deposition of the last Roman Emperor in the West, Romulus Augustulus, in 476, the successor states established around the Mediterranean coast preserved for at least the next half a century Roman culture and institutions to a quite surprising degree. In the long run, however, important structural changes in their political economies meant that their Roman character was destined to disappear.

The Codex Argenteus of Ulfila's Gothic Bible translation is a stunning symbol of the imperial and Gothic culture of Ostrogothic Italy. It was produced in Ravenna in the early 6th century for King Theoderic, on purple-dyed parchment in gold and silver inks. The vellum is so fine that it may have been made from the skin of unborn calves.

The Vandals of North Africa have become synonymous with mindless destruction and were more aggressive than many of the groups who founded successor states. As the international UNESCO excavations at their capital of Carthage have shown, however, they preserved much of the fabric of the classical city, as well as the theatre and other traditional aspects of gracious Roman living.

The first-generation successor states to the Western Roman Empire – Visigothic southern Gaul and Spain, the Burgundian kingdom of the Rhone valley, Ostrogothic Italy, and even Vandal Africa – were all born with the ruins of the Roman West smoking around them, and they continued to see themselves as part of a wider Roman world. They all maintained one fundamental institution of Roman government: large-scale taxation of the agricultural economy. This included maintenance of the administrators and record keeping at the local level (all land was registered in local city archives) necessary to make taxation work. They also maintained much of the framework of Roman law and incorporated a numerically dominant, culturally distinct Roman population, some of whose elite elements continued to enjoy access to positions of power. As part and parcel of the latter process, the kingdoms all

accepted the established Roman value system, which saw literary education and written law as essential to a civilized society. Maintaining a Roman legal system was thus an ideological statement, as well as a practical instrument of government, and most of these kings encouraged the written use of Latin at their courts. Even the kings of Vandal Africa wanted to be praised in Latin verse, and it was under their rule that much of the *Latin Anthology*, a definitive selection of older poetry, was compiled.

These kingdoms were all, however, based around the military power of the immigrant groups after whom they were named. Integrating the latter into existing Roman societies posed a number of common problems. First and foremost, the new kings needed to reward the loyalty of the immigrant soldiers who had put them in power. They did this initially through grants of landed estates, mostly found

by reallocating publicly owned assets, supplemented by annual salaries paid from existing Roman tax revenues. Only Vandal Africa saw large-scale expropriations of private property. In the Ostrogothic and Visigothic kingdoms, the immigrants were settled in a series of concentrated clusters at strategically important points. These clusters in part reflected preexisting groupings within the larger force and allowed some continuity of identity and custom to be maintained.

A second problem area was that of religion. The immigrants were all Christian, but held to a variant form – so-called Arianism – regarded as heretical by the Catholic Romans. In Africa, the Vandal kings periodically persecuted the Catholics, confiscating churches and other assets, refusing to allow the appointment of bishops, and even attempting to make the population adopt their Arian version of Christianity. Elsewhere, however, tension was minimal. Theoderic built Arian churches in his capital Ravenna, but these coexisted with Catholic ones, and the king enjoyed, for the most part, good relations with the Roman Church. He was even called upon to settle a disputed election to the papacy and was judged to have acted equitably.

History

A new strategic order evolved only slowly in post-Roman Europe. Up to the 520s, the dominant power was the Ostrogothic kingdom of Theoderic. Between 508 and 511, he took direct control of the Visigothic kingdom, adding it to lands that he had already acquired in the Balkans. He also established hegemony over the Burgundian and Vandal kingdoms, and an alliance system, with himself as the dominant partner, which stretched north into central Germany. He consider himself to have re-established the Western Roman Empire, and one of his Roman subjects hailed him as "Augustus" in an inscription celebrating economic expansion in northern Italy. But Theoderic's grand edifice did not survive his death in 526. The Visigothic and Ostrogothic kingdoms separated again, and the Burgundians and Vandals had already exploited the king's declining years by attempting to throw off Ostrogothic hegemony. The situation was transformed by Justinian, whose conquests wiped the Vandal and Ostrogothic kingdoms from the map. This allowed the Franks to swallow up the Burgundian kingdom in the 530s and the Lombards to move into Italy in 568. By c.580, of the sub-Roman kingdoms of the Mediterranean rim, only the Visigoths survived.

Structural transformation

These political changes took place on top of more structural transformations. Most important of all, orig-

Mosaic of Theoderic's palace

Theoderic, the Ostrogothic king of Italy, was determined to present himself as a legitimate Roman ruler. He continued to use the old Roman capital of Ravenna and operated a Roman palace complex there. In his Arian cathedral, St Apollinare Nuovo, Theoderic had his palace depicted in mosaic, together, originally, with himself in full Roman panoply. After Justinian's conquest, the king's figure was removed from the central arch. Theoderic was entirely typical of the successor-state kings of the Mediterranean rim in seeing himself as part of a larger, still-living Roman world and as presenting a Roman face to his many Roman subjects.

inal distinctions between Roman and immigrant, especially at elite level, steadily eroded. In a world of volatile international relations, kings needed military service above all. Romans, therefore, quickly moved from administration to military service, where there were rich rewards. Latin culture had originally been transmitted among these Roman elites, for whom it gave access to jobs in the bureaucracy. Previously, they had also been willing to pay relatively large amounts of tax because it paid for a professional army. Once they were fighting in their own defence, they ceased to be so willing, and tax gradually played a less important role in post-Roman state structures.

Intermarriage and other alliances between Roman and immigrant elites also became common, as they were present at the same royal courts. These changes were happening everywhere, but came to fruition in the Visigothic kingdom. By the 7th century, the lifestyles of the secular aristocracy concentrated on martial endeavour, and the power of the central state declined alongside its tax revenues. Cultural fusion was brought to completion by the conversion of the remaining Arian Visigoths to Catholicism at the Third Council of Toledo in 589.

Northern Worlds 500–700

The new imperial power of Western Europe emerged not from the kingdoms of the Mediterranean rim, but from further north. Here Roman ideals were lost or rejected as new immigrant elites built political systems based on warmongering and the exchange of rich gifts, rather than Latin and the efficient bureaucratic exploitation of resources.

Beyond the Mediterranean rim, there was an outright rejection of Roman ideologies. In England, all Roman villas ceased to be occupied from the early 5th century onwards, and many of them were violently destroyed. In the towns of Roman Britain, too, evidence of occupation quickly disappears in the 5th century. Among the now largely rural population, the extensive cemetery evidence shows that, by the mid-

5th century, new, Germanic cultural norms had come to prevail. From around 480–520, the same could be said of northern Gaul, too, most particularly in areas north and east of Paris.

In the past, the appearance of these new cemeteries was taken to prove that the native population had been expelled by the mass intrusion of immigrants: Angles and Saxons from the Low Countries, southern

The tomb of Clovis in the monastery of St Denis in Paris, as reinterpreted in the 13th century. Responsible for turning the Franks into one of the great powers of the post-Roman West, Clovis united previously independent warbands into one force and began to integrate them with the sub-Roman population of his new kingdom by converting to Catholicism.

Denmark, and England; and Franks from east of the Rhine in northern Gaul. In England, there certainly was some immigration. A first major influx occurred in the 440s; however, migration was still occurring in the mid- to late-6th century. The cremation burials of eastern England, in particular, clearly belong to an intrusive population of immigrant Angles. The end result was the total replacement of native Celtic languages with various Germanic dialects and the appearance of Anglo-Saxon kingdoms right across the English countryside. Some of the occupants of these new cemeteries were not true migrants, but individuals of Romano-British and Gallo-Roman descent, who accommodated themselves to new Anglo-Saxon and Frankish norms in order to prosper in changed circumstances. This makes the extent of immigration hard to estimate, but does not obscure the underlying point. Outside the Mediterranean, the old ideals of Roman civilization, such as Latin, Christianity, written law, town dwelling etc, were firmly rejected.

The rise of the Merovingians

The most important political development of the later 5th and 6th century in north-western Europe was the rise of the Frankish Merovingian dynasty. In the Roman period, the Franks were divided into a number of small warbands, but the disappearance of imperial power allowed them to unite in the reigns of a father and son: Childeric (*d.*482) and Clovis (*r.*482–511). Childeric operated as a Roman client; Clovis exploited the fall of Rome to create a dominant kingdom. By 485, he had defeated Syagrius, a Roman potentate, to add Paris and Champagne to his father's power base in Belgium. The unification of the previously fragmented Franks then gave him sufficient military power to conquer south-western Gaul from the Visigoths, establish hegemony over the Burgundians of the Rhone valley, and undertake a series of conquests east of the Rhine. These brought the German tribe of the Alamanni, in particular, under his control. Further expansion was temporarily halted by the power of Theoderic, but, after Justinian's destruction of the Ostrogothic kingdom, expansion picked up again. The Burgundians were finally conquered in the early 530s, and Frankish hegemony stretched out over all the peoples of what is now Germany: from the Saxons in the north, to the Bavarians in the south. An important side effect was that the wealth of conquest flowed into the courts of Merovingian kings, and in the later 6th century – after a gap of 75 years – they started to affect some of the trappings of Roman imperial power. Latin culture was encouraged, and efforts were made to govern both civil and ecclesiastical society by means of written law and to erect a more substantial system of taxation.

Sutton Hoo

Excavated in the 1930s, the Sutton Hoo burial site brought to life the non-Roman world of northern Europe. Instead of wearing togas and hanging about in forums, the elite of post-Roman Britain buried their dead in boats surrounded by fantastic treasure. Among the items discovered was the famous Sutton Hoo Helmet. Constructed of leather underneath, iron plates provided the wearer's head with all-round defence, while rich gold and silver inlays marked out his status. It was made for a king of East Anglia, quite likely the Redwald mentioned in Bede's *Ecclesiastical History*.

The limits of power

Behind this Romanizing façade, however, there were fundamental differences between the Frankish kingdom of the early Middle Ages and the Roman Empire. The Franks were running a structurally weaker state, with less power collected at the centre and, correspondingly, more left in the localities. The army was composed of armed local landowners, tax structures (giving the state independent financial muscle) were much weaker, the localities did not in general look to kings for written rulings, and the kings did not run the vast court bureaucracy. Frankish kings could offer court jobs to a few tens of landowners at most, where the Western Roman emperors had employed more than 10,000. In general, therefore, Frankish kings were not as powerful as their Roman forbears, unless they were engaged in military expansion, which brought them extraordinary wealth to distribute.

In the 6th century, when there were plenty of wealthy and not too powerful neighbours to conquer, Merovingian kings became very rich indeed. In the 7th century, however, the supply of suitable neighbours dried up, and kings found themselves in increasing difficulties when it came to controlling powerful subordinates. By 700, the great Merovingian Empire had fragmented. The satellite powers east of the Rhine (Thuringia, Saxony, Bavaria, and Alamannia) re-established their independence, and the central Gallic lands fragmented into separate power blocks. North-east Gaul, north-west Gaul, Burgundy, and Aquitaine all saw their own local ducal dynasties usurp most of the powers of the last Merovingian kings. Right across Western Europe both inside and beyond the old Roman frontier, states of a homogeneous non-Roman structure had emerged. The highly centralized Roman Empire gave way to early medieval kingdoms, the kings of which functioned much more on the basis of the purchased consent of local landowners.

The Rise of the Slavs

Following on from the fall of Rome, the 6th and 7th centuries witnessed another huge revolution in the European political landscape. Emerging from the woods of the East, many small Slavic groups spread across vast tracts of the continent, occupying lands as far west as the river Elbe. At the same time, social and economic transformations began which would eventually lead to the emergence of Slavic states.

Slavic origins

The origins of Europe's Slavic-speakers was a highly political issue throughout the 19th and for most of the 20th century. Western Slavic scholars insisted that the Slavs had always been a major presence in central Europe, arguing that, in the Roman period (when no Slavs are mentioned in what is now Poland and the Czech and Slovak republics), Slavs had nonetheless inhabited these territories "submerged" under the domination of a minority Germanic-speaking population. Russian scholars took the alternative view that Slavs had originated in mother Russia and that the "Slavicness" of central Europe in medieval and modern times was the result of migration. Only

with the fall of the Berlin Wall in 1989 has greater objectivity entered the discussion, the issue being decided largely in favour of the Russian view.

Slavs are first mentioned in literary sources in the 6th century AD, at which point they inhabited regions around the northern edges of the Carpathian Mountains from the southern Vistula to the Black Sea. Recent archaeological research has made a convincing identification of these groups with two related archaeological systems of the same date: the Prague-Korcak and Penkovka cultures. Early Slavs emerge from these remains as Iron Age subsistence farmers, distributed in grouped clusters of small villages composed of 10 to 20 simple log cabins, often partly sunk into the ground for extra protection against the weather. They used only handmade pottery and some very simple iron tools: a plain ard plough, for instance, which scraped narrow trenches for seed. At this point, a Slavic-speaking population in the Carpathian region was a new phenomenon. It had moved into the area only in the latter part of the 5th century, as the Hunnic empire of Attila collapsed, leaving a power vacuum. All the evidence suggests that Slavs migrated there from areas further north and east in the wooded Steppes zone of what is now southern Russia and the Ukraine.

Slavic spread

Further migrations then spread Slavic-speaking groups right across central Europe, from the Baltic to the Aegean. Byzantine literary sources describe their takeover of the Balkans, where the nomadic Avars played a crucial role. From c.560 onwards, the Avars put together a powerful empire on the Hungarian Plain, which mounted a series of campaigns into Byzantine territory. This caused huge damage, particularly in the reign of Heraclius, when the Emperor was primarily occupied with his war against Persia. As a direct result, Slavic groups moved south across the river Danube and then inserted themselves alongside the indigenous Roman population in large parts of the Balkans, even into the Peloponnese.

A critical moment in the Slavs social and economic development came in the 8th century when their early handmade pottery was replaced by wheel-made wares such as this example from None Zaluku. This reflects the major increase in agricultural productivity that supported both specialist producers and the militarized elites around whom the first Slavic states would form.

Further north and west, the spread of Slavic-speakers has to be reconstructed on the basis of archaeological evidence alone. By the 9th century, when Carolingian authors first show detailed knowledge of the Slavic world, all of central Europe east of the Elbe was Slavic-speaking, whereas, up to c.550, territories between the Elbe and the Vistula, at least, had been Germanic-speaking. Between c.550 and 800, therefore, Slavs had come to dominate vast areas of Europe.

In part, this was accomplished through direct migration. The use of pottery of the Penkovka and particularly Prague-Korcak types spread west through central European uplands as far as the Elbe in the 6th and 7th centuries. Similar pottery – known as Sukow – also spread through the northern plains of what is now Poland and eastern Germany at more or less the same time. No literary sources describe these events, but the pottery remains probably reflect the initial Slavic takeover of these lands, which, in the Roman period, had been Germanic-speaking. Further east, similar processes were also unfolding in the Russian forest world. By the 9th century, Slavic-speaking groups here had spread northwards from the Kiev region as far as Lake Ilmen, taking over a landscape which, to judge by place and river names, had originally been occupied by speakers of Baltic languages.

Slavicization

The creation of Slavic Europe involved not just migration, but also, as with post-Roman Britain, the absorption of indigenous populations into new patterns of life. Now that consensus has finally begun to emerge over origins, the big debate amongst experts in early Slavic studies now revolves around the questions of how many Slavic migrants moved into central Europe in the early Middle Ages, and the extent to which the Slavicization of Europe was based on cultural accommodation among an existing central European population.

In the past, answers were again highly political. Scholars in Cold War East Germany "found" Slavic- and Germanic-speakers living side by side on the same sites, mimicking the ideology of Germano-Slav co-operation that legitimized the state which employed them. More recent work has shown, however, that the handful of "proof sites" usually cited in support of such views were actually occupied sequentially by Germanic and Slavic groups, not simultaneously. The most useful information comes, in fact, from pollen diagrams, which show whether the basic pattern of agriculture in a given area was disrupted or not in the era of Slavic takeover. Where it was disrupted, then migration was probably significant. While the coverage of such diagrams is far from

comprehensive, it does show a mixed pattern. Slavicization was not a simple or singular process, but the product of both migration and acculturation, in different combinations in different localities.

Nor did transformation cease at the initial point of takeover in the later 6th or 7th centuries. In the 8th and 9th centuries, the archaeology of central Europe throws up Slavic pottery types (such as the Leipzig, and Tornow) of a much more sophisticated kind, characterized by a much wider range of forms, better firing, and, eventually, the use of the wheel. Agricultural exploitation also became much more intense, with more effective soil-turning ploughs and crop-rotation schemes coming into use. This greater economic productivity in turn spawned a larger population and the general development of more sophisticated political structures. These further processes culminated in the appearance of the first Slavic states of the 9th and 10th centuries.

Of all the cities of the Balkans, only Thessalonica survived the Slavic onslaught. According to a contemporary text, the Miracula *of* St Demetrius *(here pictured in a 12th-century icon), this was entirely due to the saint's intervention. It was believed that the saint prevented the city's capture in 586, 614, 633, and again in 680.*

Culture and Society

The early Middle Ages saw new cultural norms in Europe. Landowning aristocrats ceased to be trained intensively in Latin language and literature, and the Christian Church became the repository of classical learning. Only those texts were preserved, however, which were perceived to be of value for Christian purposes, and an entirely different oral culture of battle poetry was enjoyed by the secular warrior elites.

Cultural ideologies

In the Roman world, education in Latin language and literature was fundamental to being a civilized human being. Literature contained countless examples of people behaving well and badly, and was a moral database from which the civilized individual could learn to temper the barbarian desires of the body by exercising the rational influence of the mind. Literature also taught the individual to accept the civilizing influence of written laws, which were held to guarantee equal protection for all. The conversion of Rome to Christianity had prompted only minor adjustments to these long-held ideas. Some old texts fell out of use as Christian commentators such as Augustine (especially in his *De Doctrina Christiana*) added the Bible to the literary canon of vital works. But a religion with the Ten Commandments and Leviticus deep within its own ideological structure only served to reinforce the idea that written law set superior societies apart from inferior ones.

Many successor states received a Roman legacy in the form of an established landowning elite, and most embraced these Christianized Roman cultural ideologies. The *Variae* letter collection of the Ostrogothic king Theoderic stressed at every opportunity the importance of written law and classical literature, and Theoderic established some state-funded teaching posts. The Burgundian and Visigothic kingdoms, likewise, established their own functioning systems of written law. Further north, the Franks produced a more symbolic law code – *Lex Salica* – which does not seem to have been much used in practice, but showed that the Franks belonged to the club of civilized states. In the second half of the 6th century, a classical poet from Italy, Venantius Fortunatus, found an enthusiastic Gallic audience for his work, comprising both Roman and Frankish aristocrats who wanted to be written about in old-style Latin verse. As Christianity spread, the emphasis on written law continued to be transmitted, and Anglo-Saxons, Alamannis, and Bavarians all pro-

Ezra's book cupboard from the *Codex Amiatinus*

The stunning *Codex Amiatinus* was produced in Bede's monastery of Monkwearmouth-Jarrow, Northumbria, Britain, in the early 8th century. It contains richly coloured, highly naturalistic classicizing illuminations in realistic style which clearly went back to classical models. These models had probably been brought north in the collection of materials acquired in Italy by the monastery's founder, Benedict Biscop, in the 660s. The picture of Ezra, with his manuscripts collected in a cupboard, is an accurate depiction of an early medieval scholar at work. The manuscript was a luxury item. The vellum alone was made from the hides of 1700 cows.

duced symbolic law codes upon joining the new Christian world.

Literacy and education

Literacy among the secular aristocracy was widespread in the late Roman world. Parents paid for their children to receive 10 years of private education with a private teacher of language and letters – the grammarian. They were willing to do so because such an education was necessary for elite status and led to lucrative careers in the Roman imperial bureaucracy. In the post-Roman world, these careers disappeared as administrative structures reverted to a much simpler level. As a result, elite parents, even of Roman descent, became unwilling to pay for such an intense education, and the grammarians went out of business. After *c.*475, there was none north of the Alps, and they disappeared even from Italy after *c.*550. The post-Roman elite, including barbarian royal families, still learned to read some Latin, but not to write it, and they usually learned within their families, where women became the chief educators. More intensive literacy was confined to the Church, and, in *c.*500, many church leaders suddenly realized that the old educational structures were disappearing. In order to reverse this process, individual bishops started to collect libraries of important books and to establish schools within their households, to train their clergy in the literacy essential to Christianity. The *Institutes of Divine Learning* of Cassiodorus, a later 6th-century list of crucial works, was particularly influential, but there was no general pattern. The quality of post-grammarian education depended upon local initiative, with the 6th-century Merovingian, 7th-century Visigothic, and 8th-century Anglo-Saxon Churches showing particular excellence.

Art and architecture

Little architecture of the post-Roman period survives intact, making it difficult to establish general trends. In northern Francia and Anglo-Saxon England, building in stone ceased altogether, and even royal centres (such as Yeavering in Northumbria) were entirely wooden constructions. In these areas, Roman cities fell largely out of use. Further south, change was less marked. Some of the existing Roman public buildings were maintained, and new constructions in stone, particularly of churches, continued. Most of these early medieval structures were later rebuilt, although some smaller Visigothic churches still survive. The size and sophistication of construction between the 6th and 8th centuries has often been underestimated; however, as state structures brought in smaller amounts of taxation, fewer funds were available for grand architectural programmes than in the Roman period.

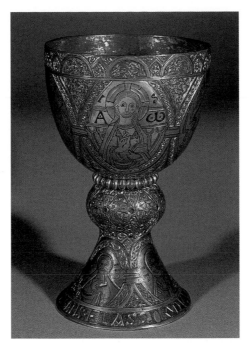

Early medieval elites were highly militarized, but also deeply pious, and the metalworking skills that produced weapons and high-status jewellery were also turned to religious subjects. This stunning gold and silver chalice was presented to the monastery of Kremsmunster by Duke Tassilo of Bavaria and his wife Liutpirc in 770.

Artistic activity throughout this period presents a similarly mixed picture. Classical realism continued to exert considerable influence, and it was seen most strongly closer to the Mediterranean. The fact that so many older manuscripts were destroyed in the Carolingian period (751–987) makes it difficult to estimate the extent of artistic activity and the predominant styles in the earlier medieval era. Further north, alongside occasional examples of the classicizing pictorial style such as the *Codex Amiatinus*, a more abstract art, the so-called Hiberno-Saxon style, was also flourishing. This was characterized by fantastic interlacing monsters and abstract patterns, and it was often used as illustration, as on the initial pages of the late 7th-century *Lindisfarne Gospels*. It manifested itself in other media: on the great standing stones of Anglo-Saxon England, such as the Ruthwell Cross, and on metalwork, such as that found at Sutton Hoo. The latter also points us towards a world that we can only begin to grasp: the rich metalwork seems to have been made by post-Roman kings to distribute to their supporters, a material expression of the generosity that was expected of them.

These elites and their kings also had their own oral culture of heroic poetry, where treasures such as those at Sutton Hoo were celebrated. *Beowulf* is a surviving example, but this tradition occasionally coincided with other forms. The Ruthwell Cross is not only decorated with Hiberno-Saxon motifs, but also inscribed with *The Dream of the Rood*, a Christian poem on the Crucifixion expressed in Anglo-Saxon poetic form.

Biographies of Key Figures

Alexander the Great (356–323 BC): King of Macedon, 336–323 BC. Became king on assassination of his father, Philip II of Macedon. Tutored by Aristotle. Took control of Greek States; embarked on war against Persians, 334 BC, destroying them at the battles of Granicus, 334 BC, Issus, 333 BC, and Gaugamela, 331 BC. Took Tyre, conquering Syria, Palestine, and Egypt, 332 BC, and founding Alexandria. Conquests in Persia took him as far as the Indus, defeating the Indian king, Porus, and marrying the Bactrian princess, Roxane. Returning to Persepolis, the Persian capital, quelled a mutiny in his troops but died of fever at Babylon. The greatest military conqueror of the ancient world; conquests spread Hellenic influence into Asia and founded cities as far as the Hindu Kush. His empire was divided among his subordinate commanders.

Archimedes (287–212 BC): Mathematician and engineer of the ancient world. Born in Syracuse. Mathematical studies led to important discoveries in mechanics. Established principles of the lever and the Archimedes Screw for raising water from a lower to a higher level by means of a screw mechanism enclosed in a cylinder. This facilitated the working of water-pumping device for drainage and was also used for grape and olive presses. Also invented military machines used in the defence of Syracuse. Died in Syracuse when the city fell to the Romans.

Aristotle (384–322 BC): Greek philosopher. Resident of Athens 367–347 BC and from 335 BC. Tutor of Alexander the Great, his influence came mainly through later period of residence in Athens from 335 BC. Opened a school, but was forced to leave in 323 BC when accused of impiety. Writings cover several categories, including logic, natural science, metaphysics, ethics, politics, and literature. Works largely transmitted through Arab translations and taken up by medieval scholars such as St Thomas Aquinas.

Augustine of Hippo, St (354–430): Major theologian of the early Church. Converted by St Ambrose and baptized, AD 387. Made Bishop of Hippo, 395. Completed his major work *De Civitate Dei* (*The City of God*), 416. He is today best-known for his *Confessions*, a long autobiographical prayer including the memorable "Grant me chastity, lord, but not yet!"

Augustus (63 BC–AD 14): First Roman emperor. Grand-nephew of Julius Caesar; claimed his uncle's inheritance, 44 BC. Was appointed triumvir with Mark Antony and Lepidus, 43 BC. Most successful of a group of competing generals and politicians. Finally defeated Mark Antony and Cleopatra at Actium, 31 BC. Victory in Egypt and its incorporation into Roman rule, his standing in Italy, and his great wealth led to dominant position in Rome. Took on an increasingly central role, with the title "Augustus". Extended the system of direct rule, reformed taxation, and doubled the size of the provincial Empire. By end of his rule, Rome had evolved from a Republican system to a virtually imperial one.

Benedict, St (480–550): Founder of Western monasticism; collected his disciples c.520–7 and founded his monastery at Monte Cassino, 529, where he drew up the rules relating to monastic life in *The Rule of St Benedict*. This set up the ideal of monastic life as one governed by an elected abbot, residence in one place, and observance of prayers. His ideal of monasticism was carried forward in the Benedictine order and later adapted by other monastic orders.

Caesar, Gaius Julius (102–44 BC): Roman soldier and statesman. Descended from a prominent family; early political career was interrupted by the antagonism of Sulla. Began to establish a political reputation upon return to Rome, 68 BC, but was more noted for his extravagant lifestyle. Sought to reconcile rivals Pompey and Crassus, becoming consul, 60 BC, in first Triumvirate. Obtained command of Transalpine and Cisalpine Gaul and Illyria. From 58 BC mounted a series of campaigns in Gaul. Defeated the Helvetii, the Germans under Ariovistus, the Belgae, and Nervii. Crushed revolt by the Veneti in Brittany; victory over the Aquitani of the south-west gave the Roman Republic complete control over Gaul. A final revolt under Vercingetorix was eventually defeated, forcing complete surrender of rebel forces and reimposition of Roman rule. First exploratory invasion of Britain, 55 BC. Defeated British under Cassivelaunus, 54 BC, forcing them into a tributary relationship. Returned to Italy, 49 BC, to power struggle with Pompey. Caesar subdued Spain then returned to Rome; was elected dictator and consul. Defeated Pompey at the battle of Pharsalus in Greece. Pursued Pompey to Egypt; remained there after the former was murdered. Wars against remaining opponents let to campaigns in Spain and Africa. Jealousy led to conspiracy and his murder in the Senate on 15 March. Great soldier and statesman, also contributed significantly as writer and historian.

Cicero, Marcus Tullius (106–43 BC): Roman orator, famous for his defence of the Republic against the threat of ambitious politicians. Letters and speeches among the most widely read and admired of classical literature. As consul, defeated and suppressed Catiline conspiracy, but was unable, as Tribune, to resist the encroachments of the Republic by Pompey, Caesar, and Crassus. After several periods of exile, returned to Rome where delivered speeches denouncing Mark Antony (the *Philippics*), as a threat to the Senate following the death of Julius Caesar. Proscribed by the Triumvirs, he was killed while trying to escape.

Cleopatra (69–30 BC): Queen of Egypt. Daughter of Ptolemy Auletes. Legendary beauty attracted attention of Julius Caesar, 48 BC. She lived with him in Rome, but returned to Egypt on his death four years later. Formed liaison with Mark Antony, who increased her domains. Committed suicide when Antony was defeated at Actium, 31 BC. The last of the Ptolemaic rulers of Egypt, her death saw Egypt's incorporation into the Roman Empire.

Clovis (465–511): Became chief of the Franks on the death of his father, Childeric, 481; defeated the Roman general, Syagrius, at Soissons and the Germans, 496. Baptized with his army, 496; defeated Alaric, King of the Goths. Fixed his residence in Paris, 508.

Constantine I, the Great (Flavius Valerius Aurelius) (274–337): Founder of Constantinople. First emperor to make Christianity a state religion of the Byzantine Empire in 324. Son of Constantine Chlorus and Helena. Earned a reputation as a brave soldier and was proclaimed emperor by the troops at York, England. Marched against his rivals, notably Maxentius, for the imperial title, AD 312. According to legend was converted to Christianity by the apparition of a cross in the sky with the message, "By this sign conquer." Establishing his power in the Western Empire, he promoted prosperity and encouraged Christianity. Defeated a rival, Licinius, in the Eastern Empire, 323, to become master of both Western and Eastern Empires. Assembled the first general Christian Council at Nicaea, 325, which adopted a settled creed of beliefs (the Nicene Creed). Transferred the capital of the Empire to Byzantium, 330, naming it after himself as Constantinople. Breifly reunited the Roman Empire and proclaimed Christianity the official religion of the Empire, 334. Baptized on his deathbed, 337.

Gregory I, the Great (540–604): Consecrated pope in 590; he propagated the faith in Italy and sent Augustine on a mission to evangelize Britain. Established the Gregorian rite to establish uniformity in the Christian West.

Hadrian (76–138): Roman emperor. Adopted heir of Trajan and, although faced with rivals, had the support of the army. Proclaimed emperor of Antioch, AD 117. Long apprenticeship in war and military affairs led him to seek reform and consolidation of the Empire. Established the Euphrates as the eastern boundary of the Empire, then conducted a major tour of Germany and Britain. Erected a continuous palisade (the Limes) on the German frontier and ordered the construction of a wall to mark the frontier of the province of Britannia (Hadrian's Wall). Further travels in Spain, Greece, Syria, and Judea followed. Revolts by the Jews and in Africa were suppressed and he promulgated important legal reforms in his Perpetual Edict of 132. An intellectual, reformer, and effective statesman and soldier, he was buried in the mausoleum he had built himself, the Castel Sant' Angelo.

Hannibal (247–183 BC): Carthaginian leader and general during the Punic Wars with Rome. Son of Hamilcar Barca; forced at an early age to swear eternal hostility to Rome. Commander-in-Chief of the Carthaginian forces at the age of 26. Appointed commander in Spain, 221 BC. Secured Spain, 219 BC; began the Second Punic War against Rome, 218 BC. Crossed the Alps to invade Italy, inflicting crushing defeats on Roman armies at Lake Trasimene and Cannae, 217–216 BC. Marched on Rome, but was deterred from capturing it and harassed by tactics of Quintus Maximus Fabius "Cunctator" (the Delayer). Returned to Africa, 203 BC; defeated by Romans, under the brilliant general Scipio, at Zama, 202 BC, ending Second Punic War. Forced to flee from Carthage, 193 BC, he took refuge in Syria and later Bithynia, where he was forced to commit suicide. A brilliant battlefield commander, Hannibal missed his chance to secure a decisive victory in Italy in 216 BC.

Herodotus (*c*.485–425 BC): Greek historian. He travelled widely collecting historical, geographical, ethnological, mythological, and archaeological material for his history of the wars between Greece and Persia. Cicero called him "the father of history".

Homer (*c*.800 BC): Greek poet. Attributed by the ancient world to be the author of two epic works, the *Iliad* and the *Odyssey*. Authorship of these earliest and greatest Greek epics has aroused great controversy, especially over whether Homer was a single figure or responsible for both works. Works are now agreed to be the product of a single author, working in the second half of the 8th century BC. Variations and inconsistencies between the works have been ascribed to the typical forms of oral poetry. The *Iliad* tells the story of the siege and sack of Troy, almost four centuries earlier. The *Odyssey* tells of the wanderings and adventures of one of the participants, Odysseus, on his way back to his homeland in Ithaca. Among the most significance pieces of world literature; nothing is known about the author.

Horace (Quintus Horatius Flaccus) (65–8 BC): Latin lyric poet. Educated in Athens, entered service of Brutus during civil war of 43 BC. Fought at the battle of Philippi. Moved in literary circles with Virgil in Rome during the "golden age" of Roman literature. His *Satires*, *Epistles*, and *Odes* have had a profound influence on Western culture.

Jesus Christ (4–33): Prophet, founder of the Christian religion and believed by Christians to have been divine. Born in Bethlehem in Judea in or about AD 4, he began to preach in 31 and was crucified in Jerusalem on the orders of the Roman governor of Judea, Pontius Pilate, in 33. Christians believe him to have risen from the dead and ascended into heaven at the Ascension. Influence was transmitted through his immediate followers, the apostles, and also by Paul of Tarsus. Life written up in New Testament, consolidating his reputation as a moral teacher and miracle worker, leading to the establishment of Christian communities around the Roman world. Roman Emperor Constantine adopted Christianity, changing its status from an often persecuted sect to a powerful force within the late Roman world, and allowing it to spread as the Roman West disintegrated. In the East, Christianity became an integral part of the Byzantine Empire.

Justinian (483–565): Byzantine emperor. Established authority with the assistance of his wife, Theodora, and his commander-in-chief, Count Belisarius, crushing the circus factions in the Nika Revolt and asserting imperial authority. Belisarius defeated the Vandals, reconquering North Africa, and overthrew the Gothic Kingdoms in Italy. In the East he established a stable frontier with the Persians. He rebuilt Constantinople, including the great Church of St Sophia. Produced his law code, the *Corpus Juris Civilis* (*The Body of Civil Law*), 529–35.

Nero (37–68): Emperor of Rome. Son of Tiberius and Agrippina. Most notorious of the early emperors, responsible for the deaths of his mother, two wives, his stepbrother, and his former tutor, Seneca. Interest in aesthetic pursuits led him to sponsor "Greek" games and to participate in artistic productions. Following the great fire which destroyed much of Rome in 64 he lavished expenditure on his "Golden House" and foreign wars in Britain and Parthia; increasingly paranoid reactions to alleged conspirators led to the Senate decreeing Nero a public enemy. Revolt against him by the Praetorian Guard forced his suicide. Died reputedly lamenting, "What an artist dies with me!"

Pericles (495–429 BC): Athenian statesman. Born in Athens of noble parents. Embarked on a series of successful military conquests, 454–445 BC. Pursued reform in Athens, widening participation, and led Athens to zenith of its commercial and imperial prosperity. Following renewed hostilities with Sparta, during the Peloponnesian War, he was attacked and died shortly afterwards, 431 BC.

Philip of Macedon (382–336 BC): King of Macedon, Philip II, 360–336 BC. Father of Alexander the Great. Instituted military reforms that enabled Macedon to assert its authority over the Greek city-states, subduing Thrace and defeating the Athenians, 341–338 BC. Assassinated at the marriage ceremonies for his daughter, Cleopatra.

Plato (429–347 BC): Greek philosopher. Originally named Aristocles; renamed by Socrates. Founded his "Academy", in Athens, 387 BC, after travel to Egypt and the Greek colonies in Italy, where had met Euclid. Remained largely in Athens after 386 BC, as a teacher and philosopher. Works consist of a series of dialogues in which his mentor, Socrates, is the principal interlocutor. Outstanding reputation ensured that his works are seen as the most famous of Greek philosophy, notably the *Symposium*, the *Ethics*, the *Republic*, and the *Laws*.

Pompey (Gnaeuis Pompeius Magnus) (106–48 BC): Roman general. Became with Caesar and Crassus one of the First Triumvirate, 60 BC. Distinguished military commander from an early age, securing triumphs for campaigns in Africa, 81 BC, and for suppressing slave revolt of Spartacus, 71 BC. Became consul at the age of 36. Suppressed piracy in the Mediterranean, 67 BC. Triumphed over Mithradates VI, securing the Eastern Empire for Rome. Returned to Rome, 62 BC. Following death of Crassus, 53 BC, rivalry with Caesar become more acute, leading to removal of his army from Italy, 49 BC, to recruit more forces in Greece and Macedonia. Pursued by Caesar, after initial success, he was decisively defeated at the battle of Pharsalus, 48 BC. Fled to Egypt but was murdered on arrival.

Socrates (470–399 BC): Greek philosopher. Born at Athens of well-to-do parents. Lived in Athens during "golden age"; served in military and political roles. Charged with impiety and corruption of youth, found guilty, and sentenced to death by taking poison. Majority of writings lost; best known through Plato's descriptions of "Socratic method" of examining arguments, regarded as the basis of formal logic. Last hours described by Plato in *Phaedo*.

Sophocles (496–405 BC): Dramatist and tragic poet. Born in Athens of noble parents. Successful in tragedian contests.

General in the Samian War, 440–439 BC, and took part in civic and ambassadorial tasks. One of a number of famous dramatists who competed in prestigious dramatic contests in Athens; younger rival to Aeschylus and later challenged by Euripides. Caricatured in Aristophanes' play *The Frogs*. Only a fraction of theatrical output survives, in seven out of an estimated 120 plays. Most famous works are *Antigone, Electra*, and *Oedipus Tyrannus*.

Theoderic the Great (455–526): King of the Ostrogoths. Succeeded to the throne 474. Defeated the Bulgarians, 485, and rival Gothic chieftains at Verona, 489 and in 493. Major figure in the establishment of Gothic "successor" kingdoms in the West.

Trajan (Marcus Ulpius Nerva Trajanus) (53–117): Roman emperor. Adopted by Nerva in AD 97 and succeeded him the following year. Reign was notable for the conquest of Dacia by 106 and the erection of Trajan's column in Rome, one of the most informative records of Roman military operations.

Vespasian (Titus Flavius Vaspasianus) (17–79): Roman emperor. Took control of the Empire after a period of turmoil. Earned his reputation as a soldier, commanding the Legio II Augusta in the south-west of Britain in AD 43–7, then suppressing the revolt in Judea in the years up to 68. Plotting to become emperor, he was proclaimed so in 69 and, arriving in Italy in 70, was given the imperial title. He raised taxation, rebuilt Rome (including the Colloseum), and restored discipline to the army. An industrious and effective emperor, he expanded the frontier of the Empire in Britain, Germany, and the East.

Virgil (Virgilus Maro Publius) (70–19 BC): Latin poet. Renowned for 12-book verse epic, the *Aeneid*, (19 BC) an account of the foundation of Rome and the travels of its founder, Aeneas. The work describes how Aeneas came from Troy to found a new home in Rome, the origin of the Roman state. Sponsored by Augustus, *Aeneid* became the founding myth of the Roman Empire and Virgil its Homer. Earlier works, the *Eclogues* and *Georgics*, were concerned with rural life.

Index

Page numbers in *italics* refer to picture captions

The Academy, Athens 46
Achaean League 53, *58,* 59, 61, 79
The Acharnians (Aristophanes) 41
Acropolis, Athens *24,* 44–5
Actium (battle, 31 BC) 93
Aeneas 72, *94,* 95
Aeneid (Virgil) *90, 94,* 95
Aeschylus 40–1
Aetolian League 53, *58,* 59, 60
Africa 26, 63, 105, 109, 113, 121, 128, 129
agriculture
Greek 12, 15, 17, 27
prehistoric 7–8, 9
Roman 80–1, 100, 113
Agrippa, Marcus Vipsanius 69, 91, 93
Alcibiades, Athenian statesman 23
Alexander the Great 6, 53, 56–7, *58,* 62, 64
Alexandria 53, 57, 63, 65
amphitheatres 88, 102, 103, 105, 109
Anastasius, Byzantine emperor 119, 120
Ancus Marcius, king of Rome 73
Anglo-Saxons *126,* 127, 130–1, 135
Antigone (Sophocles) 41
Antigonus Gonatas, king of Macedonia 59
Antigonus 'the One-Eyed,' king of Macedonia 58, 59
Antioch, Syria 111, 121, 122
Antiochus III, king of Syria 60, 63, 79
Antiochus IV, king of Syria 79
Antipater, Macedonian general 56, 58, 59, 62
Antoninus Pius, Roman emperor 110
Aqua Marcia, Rome 80
Arabs 119, 124–5
Archelaus, king of Macedonia 55
Archimedes 64
architecture

Byzantine 122
Doric style 44
early Middle Ages 135
Greek 13, 17, 25, 44–5, 53
Ionic style 44
Roman 69, 74, 94, 104–5
and science 48
Arianism 129
Aristophanes 41, 48
Aristotle *46,* 47, 56
art
Byzantine 119, 122–3
Celtic 9
Christian 119, 122–3
early Middle Ages 135
Greek 12, 13, *14,* 17, 25, 42–3, 53, 64–5
prehistoric 7, *9*
vase painting 12, 13, *14, 42,* 43
Artaxerxes, king of Persia 54
Asclepius, Greek physician 38, *46, 49*
Asculum, Italy 82–3
Asia Minor
under Byzantine empire *119*
campaigns of Alexander 56–7
colonization by Greece *20,* 21, 27, 36, 37, 54
in Roman Empire 111
Seleucid empire 63
in Trojan War 18
Athens
architecture 13, *24,* 25, *33,* 44–5
art 25, 42, 43
democracy 30, 32–3, 54
drama 21, 25, 40–1
government 21, 23, 27, 30, 32–3, 54, 62, 63
philosophy 13, 25, 46, 47, 53, 65
poetry 39
warfare 34–5, 36–7, 55
Attila the Hun 132
Augustine of Hippo *107,* 134
Augustus, Roman emperor 69, 91, 92–3, 94–5, 96, 107
Avars 119, 124, 132
Balkans 119, 125, 127, 129, 132, *133*

basilicas 105, *112,* 122
baths 91, *94,* 104, 122
Bay of Naples *100,* 102–3
Belisarius, Byzantine general 121
Beowulf 135
Book of Kells *126*
books 65, 122, *126, 128, 134,* 135
Britain
Anglo-Saxon invasion *126,* 127, 130, 131, 135
Dark Ages *126,* 130
prehistoric 7, 8
Roman conquest 84, *96,* 97, 98, 105
bronze 12, 15, 29, 34, *42, 43,* 112
Bronze Age 12, 15, *16,* 43
Burgundians 128, 129, 131, 134
burials 130, 131
Greek 12, 17
prehistoric 7, 8
Rome 71
Byzantium
Arab conquests 119, 124–5
architecture 122
art 119, 122–3
fall 125
legal system 121
and Persia 119, 121, 123, 124
Roman Empire continued 69, 119, 120–1

Caesar, Gaius Julius *see* Julius Caesar
Caligula, Roman emperor 69, 97, 107
Campus Martius, Rome 87, 91, 94
Cannae (battle, 216 BC) 78
The Capture of Miletus (Phrynichus) 40
Capua, Italy 76, *77*
Caracalla, Roman emperor 69, 110
Carneades, Greek philosopher 87
Carolingians 133, 135
Carthage *61,* 68, 74, 76, 77, 78–9, *80, 128*

Cassander, king of Macedonia *58,* 59
Cassiodorus, Roman historian 135
Cassivelaunus, British chieftain 84
Catholicism 129
Catilina, Lucius Sergius 84, *85*
Cato, Marcus Porcius *79,* 87
Catullus, Gaius Valerius 87
Celts 8, 9
Childeric, king of the Franks 131
Chosroes, shah of Persia 124, *125*
Christianity 53, 69, *106,* 109, 113, 121, 127, 129
art 119, 122–3
and legal systems 134–5
Roman Empire continued 134
Church of St. George, Thessalonica 123
churches 109, 119, 122, 123
Cicero, Marcus Tullius 65, 69, 84, *85,* 92, 106
Circus Maximus, Rome 86
Claudius, Roman emperor 69, 97, 107
Cleopatra, queen of Egypt 92–3
Clodius Pulcher 84–5
The Clouds (Aristophanes) 48
Clovis, king of the Franks *130,* 131
Codex Amiatinus 134, 135
Codex Argenteus 128
coinage
Celtic 9
Greek 13, 21, 28–9, *55,* 59
Roman *75,* 102, 112
colonization
by Greece 26–7, 37, 54, 55
by Rome 60, 75, 77, 83, 93, 102, 105
Colosseum, Rome 69, 88, *97*
Commodus, Roman emperor 89, 110
Constantine, Roman emperor 69, *106,* 109, 113, 123
Constantinople 119, 121, 122, 124
Corinth 13, 21, 27, 30, 55, 56, 61, 79

Corinthian War (395-387 BC) 54
Council of Chalcedon (451 AD) 121
Crassus, Marcus Licinius 83
Crete 6, 7, 12, 15, 16–17, 21, 59
Cycladic civilization 15, 16, 17
Cylon, Olympic victor 23

Darius I, king of Persia 36, 49
Darius III, king of Persia 57
Dark Ages
    in Britain 126, 130
    in Greece 12, 17, 19, 20, 43
death rituals see burials
Decius, Roman emperor 109
Delian Confederacy 13, 25, 35, 37
Demetrius 'the Beseiger,' king of Macedonia 59, 63
Democedes, Greek physician 49
Demosthenes 26, 45, 54
Diocletian, Roman emperor 109, 112–13
Diogenes 65
Dionysius of Halikarnassus 51
Dionysus, festival of 40, 41
Domitian, Roman emperor 98
Dorians 12, 20, 21
drama
    comedy 40, 41, 68, 86–7
    Greek 21, 38, 40–1
    Roman 68, 86–7
    satyr plays 86
    tragedy 40–1
The Dream of the Rood 135

education 13, 63, 65, 127, 128, 135
Egypt
    and Alexander the Great 53, 56, 57, 58, 59
    Arab conquest 124, 125
    Greece relationship 17, 28, 43, 49, 62, 63, 64
    Rome relationship 79, 92–3, 94, 108
    elephants in battle 78
England see Britain
Ephialtes, Athenian statesman 33
Epictetus 65
equites 80, 81
Erechtheion, Athens 24, 44–5
Etruscans 72, 73, 74, 76

Euboea 17, 21, 27, 36
Eumenes, king of Pergamum 58, 61
Euripedes 21, 38, 41, 55
Europe, defined 6–7

Fabius 'the Delayer' (Quintus Fabius Maximus 'Cunctator') 78
farming see agriculture
Flamininus, Roman general 61, 68, 79
Flaminius, Titus 88
Forum, Rome 68, 70, 71, 87, 88, 91
France 7, 9 see also Gaul
Franks 129, 130, 131, 134 see also Merovingians

Gaul 93, 97, 105, 111, 113, 127, 128, 130 see also Gauls
Gauls 68, 76, 78, 84, 94, 97
Germanicus Caesar, Roman general 96
Germans/Germany 8, 9, 81, 94, 110, 111, 113, 129
Ghassanids 124
Goths 91, 111, 113, 121
government
    Greece
        city-state (polis) 20, 21, 25, 34, 53, 62–3
        confederations 13, 25, 31, 35, 37, 53, 54, 59, 62
        democratic 13, 23, 25, 30, 32–3, 54
        monarchy 30, 31, 53, 57, 59, 63
        tyranny 23, 30, 33, 54
    Rome
        corrupt 80, 81, 82
        dictatorship 71, 83, 85
        imperial 69, 91, 96, 97, 98–9
        military 80, 82–5
        monarchy 68, 71, 72–3, 74, 91
        republican 68, 71, 74–5, 80–1, 82, 84–5, 87, 93
Gracchus, Gaius 71, 81, 88
Gracchus, Tiberius 71, 81
Great Altar, Pergamum 13, 62, 64–5
Great Fire of Rome (64 AD) 69, 97, 109
Great Mosque, Damascus 124
Greece
    agriculture 12, 15, 17, 27
    architecture 13, 17, 25, 44–5, 53

art 12, 13, 14, 17, 25, 42–3, 53, 64–5
coinage 13, 21, 28–9, 55, 59
colonization 26–7, 37, 54, 55
drama 21, 38, 40–1
games 13, 15, 22–3
government
    city-state (polis) 20, 21, 25, 34, 53, 62–3
    confederations 13, 25, 31, 35, 37, 53, 54, 59, 62
    democracy 13, 23, 25, 30, 32–3, 54
    monarchy 30, 31, 53, 57, 59, 63
    tyranny 23, 30, 33, 54
histories 13, 21, 25, 50–1
identity 20–1, 22, 25
legal system 13, 26, 27, 32, 39
Macedonian dynasty 13, 52, 53
medicine 48, 49
ostracism 33
philosophy 13, 25, 46–7, 53, 65
poetry 13, 15, 18–19, 38–9, 65
politics 12–13, 19, 22–3, 25, 27, 29, 30–1, 39 see also government
prehistoric 15, 16–17
religion 19, 21, 22–3, 24, 26, 46, 47, 63
and Rome
    conquest by 13, 23, 58, 59, 60–1, 65, 79
    cultural influence on 86–7
    science 48–9, 53, 64
    Slavic migration 127, 132
    trade 12, 17, 25, 26–7
    warfare 19, 31, 34–7, 40–1, 55

Hadrian, Roman emperor 98, 110
Hadrian's Wall, Northumberland, England 69, 98, 105
Hagia Sophia, Constantinople 122, 123
Hannibal 60, 77, 78–9
Hecataeus of Miletus 50
Hecuba (Euripedes) 41
Hellenic League 59
Heraclius, Byzantine emperor 123, 124, 125, 132
Herculaneum 69, 103
Herodotus 6, 20, 25, 49, 50–1

Hipparchus, tyrant of Athens 30
Hippias, tyrant of Athens 30
Hippocrates, Greek physician 49
Hippocratic Corpus 49
historical writing
    Greek 13, 21, 25, 50–1
    Roman 51, 86, 100
Homer 15, 18–19, 34, 38, 49
Horace (Quintus Horatius Flaccus) 86, 95
Huns 113, 132

Iliad (Homer) 15, 18, 19, 34, 38, 47
Illyria 13, 55, 59, 60, 78, 79
Ion (Euripedes) 21
Ionians 21, 33, 36
Iron Age 12, 17, 132
Isis, cult of 108
Islam 119, 124–5
Istanbul see Constantinople
Italians 68, 76–7, 78, 79, 81, 82–3, 87
Italy 25, 26, 121, 128, 128 see also Italians

Jews/Judaism 98, 109
Jugurtha, king of Numidia 81
Julius Caesar (Gaius Julius Caesar) 69, 84, 85, 88, 91, 92, 94, 107
Justin I, Byzantine emperor 113, 119, 120
Justinian, Byzantine emperor 113, 119, 120–1, 122, 123, 129
Juvenal (Decimus Junius Juvenalis) 69, 101

Kleisthenes, Athenian statesman 13, 32–3
Knossos, Crete 12, 15, 16–17
Kypselos, tyrant of Corinth 30

Laconia 21, 31
Lakhmids 124
Latins/Latium 68, 72, 73, 74, 76
law and legal systems
    Byzantine 121
    Christian influence 134–5
    early Middle Ages 134–5
    Greek 13, 26, 27, 32, 39
    Roman 68, 128
League of Corinth 55, 56
Leonidas, king of Sparta 36

Lepcis Magna, Africa 105, 110
Lepidus, Marcus Aemilius 92
libraries 13, 53, 61, 63, 65
Lindisfarne Gospels 135
Linear B script 12, 17
literacy 6, 127, 135
Lombards 121, 129
Lucretia, rape of 74
Lupercalia 86
Lycurgus of Athens *38, 39,* 54
Lycurgus of Sparta 30
Lydia 13, 28
Lysimachus, king of Thrace 58, 59
Lysistrata (Aristophanes) 41

Macedonia *52, 53,* 54–9, 58, 59, 60, 61, 62
Macedonian Wars (211-168 BC) 13, 59, 60, 61, 69
Marathon (battle, 490 BC) 36
Marcus Aurelius, Roman emperor 110
Marius, Roman emperor 81, 83, *85*
Mark Antony (Marcus Antonius) *85,* 92–3
Martial (Marcus Valerius Martialis) 69, 101
Maurice, Byzantine emperor 124
medicine 48, 49
Mediterranean rim kingdoms 127, 128–9
Melos, Greece 29
Merovingians 131, 135
Messenia 21, 31
migration 8, 9, *20,* 21, 130–1, 132–3
Miltiades, Athenian general 26
Minoan civilization 6, 12, 15, 16–17
Mithras, cult of 108
Mithridates, king of Pontus 69, 83
mosaics *50, 57, 86,* 119, *121, 123, 129*
Muhammad 124–5
Mycenae 12, 15, 17
Mycenaean civilization 12, 15, *16,* 17, 21, 30
myths
    Greek *6,* 15, 18–19, 21, 38, 43, 47, 50
    Roman 72, 94, 95, *106,* 107

Nero, Roman emperor 97–8, 100, 109

Nerva, Roman emperor 98
Numa Pompilius, king of Rome 73, 106

Octavian *see* Augustus
Odyssey (Homer) 18, 19, 38, 47
Olympic Games 13, 15, 22–3
Oresteia trilogy (Aeschylus) 40
Ostrogoths 119, 121, 127, 128, 129

palaces 12, 15, 16–17, 91, *129*
Palestine 124, 125
Panhellenic Games 22–3
Pantheon, Rome 104
Parthenon, Athens *24,* 44
Peloponnesian League 31, 37, 54
Peloponnesian War (431-404 BC) 13, 35, 36, 37, 41, 51
Pera, Iunius 88
Perdiccas, regent of Macedonia 58, 59
Periander, tyrant of Corinth 30
Pericles 13, 32, 33, 37, 44, 51
Perseus, king of Macedonia 61, 79
Persia
Arab conquest 119, 125
and Byzantium 119, 121, 123, 124
campaigns of Alexander 53, 56–7, 58
Greece relationship 25, *33,* 36, 37, 54, 55 *see also* Persian Wars
in Roman Empire 111, 113
Persian Wars (490-479 BC) 13, 25, 35, 36–7, 55
The Persians (Aeschylus) 40–1
Pheidon, king of Argos 30
Philip II, king of Macedonia 26, 53, 54, 55, 56
Philip V, king of Macedonia 59, 60, 61, 68, 78, 79
Philon's Arsenal, Athens 45
philosophy
    Cynics 65
    Greek 13, 25, 46–7, 53, 65
    Roman 65, 69, 87, 110
    Sceptic 87
    and science 46, 48
    Sophist 46–7

Stoic 65, 69, 110
Phoenicians 7, 8, 12, 20, 26, 27
Phrynichus, Greek dramatist 40
Pindar 23, 39
Pisistratus, tyrant of Athens 30
Plato 13, 25, 46–7
Plautus, Titus Maccius 68, 86
plebeians 69, 75, 81, 84
Pliny 'the Elder' (Gaius Plinius Secundus) 103
Pliny 'the Younger' (Gaius Plinius Caecilius Secundus) 100, 102, 103
Pnyx, Athens *33,* 45
poetry
    battle 134
    early Middle Ages 134, 135
    epic 19, 38, 65, 69
    Greek 13, 15, 18–19, 38–9, 65
    lyric 38–9, 65
    and politics 39
    Roman 69, 87, 95, 101, 128
    satire 69, 101
    see also drama
politics
    Greek 12–13, 19, 22–3, 25, 27, 29, 30–1
    and poetry 39
    and religion 22–3, 106–7
    Roman 68, 75, 80–1
    see also government
Polybius, Greek historian 60, *61,* 78, 87, 100, 106
Pompeii 69, 102–3
Pompey the Great (Gnaeus Pompeius Magnus) 69, 71, 83, 84, 85, 87, 91, 107
pottery
    Greek vases 12, 13, *14,* 42, 43
    prehistoric 8
    Slavic 133
Pre-Socratics 46
Procopius, Byzantine historian *121,* 122
Propylaion, Athens 44
Protagoras, Greek philosopher 46
Ptolemaic kingdom 53, 59, 60, 62, 63, 65
Ptolemy 58, 59, 63, 65
Punic Wars (264-146 BC) 68, 77, 78
Pyrrhus, king of Epirus *59,* 76–7, *78*
Pythagoras 48–9

Qusayr Amra, Jordan *124*

Ravenna, Italy *121,* 122, 123, *128,* 129
religion
    cult of the emperor 94–5, 97, 98, 107, 112–13
    Greek 19, 21, 22–3, *24,* 26, *46,* 47, 63
    and medicine *49*
    oracles 26, 47
    and politics 22–3, 106–7
    Roman 94–5, 97, 98, 106–9, 112–13
    sacrifice 47
    see also Christianity; Islam
Republic (Plato) 46, 47
roads 8, 68, 77
Rome
    agriculture 80–1, 100, 113
    architecture 65, 69, 74, 94, 104–5
    'Augustan Peace' 93, 94
    chariot races 86
    citizenship 69, 74, 76–7, 81, 83, 85, 91, 94, 110
    coinage *75,* 102, 112
    colonization 60, 75, 77, 83, 93, 102, 105
    drama 68, 86–7
    Empire decline 6, 69, 91, 110–13
    early 69, 91, 96–9
    fragmentation 91, 110–11, 113, 119, 120–1, 127, 128, 131
    festivals 86
    games 86, 88–9, 94, *97*
    gladiator shows 86, 88–9
    government corruption 80, 81, 82
    dictatorship 71, 83, 85
    imperial 69, 91, 96, *97,* 98–9
    military *80,* 82–5
    monarchy 68, 71, 72–3, 74, 91
    republican 68, 71, 74–5, 80–1, 82, 84–5, 87, 93
    and Greece
        conquest of 13, 23, *58,* 59, 60–1, 65, 79
    cultural influences 86–7
    histories *51,* 86, 100
    legal system 68, 128
    philosophy 65, 69, 87, 110
    poetry 69, 87, 95, 101, 128
    politics 68, 75, 80–1

142

religion 94–5, 106–9, 112–13
trade 7, 60, 79
Romulus and Remus 72, *73*, 107
Romulus Augustulus, Roman emperor 69, 113, 128
Rosetta Stone *65*
Ruthwell Cross, England 135

Sabratha, Tripolitania *104*
Salamis (battle, 480 BC) 36, 40–1
Sallust (Gaius Sallustius Crispus) 100
Samnites 76, 83
San Vitale, Ravenna *121*, 122, 123
Sardinia 8, 17, 77, 78, 79
Saturnalia 86
Schliemann, Heinrich 18–19
science
  and architecture 48
  in Greece 48–9, 53, 64
  mathematics 48–9
  and philosophy 46, 48
Scipio Africanus, Publius Cornelius 79
sculpture
  Etruscan *72, 73*
  Greek 13, *17*, 42, 43, 53, 64–5
  kouros figures 43
  prehistoric 7
Scythians 9, 29, 51
Second Athenian Confederacy 54
Secular Games 94
Sejanus 97
Seleucid kingdom 53, 59, 60, 63
Seleucus *58*, 59, 63
Seneca, Lucius Annaeus 69, 97, 100
Septimius Severus *see* Severus
Sertorius, Quintus 83
Servius Tullius, king of Rome 73
settlements
  Greek 12, 16
  prehistoric 8, 9
  Roman 71, 76, 81, 82, 83
  see also colonization
Severus, Roman emperor 69, 105, 110
Sicily 7, 23, 25, 26, 37, 77, 79, 82, 121
Silbury Hill, Wiltshire,

England 8
silver 29, 35, 112, 123, *131, 135*
Simonides, Greek poet 39
slavery
  freedmen 101, 102
  in Greece 17, 19, 20, 27, 28, 29, 31
  helots 21, 29, 31, 37
  in Rome 69, 75, 82, 83, 87, 101–2, 112
Slavs 127, 132–3
Social Wars 54, 59, 60
Socrates 13, 46, 47, 48
Solon 13, *26*, 27, 32, 33, 39
Sophocles *38*, 41
Spain 78, 79, 83, 113, 121, 125, 128
Sparta 21, 25, 26, 28, 30–1, 34, 37, 54
Spartacus 69, 83
St. Perpetua 109
Stonehenge, Wiltshire, England 8
Strabo 84
'Struggle of the Orders' 68, 75
Sulla, Lucius Cornelius 69, 71, 83, 102
Sutton Hoo, England *131*, 135
Syria 27, 53, 57, 59, 124, 125

Tacitus, Gaius Cornelius 100
Taras (Tarentum), Italy 26, 60, 76–7
Tarquinius 'the Proud,' king of Rome 73, 74
Temple of Janus, Rome 71
temples
  Greek 20, *24*, 36, 44–5
  Roman 71, 87, 91, 94–5, 96, 103, 104–5, 107
Terence (Publius Terentius Afer) 68, 86
Tertullian (Quintus Septimius Florens Tertullianus) 109
Teuta, queen of Illyria 13, 60, 78
theatres
  Greek *41*, 45
  Roman 86, 87, 91, *94*, 103, *104*, 105
  see also amphitheatres
Thebes 25, 31, 54, 55, 62
Themistocles 35, 36
Theocritus, Greek poet 13, 65
Theoderic, king of the

Ostrogoths *128, 129*, 134
Theodosius I, 'the Great' 22, 113, *118*
Theophrastus, Greek philosopher 48
Thermopylae (battle, 480 BC) 36
Thessaly 21, 54, 55, 63
Thucydides 13, 21, 23, 25, 37, 49, 51
Tiberius, Roman emperor 69, 93, 96–7, *99*, 107
Titus, Roman emperor 98
tombs *see* burials
Tower of the Winds, Athens *60*, 65
trade
  Greek 12, 17, 25, 26–7
  in prehistoric period 7, 8, 9, 12
  Roman 7, 60, 79
Trajan, Roman emperor 7, 69, 89, *96, 97*, 98
Tribonian, Byzantine statesman 121
Trojan War 12, 15, 18–19
Troy 18–19
Tullus Hostilius, king of Rome 73
Tyrtaeus, Greek poet 39

Umayyads *124*

Valerian, Roman emperor 111
Vandals 91, 113, 119, 121, 127, 128, 129
Veii, Italy 74, 76
Velleius Paterculus, Roman historian 83
Venantius Fortunatus, Roman poet 134
'The Venus of Willendorf' 7
Vespasian, Roman emperor *97*, 98
Vestal Virgins *87*
Vesuvius 69, 102, 103
Virgil (Publius Vergilius Maro) 69, *90*, 95
Visigoths 113, 119, 121, 128, 129, 134, 135
Volsci 74, 76

warfare
  civil war 69, 85
  hoplites 23, 34–5
  Macedonian innovations 55
  naval 35, 36, 37, 40–1
  phalanx formation 19, 34, 55

writing systems 12, 17, 18, 20, 27

Xenophanes 13, 39, 46
Xerxes, king of Persia 36

Zama (battle, 202 BC) 79
Zeno of Citium 65
Zeno of Elea 49
Zenobia, queen of Palmyra 111

Picture Credits